Y OU'RE NOT ALONE is a valuable resource of
prosthetic information and the powerful stories of
38 amputees. They share their gut level feelings
about the physical and emotional pain, as well as the courage it
takes to put pity aside and go on with life. Their compelling
personal journeys will inspire you whether you're
an amputee or not.

"For someone facing a physical challenge
like amputation, YOU'RE NOT ALONE answers many of your
questions. It's a book that is long overdue and a must for anyone
dealing with traumatic change in their life."

Teddy Kennedy, Jr.

"YOU'RE NOT ALONE is a wonderfully inspirational
tribute to those among us with limb loss. These are personal
stories of courage and overcoming. They are stories of happi-
ness. The book is excellent reading for all of us, and especially
those who are involved in disability rehabilitation."

Ernest M. Burgess, MD

"I found YOU'RE NOT ALONE a stimulating and
skillful combination of technical information
and human interest."

Sidney Fishman, Ph.D.

ONE SECOND I WAS STANDING; *the next I was on the ground. I'll never forget the crunching sound of the wheels as they ran over me. I knew exactly* what had happened. Both my legs had been cut off. *I raised my head and saw one of my legs a few feet away in the middle of the track . . . I* thought I was going to die . . . As I lay in the hospital, I *wanted to kill myself. If there had been any* way — a pair of scissors or a gun — I would have done it . . . But, I talked with Roger Charter, another amputee. *I saw a video tape of him running. "My God, look at that guy. He's lost both legs above the knees,* and he's not walking — he's running." I saw Roger *and other amputees who had faced the same* kind of catastrophe, and I knew I wasn't alone. I knew *if they could make it, so could I . . . And now* I'm just living for the day when that phone will ring, *and it's going to be someone calling me like* I called Roger. It's going to give me the *opportunity to tell that person what I went through,* and I'll be able to help someone like *other people helped me.*

Brent Polanchek

You're Not Alone

BY JOHN SABOLICH, CPO

With the Stories of 38
People Who Conquered
the Challenges of a Lifetime

Linda Adlof, Editor
Carol Sorrels, Managing Editor
Emily Remmert, Contributing Writer

Introduction

*This book is dedicated to the
millions of amputees, young and old,
who have faced losses of limbs and struggled
to find new direction for their lives.*

Y*ou're Not Alone* is a compendium of prosthetic information accompanied by a collection of personal
stories from 38 amputees who share gut-level
feelings. Those who chose to share their stories are candid
about the physical and emotional pain of amputation, grief
over losing an arm or leg, frustrations and triumphs with a
prosthesis, as well as the courage it takes to put pity aside
and go on with life. They share their experiences, successes,
inner strengths, hopes and dreams . . . many times things
most of us take for granted. I believe their compelling stories
will inspire everyone — whether you're an amputee or not.

As a resource, this book is designed to provide basic
information for amputees, those who may be facing an
operation to remove a limb, along with their friends and
families. I've had the idea for the book in the back of my
mind for a long time. It became a kind of nagging thought
as I visited countless patients in the hospital. Here were
people frantically searching for answers, trying to piece
their lives together and finding little — if any — helpful

information. Many were literally in tears, crying out for someone to talk to . . . another amputee . . . someone who understood . . . or something they could read that would give them some answers. My hope is this book will fill part of that void.

Some people may not agree with the opinions expressed in this book. That's all right. *You're Not Alone* is a collection of opinions. Many of the stories are by our patients; some are not. Not all of the feelings of individual amputees represent my personal opinions, nor would their suggestions necessarily be the advice I'd offer. But each person was asked to share his or her personal experiences.

The stories of these amputees and others have touched my life since I was a young boy, when my father started the Oklahoma City-based prosthetics clinic. I've seen the frustration of many amputees whose prostheses were ill-fitting, causing pain and keeping them from leading active, fulfilling lives. I also have seen old wooden legs evolve into lightweight, flexible, high-tech and more usable limbs. I've been there to see the faces of young children light up when they were able to run for the first time.

Over the years, amputees have shared with me the grief and bewilderment of waking in a hospital bed, missing a limb, and not knowing what to do next or who to turn to. They have so many questions, and there's just too little information available. Amputation is not something you think about unless it happens to you, a loved one or a friend. In the midst of such a life-changing trauma, it's hard to comprehend all that needs to be considered. (In a special section, I've attempted to answer some of the common questions.) Every amputation is different, and not all the suggestions will apply to every amputee. But I hope it will serve as a guideline for what to do before the amputation if you have a pending operation . . . to what you may feel upon waking and how to deal with those emotions . . . to proper fitting of a prosthesis and prospects for future improvement in artificial limbs . . . and finally, how to mainstream back into life again.

My goal in compiling *You're Not Alone* is to encourage amputees not to give up and to keep asking questions until they are satisfied with the answers. Ask other amputees for advice. Find a support group. Many amputees have shared the discovery of spiritual journeys. They found that their unwavering faith in God has led them to a new, deeper understanding of life. I encourage you also to call upon that inner strength and never give up.

Once you have read the personal accounts in *You're Not Alone*, I think you'll agree these amputees have very human and encouraging stories to share. They are people who have confronted one of life's toughest challenges and have gone on. They told their stories for this book because when they faced their amputations, they longed for something to read . . . something to hang on to . . . something to tell them that they were not alone.

John Sabolich, CPO

Acknowledgments

*"No man is an island," John Donne wrote in 1624
and it rings true for me today. There are
many people whose guidance and inspiration have
impacted my life and career. This book
reflects some of the things I have learned over
the years from my family, teachers,
colleagues and, most importantly, patients.*

No one person has been a greater influence in my life than my father, Lester J. Sabolich, CPO. His strength and encouragement nurtured my interest in prosthetics. He taught me many valuable lessons about being a prosthetist, including that the patient — the person — always comes first.

My professors and instructors at New York University also shaped my vision of what a prosthetist ought to be. Norman Berger; the late Ivan Dillee, CP; Dr. Sydney Fishman; and Dr. Richard Hans Lehneis, CPO; were among my mentors and profoundly influenced my career.

I also want to thank a number of colleagues who have challenged my thinking and forced me to grow over the years, many times inspiring me to dig deeper and research further. Thanks to George Breece; Dr. Ernest Burgess; Kevin Carroll, CP; the late Chuck Childs, CPO; Jack East; Alan Finnieston, CPO; Bob Gailey; Ed Gormanson, CP; Tom Guth CPO; Sam Hamontree CP; Glenn Hutnick, CPO; Lloyd Keller; Joseph Leal, CP; Ivan Long, CP; Dan Morgan, CPO; Alvin Muilenburg, CPO; Al Pike, CP; Charles Pritham, CPO; Roy Snelson, CPO; Timothy Staats, CP; Jan Stokosa, CP; Michael Wilson, CPO; and Keith Vinnecour, CPO; to name a few. To Steve Shepherd, who has been a spiritual mentor to me for many years, I am grateful.

The great strides in prosthetic technology would never have been accomplished without the dedicated work of the entire Sabolich staff. Their commitment to clinical leadership and prosthetic excellence has set the standard for effectively meeting the rehabilitative needs of their patients. Simply put, they take our patients into their hearts. Without these people, the research and advancements would not be achieved. Only they can understand the long hours, the mangled hunks of plastic in the trash and grit it takes to work through the failures that finally lead to a single breakthrough. I thank each of them for their daily sacrifices and devotion in caring for the needs of our amputee patients. I especially want to recognize some of our staff who read this manuscript and gave me important feedback: Phyllis Bell Stong, Bill Copeland, Mae Hickam, Marge Pittenridge, Emily Remmert, and certified prosthetists Kevin Carroll, Ed Gormanson and Tony van der Waarde.

Special credit should go to Managing Editor, Carol Sorrels, whose enthusiasm for this book was contagious and whose persistence, insight and vision helped make this book a reality. Also to Editor, Linda Adlof, who worked closely with the amputees on their stories and whose commitment to this project was unfailing.

In addition, there are two women who have greatly influenced my life. I want to say a special "thank you" to my mother, Lorene Sabolich, who read this manuscript and offered suggestions. She has been a constant source of support and spiritual influence throughout my life. I also want to express my gratitude to my wife, Lee, whose patience and kindness endures, project after project. She is always there to lovingly encourage me, even in my moments of frustration.

The willingness of 38 amputees to openly share their struggles, triumphs and hope clearly sets this book apart. Integrating what they have learned into our lives can leave us changed, forever.

Finally, in the past few years, I have come to realize how important God's grace is in my life. Without it, this book would not have been possible.

Contents

Frankly Speaking

PRACTICAL ADVICE
FROM JOHN SABOLICH, CPO

"I awoke in my hospital room. Still groggy, a flat sheet was all I saw — a flat sheet where my leg used to be. What was I going to do? How could I go on? It just wasn't fair. Why me, oh God, why me?"

These thoughts from one amputee tell the story. It's a story of pain, bewilderment, and searching. It's a story that countless amputees have shared. I've heard it over and over in my years as a prosthetist.

Those first feelings after waking from an amputation can be overwhelming. Questions, shock, changing emotions, loneliness, pain from the surgery, as well as phantom pain from the loss of a limb — an amputee may experience them all. And there may be anger or even ambivalence about going on with life.

An amputation is a life-changing experience. Unlike other operations, it is very visible. That fact becomes a major roadblock for some people. I'm frequently asked why one amputee seems to do so well, while another does not. I

1

believe the answer is acceptance. Perhaps you are familiar with the first part of the Serenity Prayer: "God grant me the serenity to accept the things I cannot change, the courage to change the things I can, and the wisdom to know the difference." This prayer offers good advice for each of us — amputee or not. But it holds an especially important message for amputees.

We all struggle with acceptance. All of us face changes in our lives which we must learn to accept if we are to be emotionally healthy and lead fulfilling lives. In the case of a person who must confront the loss of a limb, acceptance is crucial. Sometimes it's easier to place the blame or take out the hurt for a loss on other things or other people. It's easier to focus on the external and try to avoid dealing with your own inner feelings. Acceptance of an amputation may be difficult because the loss of a limb is so final. As with any loss, there is a grieving period when you may want — and need — to scream or cry. But once you get through the grieving, the choice is yours; you can accept the change or fight it. But fighting it only leads to frustration and bitterness — and it's very emotionally draining. For some, the road to acceptance is a long, arduous one. Others, who choose to face the change and work to accept it, are better equipped to move on with life. They focus on the change as a challenge.

Don't misunderstand. It doesn't happen overnight, and it isn't easy. An amputee has to take it one day at a time, sometimes maybe five minutes at a time, step-by-step. But if you can maintain a positive attitude — and focus on the solution, rather than the problem — life does get better. Everything in life can be looked at two ways — positively or negatively. A person who seems to have it "all," but has a negative attitude can still be a miserable person. Cultivating a positive attitude about what life has to offer will pay off in the long run. I will more fully discuss grieving and mainstreaming back into life later in this section. But as I begin to share the process of change an amputee faces, I

Ivy Gunter, above-the-knee amputee.
International Model's Hall of Fame, model.

want you to understand that accepting yourself as you are is the all-important first step. Whether you decide to wear a prosthesis or choose not to, your first goal has to be to accept yourself as a whole being — just the way you are right now.

Perhaps fashion model Ivy Gunter sums it up best when she says: "Focus on what you have, not what you don't have." Ivy was at the pinnacle of her New York modeling career when cancer forced amputation of her leg above the knee. Determined not to let the amputation put an end to her career, she was fitted with a highly cosmetic prosthesis and returned to modeling. It was after the amputation that she became a real model — a role model for other amputees. Her positive attitude has given inspiration to amputees around the world. She reaffirmed that there is life after amputation — there is hope. In fact, there can be an even more complete life as you refocus your perspective after a tragedy.

TOUCHING PEOPLE OF ALL AGES

While more than 75 percent of all amputees are over age 50, sex, race, or age make no difference when it comes to losing a limb. Generally, amputations result when there is:

1. An accident. The accident may actually sever the limb, or crush major arteries or bones, and may force later surgical removal of the limb.

2. A life-threatening disease. There are many patients with diabetes, vascular disease, circulatory problems, or cancer. A patient may face the alternative of giving up an arm or leg — or losing his or her life. A parent may confront a heart-wrenching decision when asked for permission to remove the limb of a young son or daughter who might otherwise die.

3. A congenital anomaly. Some infants are born without arms or legs, or with partial limbs, because of birth defects.

William Carroll, age 66, above-the-knee amputee from
Norman, OK, keeps fit by working out at the gym.

In some cases, amputation of a deformed limb may one day become necessary to properly fit the child with a prosthesis.

4. A painful or paralyzed limb. An amputation is sometimes done to remove a withered arm or leg.

I know no one likes to talk about it, but the thought of cutting off a limb is difficult. The very idea may sound ghoulish and make you uncomfortable. You may not want to think about it. In fact, if you are facing a life-threatening situation, exactly what shape your residual limb is going to be in after the amputation may be the last thing on your mind. But maybe you need to refocus on what life holds for you once you survive. With that in mind, it is important to realize the way your amputation is done will significantly impact the rest of your life.

LIMBS FOR THE OLDER AMPUTEE

When a person gets into their sixties, and especially into their seventies or eighties, it is important for the prosthetist to take a different approach in fitting techniques that accommodate the changes of aging. Consideration must be given to sitting comfort as well as walking comfort.

It is vital for the older amputee to be able to put the prosthesis on easily. Older patients are sometimes told a suction limb is best. This is not necessarily true. Many times I find it best to use a "slide on fit" which is easy to slip on with a light-weight activity belt.

The older amputee usually has more movable, loose tissue in the residual limb. Therefore, the flexible socket needs to have adequate bone and muscle contouring so it is stable and won't rotate on the patient's leg. Otherwise, the foot will move in and out while the person tries to walk which is both unsafe and uncomfortable.

The newer advanced plastics and modern materials now make it possible to reduce the weight of a prosthesis to about half of the conventional type. Therefore it takes less energy to walk.

Many times older amputees are advised not to consider a prosthesis in cases where they have poor balance. However, with a contoured socket that fits accurately, gait training and therapy, they can do quite well, to the surprise of many therapists and doctors.

Lack of circulation is a major reason for amputation in the older population; therefore, it is important the socket be shaped in a manner to aid circulation, not restrict it. This is another reason for vascular and muscle contouring which is not present in conventional socket designs. In fact, some sockets may restrict blood flow.

In choosing componentry, one needs to consider a stance control or more stable, locking knee on above-knee cases to help prevent falls. A light-weight foot that has good energy absorbing qualities should also be used. There are many component choices, but these are the two most important.

It is important the older amputee receives adequate gait training by a qualified physical therapist. The therapist can aid the patient in deciding if a cane or walker is needed, or if they can eventually walk unassisted.

Above all, the amputee needs to be heard and listened to carefully throughout their entire prosthetic management program. Older amputees have more alternatives in prosthetic care today than ever before. Those who have been confined to a bed or wheelchair before, may be able to walk again and enjoy more independence.

WHEN YOU'RE FACING AMPUTATION

Historically, the medical community has viewed amputation as destructive. That view has a negative psychological impact on patient and surgeon. If you change your mind-set and look at it as reconstructive, then you can focus on what the residual limb will do for you after the surgery. In other words, think of the surgery as fashioning the end of your limb to make it more capable of bearing weight —

whether it's an arm or a leg.

If it's a non-emergency and you have time before your operation, I strongly suggest that you consult a prosthetist. Working as a team, the patient, surgeon, and prosthetist can discuss the surgical options and decide what will best complement your future prosthetic management program. The idea of contacting a prosthetist before surgery is a concept beginning to be embraced by physicians, allied health organizations, and amputee support groups across the country. Amputees who have gone through the heart-aches and physical pains of amputations that make it difficult to wear artificial limbs, recognize the need to contact a prosthetist early in the process as they begin to reshape their lives. But don't be surprised if your surgeon questions the idea. One amputee recently went back for revision surgery. Her doctor wanted to know why she wanted him to consult her prosthetist. "Because he is going to have to work with what is left for the rest of my life," she explained to him.

Exactly how much of a limb should be removed has recently become an issue of controversy. Many people, well-meaning doctors included, think the less removed, the better. They feel the longer the limb, the better the lever-age, which may sound like the most logical approach. In reality, this may not be the best option when it comes to fitting an amputee with a comfortable and functional prosthesis. Some physicians tend to leave all possible length of a limb — even when the person has no feeling in the lower part of the limb or there will be a lot of severe scar tissue. Those types of amputations generally set up a series of future problems for the amputee who wants to wear a prosthesis and become independently mobile again.

There are many things to consider when deciding on the level of amputation. Where an amputation is done may affect your mobility, as well as the cosmetic look of your artificial limb.

*J.B. Richard, 73, above-the-knee amputee, and wife Beulah
taking a leisurely stroll.*

Let's take the case of a knee disarticulation, or a very long above-the-knee amputation. The surgeon amputates at the knee, leaving a long residual limb. In the past, amputation through the knee has been considered best for leverage and weight-bearing, as well as for a simple, clean surgery. (The limb is disjointed instead of being cut through a bone.) But many knee-disarticulation amputees find the long residual limb to be both functionally and cosmetically undesirable. The extra length creates several problems. Bulky knee width and unequal joint centers can cause severe cosmetic problems in the artificial limb, while sharp, bony protrusions can cause chronic prosthetic fitting problems.

Additionally, the prosthetic knee component takes up considerable space, which adds to the overall length of the prosthesis. What you end up with is a very long thigh. To compensate, the calf portion of the prosthesis must be shorter so the overall leg length will match the sound leg. Consequently, when the amputee with a knee disarticulation sits, the knee projects too far out and the foot doesn't touch the floor. When the amputee walks, the swing of the knee looks uneven. And because the knee joint protrudes so far, it can be difficult to get the necessary leverage to get up out of a chair, especially for a person who has had both legs removed. You should understand that the extra length in a residual limb may actually prohibit use of the type of knee joint you may want. Again, this is because of the space required by the knee component.

Other disarticulations (ankle, elbow and wrist) and amputations which leave very long residual limbs sometimes cause similar problems. Patients usually object to the width of the prosthetic socket required by these amputations. The prosthesis often looks bulky, and there is usually no way around that. I've seen many patients with tears in their eyes because of the bulk of the finished artificial limb. Most women, and many men, find these levels of amputation cosmetically displeasing. However, I have seen a few disarticulation amputations where the surgeon trimmed down the large part of the bone, shortening it slightly, and the finished prosthesis looked reasonably good. Still, these may never look as good cosmetically as shorter amputations.

I am not saying that all amputations that leave longer residual limbs aren't advantageous for some patients. In the case of a child, concerns about bone growth and spur formation may outweigh the negative aspects of a disarticulation. But I believe it is imperative, especially in non-emergency situations, that the implications of the various surgical options be discussed thoroughly with the patient.

Leaving a very long residual limb is not as necessary as it once was because of advanced socket techniques and high-tech prosthetic componentry. In fact, many ankle-level (Symes) or long, below-the-knee amputees may do better with a somewhat shorter limb that is protected by the softer, thicker calf muscles. And blood circulation is normally better in the shorter limb. Over the years, I've noticed that few Symes amputees run on their prostheses, but running is relatively common among those with shorter below-the-knee residual limbs. One reason may be that the longer limb does not leave room for the shock-absorbing foot and ankle componentry, so the amputee receives an uncomfortable jarring with each running step.

There are a number of other factors that should be discussed, including rounding of bony prominences, scar placement, and vascular viability (blood circulation) at various levels of amputation. If possible, it is important that the surgery does not leave you with a lot of limb in which there is no feeling. You need to have feeling in the residual limb.

Other special procedures such as myodesis (muscle-to-bone reattachment), myoplasty (tying muscle to muscle), syostosis (bone-bridging), and prosthetic joint space requirements should be considered. It is also important that the doctor pay particular attention to the nerve endings during the operation. You may want to check with your surgeon on how that will be done. One surgeon with whom we work says that

11

anytime a nerve is cut, a neuroma is going to form. But how the nerve is cut may make a difference in the amount of pain the neuroma causes later. Painful neuroma formation can be decreased if the surgeon gently pulls the nerves down, clips them cleanly and allows them to retract up into the soft tissue or muscle bed, according to the surgeon. This surgical procedure helps keep the neuroma away from the scar tissue that forms naturally inside the end of the residual limb.

And again, in some cases where a surgeon tries to save the length of the limb at all costs, an amputee may be left with a lot of undesirable, non-sensitive scar tissue. Scar tissue may not only adversely affect how well you function on your prosthesis, but also is often a source of constant skin breakdown. This is especially true if the scar tissue is stuck to a bone, preventing the tissue from moving freely over the bony areas.

The bottom line is to find out as much as you can from your surgeon and prosthetist before the operation. The fewer surprises, the better. I have worked with many amputees who overcame pain from initial operations only to face revision surgeries because their limbs were not amputated at levels for best prosthetic use.

Communication among patient, doctor and prosthetist can make a difference — the difference between an amputee struggling through life on crutches, dealing with unnecessary pain, or getting on with life using a prosthesis. As an amputee, you need not feel powerless. Through research, you can gather the knowledge to participate in the decisions that will affect your life.

So, how do you choose a surgeon and a prosthetist? Chances are you have no idea where to start. The best answer: ask for recommendations. Ask family, friends and other amputees. Find out how many amputations your surgeon has done. The more experience, the better. Ask if you can talk to several of his or her amputee-patients. It's helpful to talk with an amputee who has the same type and level of amputation.

The same goes for a prosthetist. First, consult only with

12

a certified prosthetic facility. The American Board of Certification in Prosthetics and Orthotics monitors the profession and regularly reviews facilities to make sure they meet minimum standards. The American Prosthetic and Orthotic Association in Alexandria, Virginia, can provide a list of certified prosthetic facilities.

But beyond certification, experience counts. You need a prosthetist who is experienced in dealing with your particular level of amputation. One prosthetist may serve a lot of below-the-knee amputees, but may not have a great deal of experience fitting an amputee with a hemi-pelvectomy or hip disarticulation. And there is a significant difference between fitting a long above-the-knee and a short above-the-knee amputee. When it comes to getting a proper fit, it can make a difference whether a prosthetist makes 10 legs or as many as 100 each year for your level of amputation. Some prosthetists are more open to using new technology and advanced materials than others. Again, ask to talk to several of the prosthetist's patients, especially amputees whose amputation level is the same as yours is to be, and those who are as active as you want to be. Most amputees are more than willing to share what they have learned.

When it comes to selecting a surgeon or prosthetist, ask questions until you get the answers. If your prosthetist or doctor seems annoyed with all your questions, find another one who will listen to you. There are a growing number of amputee support groups that can provide valuable information, and be an on-going source of encouragement as you begin life as an amputee. For a list of amputee support groups, you can call our toll-free number: 1-800-522-4428.

For the most part, there isn't enough communication between physicians and prosthetists, who are both earnestly trying to serve amputees, but face daily time constraints. Still, the amputee is best served when the physician and prosthetist take the time for consultation. A real effort to communicate can only benefit the amputee.

After Surgery . . . Is My Leg Still There?

What can you expect after the amputation? Amputees often complain they weren't told before surgery what they'd feel after the amputation. You may awaken after the operation and think your arm or leg is still there . . . that the doctor didn't amputate. No, you're not imagining it. It's a phenomenon called phantom limb. It can be merely a sensation, or it may be pain.

It's common, but some amputees hesitate to even mention the sensation or pain to anyone because they rationalize that it just couldn't be . . . and maybe worse, someone might laugh at the very idea. But many amputees have told me that phantom sensation and phantom pain are very real indeed.

Initially, the pain from surgery will be the most overwhelming. Doctors often prescribe heavy sedatives, like morphine, for the pain. There may be side effects when the pain medicine is tapered off, and you can discuss these with your doctor.

Phantom pain is generally worse immediately following the amputation. Depending on how you lost your limb, you may feel as though your arm or leg is being twisted or bent in an awkward position. Amputees who have been through extended pain or very traumatic accidents seem to experience greater phantom pain, but it depends on the individual. For some, it feels as mild as a tingling sensation. Others describe it as a stabbing, burning pain that comes in intense waves. The good news is that it normally gets better with time. Still, many amputees will experience episodes of phantom pain, ranging from mild to severe, throughout their lives.

One problem is that people, including some well-meaning doctors and nurses, tell the patient to forget about the leg or arm that has been amputated. The reasoning is "it's not there anymore, so it can't hurt you anymore." I feel this makes phantom pain more difficult and harder to accept. It isn't necessarily healthy for the amputee.

Let's take the case of a leg amputation. After the surgery,

14

the brain doesn't know that the leg is gone and continues to crave information from the floor. I ask amputees not to forget their leg or their foot . . . but rather, to imagine feeling the foot hitting the floor and the toes bending, even though they are gone. Cerebral projection — visualizing the amputated limb as if it is still there — is something I've been experimenting with. I've found that patients who visualize their amputated limbs intact are usually the ones with the best gaits. And visualization also seems to help them deal with phantom pain.

As an extension of that theory, I have developed the Sense-of-Feel System, designed to give amputees feeling through their artificial limbs. Currently, the system is being tested, and preliminary findings seem to indicate it eases phantom pain while providing other benefits. I will more fully discuss the prospects for Sense-of-Feel in the section on Regaining Feeling.

If phantom pain continues to be a problem, you may want to ask your physical therapist or physician for treatment suggestions. Other amputees often have "home remedy" tips on how they handle pain. And pain management centers offer a variety of approaches to deal with phantom pain. Here are some ideas for pain reduction, but not all of them apply to a new amputee. You should check with your doctor before trying these, and remember, what works for one amputee may not ease the pain of another.

1. Try some mild, total-body exercise to increase circulation and/or exercise the residual limb.

2. Visualize the missing limb and mentally exercise it.

3. As you physically move the limb on your sound side, mentally move the missing limb in the same fashion in unison.

4. Using basic relaxation techniques, tighten and then slowly relax the muscles in your residual limb.

5. Massage your residual limb with your hands or with a shower massage.

6. Soak in a warm bath, hot tub or whirlpool — or try

wrapping your residual limb in a warm towel, or a heating pad. Warmth often increases circulation and reduces pain.

7. Wear an Ace bandage or shrinker sock. If you have your prosthesis off, try putting it on and taking a short walk.

8. If you are wearing your prosthesis, take it off for a few minutes. Then, put it back on. Sometimes the residual limb is being pinched, and changing the position of the prosthesis may relieve the pressure.

9. If you have been sitting for a period of time, change positions or stand to increase blood flow to the residual limb.

10. Keep a diary of the pain. Some people find a relationship between the pain and certain foods.

Some amputees also use self-hypnosis, chiropractic treatment or a Transcutaneous Electrical Nerve Stimulator (TENS) unit. If phantom pain persists, you may want to ask your doctor or prosthetist for more information about pain management clinics.

Another area under investigation is Biomagnetic Technology where special concentric, alternating-poled magnets are incorporated into the prosthetic socket. There is some evidence that this special magnetic affect results in increased circulation for the patient and may have a positive effect in reducing phantom or neuroma pain.

In addition to pain, the personal realization that you are now an amputee may hit you following surgery. "No matter how prepared you are for the operation, you're never prepared for waking to see a flat sheet where your leg used to be," says one amputee. Pulling back the sheet that first time can be a real emotional trauma — one that those of us who aren't amputees can't really describe or understand. It helps if you have someone to talk to, whether it's a family member, a doctor, nurse or friend. Other amputees can be especially helpful in understanding the feelings you are experiencing. Your doctor, prosthetist or local amputee support group can give you names of amputees to call.

Some amputees will awaken after surgery to find a rigid cast, or a cast with a pole, knee and/or foot attached to their residual limb. There are pros and cons to this immediate post-operative fitting, and you may want to discuss these with your doctor and prosthetist. Many doctors dislike this type of fitting because the limb cannot be viewed through the cast during the healing process, and they prefer an early prosthetic fitting a few weeks after the surgery. Most amputees will find only a soft dressing covered by an Ace bandage on the residual limb.

You may be surprised to discover your limb is very swollen, rather bulbous and quite a bit larger than your other arm or leg. The swelling will go down, and the residual limb will shrink significantly over the first three to four months after the amputation. The muscles tend to atrophy because they are not being used and the fluid build-up slowly goes away. Eventually a mature residual limb will usually be smaller than the other arm or leg.

However, if you are fitted with a bone and muscle contoured socket that allows for muscle growth (hypertrophy), your residual limb can build back much of the muscle it lost. Using that muscle can help improve your gait.

The average hospital stay for a new amputee is seven to ten days, if there are no other medical complications. You can expect your medical staff to have you up and out of bed as early as the first day after surgery. You should consider beginning physical therapy that will prepare you for wearing a prosthesis. Your physical therapist or nurse can show you how to properly wrap your residual limb in a figure-eight configuration with an Ace bandage. This is important to help keep the swelling down.

A physical therapist can play a significant role in your recovery. The forward thinking would be to include the therapist in the doctor-patient-prosthetist team, even before surgery. After surgery, a physical therapist can help prevent flexion contractures, a sometimes permanent shortening of the muscle or tendon that may cause deformity or stiffening of a

17

joint in the residual limb. As an example, some amputees develop a "frozen" joint that prevents successful prosthetic use. Make sure your physical therapist checks for the onset of flexion contractures.

The therapist can also help you learn to desensitize your residual limb. Limb desensitization is very important, yet frequently overlooked. An amputee who can't stand to have the residual limb touched will not be able to tolerate a prosthetic fitting. Once you can massage the limb, work up to patting it, rubbing it with a towel and even lightly slapping it. This will prevent the development of adhesions, and you will feel less and less nerve irritation.

After hospitalization, you may be referred to a rehabilitation facility, depending on the severity of the amputation and other medical problems. However, most amputees will be allowed to go home.

GETTING TO KNOW YOUR RESIDUAL LIMB AND TEMPORARY PROSTHESIS

You should get a temporary prosthesis as soon as your doctor says it is okay. Usually, an amputee can wear a temporary as soon as the stitches are removed — about two to six weeks after the amputation. In the meantime, you should be getting acquainted with your residual limb — massaging, desensitizing, exercising and working with it. You will hear the residual limb referred to as a "stump." This is a blunt and sometimes shocking term that may be offensive to some people, particularly new amputees. Although the word stump has been used historically, I prefer the term residual limb.

Learning to accept, or bond with, your residual limb is an important step for amputees. After a time, some amputees even choose to name their residual limbs — like "short arm" or "my little leg." One fun-loving teenager, Leslie Wilson, draws a face on her short leg to make it a conversation piece when she is at the beach. Sometimes a spouse or companion affectionately nicknames the residual limb.

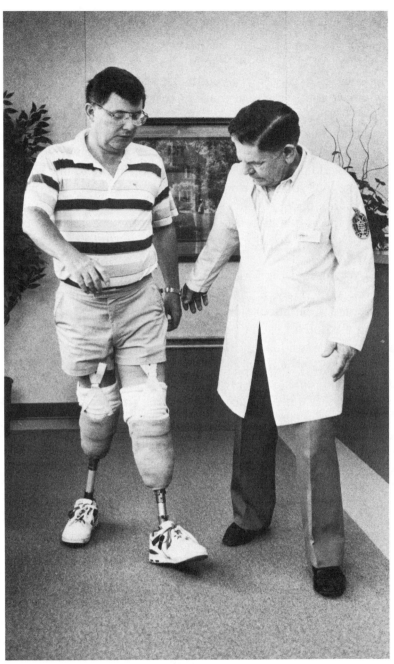

Lester Sabolich, CPO, with patient, John Patterson, bilateral below-the-knee amputee, trying out his new temporary prostheses.

For some, it is all part of the healing process as you learn to accept your amputation. The journey to acceptance can be a spiritual healing, according to amputee Phyllis Bell Stong, who lost her leg to cancer as a youth. She and other amputees say you have to first get over thinking that the residual limb is ugly. Phyllis admits that even after 20 years, there is an occasional twinge of sadness when she catches a glimpse of herself in a full-length mirror. She says you have to acknowledge that sadness and go on from there — you don't have to like what you see, but you do have to accept it and move on. Learning to look at, touch, and massage the residual limb will help you accept the amputation. After all, it's part of your body. As far as you are concerned, it is your arm or leg — not just a stump or residual limb.

You should continue wrapping the leg or arm with an Ace bandage each day. If you forget how, there are a number of amputee publications which will show you the proper wrapping method for each type of amputation. It is important not to wrap the residual limb too tightly above the end of the amputation, which will restrict circulation. The bandage should be removed and rewrapped several times each day, because it will become loose as the limb shrinks and fail to provide adequate support. I do not recommend using the shrinker or reducer socks until after the stitches are removed and the surgery is more healed. When donning a shrinker sock before the surgery has healed, it can hang on the bulbous end of the limb and pull on the incision. Once the incision has healed, a shrinker sock is more convenient and helps further reduce the residual limb for prosthetic use. Even after you get your temporary prosthesis, you should use a shrinker when not wearing your artificial limb to keep swelling to a minimum. Some amputees continue to wear them throughout life, finding the shrinker support particularly comfortable at night.

Getting your temporary prosthesis can be exciting and a little frightening. You will have lots of questions, and you shouldn't be embarrassed to ask your prosthetist about whatever concerns you. You may want to make a written list so you don't forget important questions. If you have talked with your prosthetist prior to surgery, you will already have a working relationship. If not, as you go for your first fitting, be sure to communicate your needs. A prosthetist is neither a mind reader nor a magician — but can become an important part of your life. An amputee-prosthetist relationship differs from a patient-doctor relationship because of the amount of time you spend with the prosthetist. You will spend hours and days with your prosthetist during the fitting process, and for the rest of your life.

The fitting process will begin with the prosthetist taking an impression or cast, along with measurements of your residual limb, so a socket can be properly designed. Taking a cast involves wrapping a wet plaster of paris bandage around the residual limb. After the material hardens, it is removed and used to make your first socket.

Do not be shocked when your temporary isn't light and attractive like other prostheses you may have seen. Usually, a temporary is somewhat bulky, heavier, and less cosmetic than a permanent, or definitive prosthesis. Normally, there is no cosmetic covering, so you will see the socket attached to various componentry. It probably will be held on with a light belt/harness, or occasionally by an elastic sleeve.

You may ask, "Why do I need a temporary . . . why not just get a permanent artificial arm or leg?" The reason: your residual limb will continue to shrink, necessitating socket changes. A temporary saves time and money, and changes can be made that will provide a better-fitting permanent prosthesis. That's the primary purpose of a temporary prosthesis. If you've lost your leg, it lets you be up and mobile, learning to walk and balance while your residual limb continues to shrink. Bearing weight helps shrink the residual limb faster. If you've lost an arm, it allows you to pick up objects and manipulate your world. Many people are anxious to get into permanent, more cosmetic prostheses quickly. Going to a permanent prosthesis too early is a mistake in many cases because it doesn't give adequate time to let the temporary do its work. I advise patients to wear a temporary for a minimum of three months.

You may even get more than one temporary, depending on shrinkage. After you are fitted with a temporary, and as the limb shrinks, you will use prosthetic socks to take up the extra space in the socket. You will continue to add socks to help the socket fit properly. Sometimes the residual limb will shrink so much that another socket will be necessary. At that time, if the arm or leg has matured, you will be ready for the preparatory stage. It depends on the individual.

In addition to shrinking the residual limb, the temporary leg or arm toughens and desensitizes the limb to prepare you for wearing a permanent prosthesis. If you've lost a leg, it helps you regain balance and relearn how to walk. At this point in the prosthetic fitting process, it is important for the amputee to learn to tighten the muscles in the residual limb while walking on the temporary prosthesis. It is one of the most important things I ever discuss with an amputee who is relearning to walk. Mastering the muscle control may take a while, but the benefits include better stability, more comfort and less limp. If you have lost an arm, the temporary prosthesis increases range of motion and strengthens the muscles. Most importantly, however, it encourages you to keep using both hands — preventing you from becoming one-handed.

Your temporary may cause you some initial pain, but the pain should not be excruciating. Some patients are more sensitive and will experience more discomfort. In lower extremity cases, you should be up and walking in a day or two, if there are no additional medical problems. If you are in pain for a long period of time, there is a good chance something is wrong. You may need to see your doctor — there may be a medical problem that has gone undetected. You may also need to talk to your prosthetist, or maybe another prosthetist, if you don't get your problem solved.

Whether you've lost an arm or leg — if you don't already

have a physical therapist, your prosthetist should be able to recommend one who has experience with amputees. I prefer patients to get as much physical therapy as possible — at least once a day at first. But each individual is different, and it often depends on the type of amputation. Some amputees need little physical therapy, while others need a great deal. Occupational therapists are especially helpful in training upper extremity amputees to be more functional, with or without prostheses.

After the temporary comes the preparatory stage. It is often confused with the temporary stage, but a preparatory is usually a prerequisite to the final prosthesis. Not all patients get preparatory legs or arms, but I believe it is, many times, essential for a more accurate fit and alignment. Your residual limb will be cast, just as it was when you were fitted for a temporary prosthesis. Usually, a transparent, diagnostic test socket is used so the prosthetist can see through it to determine the fit. The clear socket is to a prosthetist what an X-ray is to a doctor — an opportunity to see what is happening inside. The idea is to get the fit, contour, and alignment as accurate as possible before the final prosthesis is cloned. It gives the prosthetist a chance to make custom-fitting adjustments, taking into consideration weight-bearing areas and relief for sharp, protruding bones, scars, or sensitive tissue. The preparatory stage may last from a few days to a few weeks, depending on the amputee.

If you are unsure about the fit, tell your prosthetist. You may need to wear the preparatory longer to pinpoint needed changes. You certainly don't want to go ahead with making a cosmetic, permanent prosthesis until the fit is complete and as accurate as possible.

At this point, I would like to touch on the need for daily hygienic care of your prosthesis. Many amputees notice they seem to perspire more heavily after an amputation. Sometimes this scares them — they think there is something wrong — but you need not worry. One reason the perspiration may appear greater is that after an amputation, there is less body surface from which to perspire. You're not necessarily perspiring more, but it is now concentrated over a smaller area.

You will notice that your residual limb perspires a lot inside the socket — naturally anything encased in plastic would. Perspiration inside the socket can be both a source of odor and bacteria, as well as the culprit behind skin problems. But there are a variety of products available to help manage this problem. Using an anti-perspirant on the residual limb is one answer. There is also a special prescription anti-perspirant called Dry-Sol. But if you use Dry-Sol, it should be applied at night and washed off in the morning before donning your prosthesis. You need to ask your prosthetist or doctor for additional information on the proper use of Dry-Sol. Some amputees say that powdering the residual limb with baking soda is one simple solution to the moisture problem. However, others don't like powder because it builds up in the socket, making it more of a chore to clean. It's a personal preference. Regardless of your choice, your prosthesis is now a part of you and should be cleansed daily, just as you care for the rest of your body. The socket should be thoroughly cleaned every day with alcohol or anti-bacterial soap and water. Many amputees prefer to bathe and clean the socket at night, so both the skin and the socket are completely dry when donning the prosthesis the following morning.

Stump socks also need to be laundered regularly. Most amputees report hand washing and line drying is preferable to prevent sock shrinkage and a must if you use a soft, woolen sock. Some amputees find they even need to change socks more than once a day because of perspiration. Each amputee develops a personal hygiene regimen that fits individual needs and schedules. You can find more hygiene tips in many amputee publications, or ask your prosthetist.

DRAMATIC CHANGES IN PROSTHETICS

As you look forward to your permanent artificial limb, you should realize that the world of prosthetics has changed dramatically in recent years. Amputees are now able to do

*Roger Charter, the first bilateral above-the-knee amputee,
to run step over step.*

things that were only dreamed of prior to the 1980s. Lightweight and flexible materials, advanced socket designs, and high-tech componentry have expanded the possibilities for amputees. For those who have lost legs, there is hope for even very short above-the-knee, hemi-pelvectomy and hip-disarticulation amputees who have been told they would never walk. They are discovering what it is to be independently mobile again. For those who have lost arms, myoelectric arms offer a functional and cosmetic replacement for hooks, previously the only choice for upper extremity amputees.

The technology is available, but the individual amputee possesses the key ingredient for prosthetic success. Attitude. You must have the desire, commitment, and motivation to try to make your artificial limb work for you. What each individual amputee can do with a prosthesis depends largely on the person. Sure, the type of amputation and other physical problems are important, but to a great extent, what you will be able to do depends on you. Technology is only a secondary factor in the successful use of a prosthesis.

Many of the improvements in prosthetics can be attributed to the inner desires of amputees. It was 1982 when 3-year-old Sarah East, wanting so badly to run and keep up with her playmates, inspired the development of the Oklahoma City (OKC) Running Leg. I saw a movie of above-the-knee amputee Terry Fox running with a hop-skip motion and, knowing Sarah's desire, that night I sketched the design for the running leg. Initially, I just took a piece of elastic cord, wrapped it around her leg, came up in front of her knee and behind her hip, and tied it around her waist. This was primitive, but after further research and development, the OKC Running Leg was completed. Sarah put it on and she took off running. To my knowledge, she was the first above-the-knee amputee to run step-over-step. Sarah's run was first documented on videotape and later by *CNN*.

That development spurred us to further research, until in 1988, Roger Charter became the first bilateral above-the-knee

Doug McCormick, above-the-knee amputee, thrilled to be running again.
(Doug has a very short residual limb, only a 3" femur)

amputee to run step-over-step. It was a feat previously thought impossible, but he proved it could be done. However, not every amputee wants to run. For many, the goal is to walk comfortably. But thanks to advances in technology, now the option exists. It's like Roger says: "I may never run a marathon. But if it starts to rain, I can pick up my pace and jog to the car." With technology and determination, there is no longer a stereotype of what an amputee can or cannot do.

In fact, there is so much available to amputees today that it may be confusing. I cannot stress enough that the socket is the most important element — more important than a hydraulic knee, an electric hand, or a cosmetic covering. If the socket doesn't fit accurately, the prosthesis is going to be painful to wear, and you'll be tempted to put it in the closet. All the high-tech "bells and whistles" won't help you if you don't have a socket that fits.

As you become a prosthetic consumer for the first time, I would encourage you to have realistic expectations about the look, feel and function of your artificial limb. And remember, not every amputee is the same — no two amputations are exactly alike, so fitting requirements differ. People vary in physical strength, as well as in the time it takes to adapt to a prosthesis. Try not to be overly-critical of yourself, but set realistic goals and expectations.

I should also add that the terms "permanent" or "definitive" prosthesis can be misleading. No artificial limb is going to last the rest of your life. Depending on how active you are, you can expect a prosthesis to last two to five years; with children even less. It is mechanical, and mechanical things eventually break down. Major fluctuations in weight or volume can also necessitate a new socket or other changes in the prosthesis.

For the purposes of this discussion, I will answer some questions about sockets and prosthetic fittings for the most common amputations. Again, please realize each case is individual, and each person will have special fitting needs.

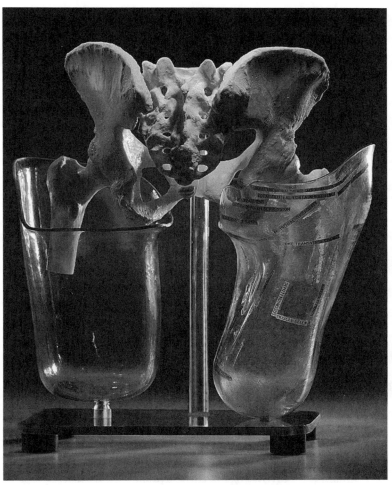

Side-by-side comparison of the shape and fit of the Sabolich Socket (right) and the conventional quadrilateral design. Note the bone, muscle, vascular and nerve contouring, and the full containment of the lower pelvic bones.

ABOVE-THE-KNEE

Sockets have come a long way from the early days of artificial limbs. I began experimenting with different above-the-knee socket designs in the mid-1970s. Then, the quadrilateral, a square-looking, hard socket was the current above-the-knee socket design. The old plug socket was also still used sometimes. It was largely a predetermined cylindrical shape into which you "plugged" your leg.

The quadrilateral was made of hard, heavy plastics or wood, designed very wide from side to side and narrow from front to back. The theory was that for weight-bearing purposes, the large bone you sit on had to be placed on a seat or shelf-like structure near the back of the socket. The socket squeezed the leg from front to back, helping force that bone back on the socket shelf. This left little room in the groin, and the bones in the crotch area tended to strike the top of the square socket, often causing pain.

There were other problems with the quadrilateral socket. It didn't encompass and contain the lower pelvic bones, so you had to sit up on a hard ridge, increasing instability. The socket usually gapped along the upper outside part of the leg as weight was applied, contributing to malalignment of the thigh bone and leaving the amputee with a noticeable limp. After experimenting with a combination of the plug and quad sockets, a shape not as wide from side-to-side as the original quad socket evolved. Known as the quadraplug, it was an improvement, but remained far from the sophisticated socket designs of today.

Yet another socket design that was very narrow from side to side, called the narrow ML, became available in the early 1980s. With this socket, the sitting bone was still mainly on the shelf, but it was forced more to the inside rather than the back of the hard socket. Unfortunately, even at best, only the tip of the sitting bone was contained inside the socket. This concept of placing part of the sitting bone inside the socket originally came out of German socket design efforts in the early 1950s and was revised by American prosthetists. The shape of the socket remained rounded and very generic, with no distinct muscle, bone or vascular contouring.

After much study, I developed a design known as CAT-CAM, which stands for Contoured Adducted Trochanteric-Controlled Alignment Method. My aim was to capture as much of the pelvic bone as possible within the socket and help bring the thigh bone into better alignment under the amputee. The original CAT-CAM was wider than the narrow ML at the top to lock against the pelvic bone, and then narrowed down from the middle to the end of the socket. The advantage of the pelvic containment was that it helped keep the thigh bone from drifting out from under the amputee. In addition, it helped stabilize the residual limb within the socket by locking the bones along the top of the brim, reducing inadvertent movement between the socket and the residual limb. This socket was an improvement over the quadrilateral socket and the narrow ML.

CAT-CAM evolved into a totally flexible design, with bone and muscle contouring. Tom Guth, CPO, collaborated with me on the design and development of the flexible CAT-CAM socket in 1984. The soft, flexible socket allowed a more intimate fit—especially around the pelvic bone—which increased comfort and control. We taught the CAT-CAM concept at the University of California, Los Angeles, in 1985. But my research did not stop, and much of what was taught then is now obsolete. Unfortunately, some amputees are still being fitted with variations of the narrow ML socket when they ask for a CAT-CAM. But the sockets are not the same. The narrow ML design is not bone-and-muscle contoured, nor does it contain the pelvic bone in a significant way like later socket designs.

In recent years, further refinement of CAT-CAM led to SCAT-CAM and ultimately, the Sabolich Socket. The totally flexible socket has anatomically-designed channels and grooves for various muscle, bone, tendon, vascular, and nerve areas. It also has built-in reliefs for concentrated pressure spots. Years of experience with hundreds of patients and extensive

31

cadaver studies led to the logically-applied, bio-mechanical principles incorporated in the Sabolich Socket. Because it is totally flexible around the top, a higher, more intimate fit is possible. This higher fit is very important for rotational stability and better side-to-side control. It also aids in command and alignment of the thigh bone, preventing it from shifting as much as in other socket designs.

Most recently, we began using an ultra-flexible rubberized plastic in socket designs for all levels of amputation. The soft, pliable plastic is more flexible and comfortable than any material previously used. It is still in the early stages of use, but amputee response has been encouraging.

Hip-Disarticulation and Hemi-Pelvectomy

Advanced CAT-CAM technology, originally designed for above-the-knee amputees, spilled over into socket designs for hip-disarticulation and hemi-pelvectomy amputees. In the past, anyone with a leg removed at the hip or pelvis had a hard, bucket-style prosthesis.

The latest breakthrough for hip-disarticulation amputees is the Sabolich Femurless Socket (SFS), but it's not for everyone. It can only be used when there is sufficient tissue mass extending down from the hip area. We have been able to draw this tissue into a socket resembling an above-the-knee socket. Consequently, the gait of the amputee is better and similar to an above-the-knee amputee. And no longer is the amputee forced to wear the pelvic bucket-style girdle. This new socket design is only in its infancy, but appears to hold promise for some hip-disarticulation amputees.

The more conventional hip-disarticulation socket developed at our facility is still far advanced over earlier designs. The socket wraps around the hip area and sitting bone in a new way, but it is anatomically contoured to contain and support the pelvic bone, rather than forcing the amputee to sit on a flat, hard surface. Patients report they no longer feel like they are "sloshing around in a bucket," and there is more security and stability. A special silicone interfacing that cushions the bones has been developed, providing much greater comfort.

All of these technological advances have resulted in a new generation of prosthetics for those with very high level amputations. It makes walking a reality for many who would have given up in the past. Of course, in the case of a hemi-pelvectomy, even the pelvic bone for sitting is removed. The latest socket design provides the necessary containment in a flexible socket with a special silicone interfacing but still emphasizes anatomical contouring.

Both hip-disarticulation and hemi-pelvectomy amputees are totally dependent on a mechanical hip joint and the general mechanics of a prosthesis to walk, since there is no residual limb to move the prosthesis or stabilize an artificial knee. Attached to the socket is a modified, energy-storing hip joint. The joint has a self-activating spring which triggers flexion of the hip and knee, allowing an amputee to walk with less energy. In the latest design, the hip joint has been recessed into the socket to keep it from striking the chair when the amputee sits.

Below-The-Knee

A below-the-knee amputee usually has an easier time adapting to a prosthesis because the knee joint remains intact, making it easier to walk. But even below-the-knee prosthetics have seen significant advancement in recent years. A below-the-knee prosthesis used to be made very tight from front to back. The person's weight was concentrated on selected areas of the leg. But I've found success relying on bone and muscle contouring to distribute the weight properly. The latest below-the-knee socket does just that. The improved socket design now is being made even more comfortable with a silicone interfacing. And below-the-knee sockets continue to evolve.

Earlier designs used belts and straps to hold the leg on, but the trend is toward elastic sleeve suspension. The sleeve, which

*Bill Copeland, above-the-knee amputee, giving a new
prosthetic foot in research, a rugged test.*

resembles an athletic knee support, holds the leg in place with
tension and creates a slight suction effect that holds the leg
on. It provides better support and stability, while also allowing greater range of knee movement. One earlier design, still
in use, is called supracondylar suspension. The socket comes
up over the knee and clamps on above the joint. This design
isn't used as much because it limits knee flexion, and the
high trimline shows through trousers or pants.

Some below-the-knee amputees use suction sockets to
suspend the prosthesis, but this is rare. These usually only
work well on a more fleshy residual limb. Most amputees
prefer the other suspension options. Some even choose the
old belt and cuff suspension, especially those who do a lot of
manual labor.

Legs In Motion

I, again, want to emphasize that componentry is secondary.
Some amputees get very excited about all the advanced hips,
knees and feet. Sometimes an amputee goes looking for a

mechanical miracle when the real problem is the socket. A socket has to fit accurately and be comfortable before man-made gadgetry is going to help.

Having said that, there are a wealth of components that will aid individual amputees with their special problems. I want to touch on the main components, so you have a starting place. But if there is something special you want to be able to do, like sit Indian-style on the floor or rotate the ankle for a golf swing, there is a component that will allow you to do that. However, these "extras" usually add weight to your prosthesis. If doing one particular thing is important to you, ask if there is a component that will help you do it. But realize there may be trade-offs, like the additional weight and extra maintenance. A prosthetist will never be able to duplicate what God originally created, but technology is making more things possible.

When you start looking at the various components, you will find there are two major types: endoskeletal and exoskeletal. Endoskeletal means the components are inside, much like the human leg, with a cosmetic covering on the outside. The older, conventional legs were all exoskeletal—hollow inside, with the strength built into the outside wooden and plastic surface. Today, most legs are endoskeletal, but occasionally look exoskeletal because of a semi-soft covering. I'll talk more about coverings in the section on cosmetics.

Hydraulics have played a large role in helping amputees walk more naturally. Hydraulic knees have been on the market for years, but they weren't always popular. Their main drawbacks have always been weight and maintenance. A hydraulic cylinder is heavy, and when that heavy cylinder is put into a leg that is already heavy, the total weight becomes prohibitive. Now that the other parts of the leg—the pylon, socket and foot—are made with lightweight composites and plastics, an amputee can better tolerate the weight of a hydraulic knee. Improvements in hydraulics have also made the artificial knees more reliable.

A hydraulic knee offers cadence and gait control. When

35

you walk or run, it makes the swing movement of the knee more fluid and natural-looking. Hydraulics allow you to change your pace quickly and easily. Some hydraulics also provide a braking aid, which slows the knee if you start to fall. The knee will not always stop a fall, but it will slow it and may give you time to catch yourself and prevent the fall.

There is a knee that can prevent falls—one which often is used with weaker or older patients. It is known as the weight-activated safety knee and provides an extra measure of safety by acting as a mechanical brake.

A third, commonly used knee component is the manual locking knee, which has a switch to lock and unlock the knee. It is especially good for the hunter or fisherman who travels uneven, rough terrain or the older person who doesn't want to take any chances with a knee that automatically flexes. There are a variety of other knees, but these three are the most-common types.

As far as feet are concerned, the latest are flexible and energy-storing. They offer extra cushioning and shock absorption, which make walking easier. Several feet on the market incorporate the multi-axis principle. They adjust better to uneven surfaces and are especially useful to people, like farmers, who walk over rough terrain.

The Sabolich Foot is the first to bio-mechanically mimic the action of the natural arch in the human foot. Still in research and development, it will offer greater shock absorption than other prosthetic feet, and will help conserve energy, promote a natural gait, and allow side-to-side motion. Roger Charter tested the foot when he became the first bilateral amputee to run step-over-step.

One other foot option is an adjustable foot. Women who have had amputations frequently ask: "Will I be able to wear high heels again?" Years ago the answer was "no," but the latest designs in feet allow women to wear a variety of shoes, from flats to high heels. Some women even choose to have a number of feet to accommodate different heel heights. The choice

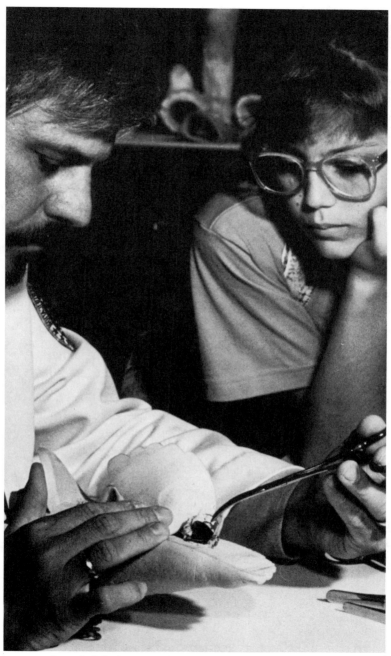

*John Sabolich shows Sarah East, above-the-knee amputee, the
transducer in the Sabolich Sense-of-Feel System.*

is up to the individual, but you should remember that the lower the heel, the easier it is to walk with your prosthesis.

Again, these are just a few of the options in feet. You could write another book just listing all the available components. All the different components that we are not describing further reinforces the need for good communication with your prosthetist. During your evaluation, make sure you discuss your needs and options.

REGAINING FEELING

Perhaps one of the most exciting things under development for amputees is the Sense-of-Feel System, introduced in 1990. The idea of an amputee actually "feeling" the foot on the floor or pressure against the fingers is something I'd thought about for a long time. Testing has been primarily on lower extremity amputees up to this point. As I mentioned earlier, I hope in addition to a new sense of security and balance, it will give amputees some relief from phantom pain.

In the early 1980s, I began to work with amputees on gait training, using a beeper system. The beeper would tell the person when the foot was on the floor. It became apparent that when the beeper was turned off, some would stumble. Sense-of-Feel takes that concept further. With the beeper, the amputees became reliant on the beep for the timing of their walk and heel-toe sequence. It was reasoned that if a mere beeper had that kind of effect, then what effect would actual feeling have? The Sense-of-Feel System consists of pressure transducers incorporated into the sole of the artificial foot. The transducers respond proportionally to pressure on individual areas of the foot and send signals to electrodes in the socket. The sensors give the amputee a tingling sensation in the residual limb — the greater the pressure, the greater the sensation.

In effect, the brain is once again in communication with the floor via the artificial foot. Several different sensors, incorporated into the sole of the prosthetic foot, tell the amputee which part of the foot is experiencing pressure. For example,

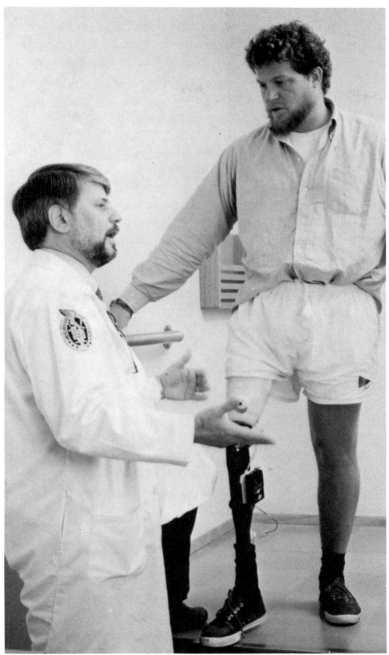

Teddy Kennedy, Jr., above-the-knee amputee, and John Sabolich discussing the Sabolich Sense-of-Feel System that Teddy was testing.

when pressure is placed on the transducer in the ball of the foot, signals are sent to the skin on the forward section of the amputee's residual limb. When improved communication with the brain is established, the amputee has better balance —making walking or running easier.

While researching Sense-of-Feel (SOF), an interesting phenomenon surfaced, which is called "cerebral projection." We discovered that in some instances, when patients began to really visualize their legs and feet, the image became so real that they could actually "feel" toes bending and heels pushing against the ground. With cerebral projection, the amputees felt more comfortable with their prostheses. This phenomenon made the amputees feel like they had "life" in their artificial limbs. They had less limp, their gaits improved, and they walked more naturally.

Exactly to what degree Sense-of-Feel will help phantom pain remains to be seen. But judging by what amputees who have tried the system tell me, I believe it has promise.

Additionally, Sense-of-Feel has several other applications. For new amputees, it may help prevent damage to delicate tissue immediately following an amputation. Because the amputee feels a greater tingling in proportion to the amount of pressure being placed on the foot, it sends an early warning if too much pressure is being placed on the prosthesis. Consequently, the amputee can adjust the pressure, so the residual limb will not be damaged. Aside from amputees, the system may be helpful in the treatment of head injury and paraplegic patients, as well as diabetics who have little or no feeling in the soles of their feet and need some type of warning device or aid to help them gain better balance.

The National Institutes of Health's (NIH) new National Center for Medical Rehabilitation and Research has awarded a Phase I and Phase II grant for funding of research and testing on the SOF System. Balance and gait are being evaluated to determine if the SOF device improves these functions, as previous subjective testing has indicated. Computerized gait lab analysis studies will provide quantified measures for both balance and ambulation with and without the SOF device. One of the spinoffs from this testing has been the Hot and Cold Sensory System, which allows an amputee to feel fluctuations in temperature on their residual limb.

It is very encouraging to have the federal government recognize and support the need for prosthetic and orthotic research in the private sector.

Research on the SOF and Hot and Cold Sensory Systems has implications for other areas of disability. We have also received a Phase I grant from the NIH for a study with the Sense of Feel System as a Neuropathic Foot System, which will provide a protective sensation to patients with insensate feet.

Research on adaptation of SOF for use with myoelectric arms and hands has begun. This is especially important for hands since it enables the person to feel how much pressure is being applied when doing a variety of things, from shaking hands...to holding a delicate object like an egg.

THE SHAPE AND FORM OF THINGS

Shape and form of a leg is important to a lot of amputees, especially women. Some women want a leg to look good so they can recapture their feelings of femininity after an amputation. The size and shape of a leg is important to many men, as well.

Some people may tell you, "Well, you've had a leg amputated, so you'll just have to get used to the look of a prosthesis." Cosmetic coverings have come a long way, but they still have a long way to go. Frankly, even though our lab was able to create a leg for model Ivy Gunter that allowed her to return to her career, much research is still needed in the area of cosmetics. Sculpturing something that closely resembles a human limb is an art form. Further studies with various silicones that will improve shape, skin texture, and coloration are now underway at our research lab.

If cosmetic appeal is especially important to you, you

need to tell your prosthetist early in the fitting process. You need to start thinking about shape long before the covering goes on. Sometimes, you may have to choose between a small bulge in the shape and the perfect alignment of the prosthesis. It may mean a sacrifice in the way you walk if you want a more perfectly shaped leg. But it is a decision you have the right to make.

The highly-cosmetic coverings are soft, one-piece designs and can be damaged if you lead a very athletic lifestyle. That doesn't mean you can't take a hike or bike ride, but if you want to run competitively or play regularly on a softball team, I recommend a hard or semi-soft, two-piece cover. It isn't as cosmetic, but it is more durable. This cover has to be split at the knee for above-the-knee amputees, forming a two-piece covering. For that reason, it sometimes is mistaken for an exoskeletal leg even though all the components are inside the cosmetic shell. Also, the two-piece leg design tends to allow a smoother walk since there is no foam covering to interfere with knee action. Of course, many amputee athletes choose not to wear any cosmetic covering at all since it's lighter and doesn't inhibit knee movement.

For men, simulated hair and veins can be added to the leg. The technology is available to apply real hair, but it is rarely done because it is costly and time-consuming.

Many of the same cosmetic principles used for artificial legs apply for upper body prostheses as well. You will want to discuss these options with your prosthetist. As I conclude this discussion on cosmetics, I want to point out that even with as much as a prosthetist can do to improve the looks of an artificial limb, the prosthetic leg or arm still isn't flesh and blood. If you have extremely high expectations for the look of the arm or leg, you may be disappointed. Computer-aided design may one day take the guesswork out of sculpting an artificial limb, but this technology is still in the primitive stages.

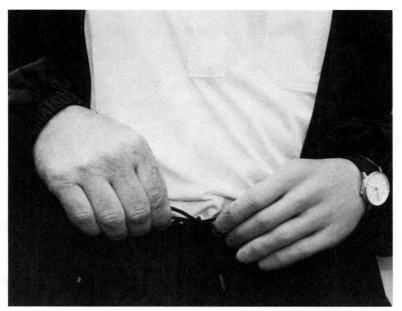

The myo-electric hand resembles the human hand cosmetically.

UPPER LIMBS: REACHING FOR A NEW WORLD

The loss of an arm or hand may be more difficult to adjust to than the loss of a leg. Not only is it more visible, but the complicated function of a hand is much harder to duplicate than a leg or a foot.

The good news is that even upper extremity amputees have more options today than ever before. At one time, a hook was the only prosthesis available to someone who lost an arm or hand. Myoelectric arms more closely resemble the human arm and hand, and are more cosmetically pleasing than hooks. Powered electronically by muscle movement, myoelectrics were developed in the 1960s and have recently become available in proportionally-controlled designs. The proportional control allows movement of the arm and hand at different speeds, depending on the amputee's muscle movement.

Early fitting is the key to successful prosthetic use for those who have lost arms, whether you choose a hook or a myoelectric arm. Going more than a few months without a prosthesis greatly reduces the amputee's success rate. Why? You become mentally one-handed, learning to do everything with the remaining hand. Then, it becomes a chore to relearn everything with a prosthesis. If you learn initially with a prosthesis, it becomes more second nature.

Early fitting with a passive hand is especially important for babies born without limbs. A baby needs to start wearing a prosthesis by three to four months and no later than six months. Fitted after that, a child often rejects the prosthesis as a foreign object and resists wearing it.

Just as with lower extremity amputations, the more joints that are removed, the harder it is for the amputee to adapt. Generally, a below-the-elbow amputee will have an easier time learning to use a prosthesis than an above-the-elbow amputee. The elbow function and the rotary movement of the shoulder are both lost when the amputation is above the elbow.

Also, if the residual limb is left excessively long — as with disarticulations at the wrist and elbow — there is a problem with the space required for the artificial joint. Often the lower forearm must be made shorter to compensate for the length after a joint is attached to the prosthesis. Shoulder disarticulation amputees have problems similar to those with hip-disarticulations — a big shoulder socket normally has to wrap around the shoulder. Recently, however, smaller shoulder cap designs have been developed, reducing the size of the prosthetic shoulder socket.

Hooks, switch-controlled electronic arms, myoelectric arms, and combinations of the two are all available. Hooks are usually body-powered and are operated by cables attached to a harness strapped around the shoulders. Movement of the shoulder opens and closes some hooks, while others are electronically-powered. Alternatively, myoelectric arms are muscle-controlled. A small electrode in the arm socket picks up electrical signals as the muscles in the residual limb contract, which in turn triggers operation of the elbow, wrist and fingers. For instance, one muscle group initiates opening of the hand, while another group closes the hand. It takes some training and effort to learn to use the muscles that operate the arms and hands. I recommend physical and occupational therapy for most patients who have lost arms — especially for those with high level amputations, like shoulder disarticulations. It is often difficult to find a physical therapist who has experience with myoelectric arms, since these amputations are not as common. It may take some research to find an experienced therapist.

The elbow can be myoelectric or switch-controlled. Frequently, hybrid (combination) systems are used, with a switch-controlled elbow, but myoelectric wrist and fingers. Many adaptations can be made to a myoelectric prosthesis.

I prefer myoelectrics over hooks for two simple reasons: if you're going to wear an upper body prosthesis, an arm is more accepted than a hook in our society, and most things are made for hands — not hooks. With advanced technology, myoelectrics are much more functional as well. The grip of a myoelectric hand is much stronger than a hook, which usually depends on rubber bands to close it. Amputees also find they can do many things with myoelectric hands that they can't do with hooks. However, even the best myoelectric hand is only able to duplicate a small portion of what the actual human hand can do. Yet what it can do is significant and practical for a person who has lost a hand.

Frankly, hook versus hand is a center of controversy. Many physicians, prosthetists and patients debate the issue. Some professionals are dogmatic about prescribing use of a hook because they are used to hooks and feel myoelectric hands are too expensive and break down too frequently. While the trend is to myoelectrics, many people are able to use hooks effectively in their work and do not want to change.

Ken Whitten, who lost both his arms, and Chuck Tiemann, who lost one, both say it's important to them not to look like "Captain Hook". For that reason, they both

45

*Jamila Mohammad, above-the-knee amputee,
enjoying summer fun.*

chose myoelectrics over hooks. Both like their myoelectric arms and hands because they look more natural — but both have gone through the frustration of breaking the mechanical arms as they tested the limits of the prostheses. Myoelectrics work well but are far from perfect. Mechanical failure is one of the drawbacks. Upper extremity prosthetics have come a long way and are constantly being improved. But there is still much research to be done to even begin to come close to mimicking the function of a real human hand. Despite that, many people have found a great deal of success with myoelectric arms and hands. And with the right attitude, you can learn to use and accept a myoelectric arm or hand as a part of your body.

CHILD AMPUTEES

One mother says she couldn't bear to look at her new baby who was born without a leg. Another fears what family and friends will say when they see the tiny limbless infant. Yet another blames herself and is so angry that she can only sit and cry. These feelings are not uncommon, most parents are devastated when a child is born without an arm or leg. Initially, there is a lot of guilt and soul searching. Every parent expects nothing less than a "perfect" newborn.

It is equally traumatic when a child is diagnosed with cancer or injured in an accident. A parent probably faces no greater emotional dilemma than that of deciding whether the arm or leg of a son or daughter should be amputated. In the final analysis, it may come down to amputating the limb or losing the child. And there are no easy answers. In many cases, the child handles it better than the parents.

I guess the best advice is to realize that you're not alone, and there is hope. Parents who have gone through the experience say watching their children grow up as amputees isn't nearly as bad as they originally imagined. Many times parents anticipate problems that never even materialize. The toughest part is accepting the amputation and treating a child amputee as you would any other child. Love your son or daughter with all your heart and offer the support that's needed, but don't become overindulgent just because of the loss of a limb. Coddling and spoiling will only slow the child's journey to acceptance of the amputation and deny growth of healthy, positive self-esteem.

Children who are fitted early with prosthetic limbs almost always accept them and do quite well. They run, jump, bike, participate in sports, hang out with their friends, and grow up too fast — just like other kids. Generally, they learn to do most everything, even though sometimes they have to do it a little differently.

In recent years, I have developed a cosmetic and functional infant prosthesis that weighs as little as two ounces. That compares with the older prostheses which weighed two to four pounds. It's called the Oklahoma Infant Leg (OIL) and utilizes expanded polyethylene to form a one-piece, ultra-light jointed leg. It provides flexibility in the socket, as well as the joints, and is available for all amputation levels. Designed for the 3-month to 24-month age group, it is great for those early developmental stages of infancy, crawling, and later, beginning walking. The prosthesis is soft, waterproof and can be made to smell like baby powder, which seems to make acceptance of the artificial leg a little easier.

It's critical that mom and dad accept the amputation, too. Many parents spend years blaming and questioning themselves — wondering if they did something that resulted in the amputation. But the "why" isn't really important. The solution is what is important. Parents need to get past the self-blame and pity stage if they are going to help their child. Sometimes that means counseling. One parent says she couldn't have gotten through it without help from a child psychologist. If that's what it takes, it's certainly appropriate. But, by all means, find someone with whom you can talk. You can't help your child if you remain bitter about the loss. A parent who has been through the experience can be especially supportive. Ask your doctor or prosthetist for the names of parents you might call, or check out the special support groups for parents.

WHAT ABOUT FINANCIAL COSTS?

In the midst of all the emotional trauma of amputation, you also are forced to deal with the financial picture. The cost of a prosthesis varies, depending on the level of your amputation. Generally, the higher the amputation, the greater the cost. High-tech componentry, advanced designs, and special technical procedures also add to the cost. The cost of an electronic arm can be significantly higher than a leg. The same consumer rules apply when you purchase a prosthesis as when you buy anything else: if someone offers you a deal that sounds too good to be true, it probably is.

When you buy a prosthesis, realize that you are purchasing both a service and a product. Just as you want to make sure an auto dealership will be able to service your car, you need to have confidence in your prosthetic service. Service is especially important because it is not only the future service, but proper fitting when you first get your prosthesis. You are paying for experience, knowledge and expertise more so than you are with your car. You'd never buy a car without asking questions, so ask questions and get the answers before you settle on a prosthesis.

The bottom line is that you want a prosthesis that is comfortable, functional and fits your lifestyle. You can take charge of your prosthetic care by understanding a few basic things. The good news is that many insurance plans, including Medicare, pay for a portion of the cost of a prosthesis. To determine what your policy will pay, contact your insurance agent or group health plan division. Ask if prosthetics are covered and if there are any limitations. Your prosthetic center may even have a financial counselor or business office that can check on your insurance coverage for you.

Most importantly, find out what type of documentation

you need to submit with your claim. All insurance companies require documentation of need. Your doctor will write a prescription for your prosthesis, and it will be the primary source for documentation. For that reason, it is important to communicate your lifestyle needs to your doctor and make sure he understands your entire health background. For instance, a heart condition or other medical problems that necessitate regular exercise certainly would justify your need for a particular type of prosthesis. Just saying that you dream of running again will not get the insurance company to pay for a high-tech running leg. You and your doctor will want to discuss your needs at home and on the job as a part of documenting the need for a prosthesis. Documentation from allied health professionals, like your physical therapist and perhaps your prosthetist, also may be beneficial in establishing your case for payment. You should realize that with rising health costs, insurance companies are constantly looking at cost containment, so your case of need must be well documented if you expect payment.

You may also want to find out what your avenues of appeal are if payment is denied. You are fully justified in asking "why" if your insurance company refuses payment for a portion of your prosthetic care. It may be a simple breakdown in communication of your needs. If you are covered by a group plan, ask your employer to go to bat for you. Insurance companies are highly competitive, and their clients tend to have some leverage in payment of justified claims.

Medicare will pay for prosthetics, although benefits are restricted. Currently, benefits through the Veteran's Administration are also limited.

So, what if you don't have insurance or your insurance benefits don't cover prosthetics? There is still help available. Check on medical assistance through Medicaid or your state vocational rehabilitation program. In some states, medical assistance is also available through non-profit agencies or charities.

GRIEVING AND GETTING ON WITH LIFE

There are no simple formulas for dealing emotionally with the loss of a limb. And there is nothing wrong with grieving. In fact, it is a healthy part of inner healing after an amputation. Everyone grieves in his or her own way. Some amputees say crying, or even screaming at the top of their lungs, helps release a lot of anger and frustration that accompanies tragedy.

Grief and denial are very natural first steps for an amputee. Acknowledging the grief and anger is important as you begin the journey to acceptance of the amputation. And, again, it all boils down to acceptance. You need to admit to yourself that you have suffered a loss and that it is painful. Grieve over the loss. Then, put it behind you. Look toward the future with hope, but live in today.

I know that sounds simple for me to say, but it is all part of the process that many amputees have shared with me over the years. Initially, you may be haunted by the questions "Why me, God?" or "Why did this happen to me?" These are common questions, but they can also become barriers to getting on with your life if you dwell on them. The real question is not "Why did I deserve this?" but "How am I going to deal with what has happened?" As an old farmer once said: "It doesn't matter how the horse got into the ditch. What matters is how you get him out."

How you feel about yourself should be controlled by only one person — you. Don't let a stubborn sense of pride stand in your way, and don't let someone else's yardstick of success measure your life or sense of self-worth. Sometimes we are too self-critical and try to measure up to someone else's definition of what we "ought" to be, which is self-defeating. More so than at any other time in your life, you need to learn now to value yourself for who you are — and never forget that you are okay just the way you are.

Don't be surprised if just when you think you are getting a grip on the situation, you suffer a set-back or two. During your hospital stay, where a round-the-clock staff

51

serves your needs, you may be lulled into a false sense of independence. Things seem easier then. Many amputees report that returning home is a real shock when they suddenly discover their house and previous way of living doesn't necessarily fit the lifestyle of an amputee. You may have a two-story house, your bathroom may not be arranged so you can easily maneuver, and even getting up out of that easy chair to go to the kitchen may now seem like an enormous task. But it's nothing you can't manage with time. Remember, time is your ally — emotionally and physically, you are going to get better with time.

You may face depression and anxiety over the changes you need to make in your life. You may feel like your life is out of control. There may be a feeling of helplessness and even shame over your new physical appearance. That's all very common. You may need counseling. Despair or extended depression can lead to thoughts of suicide in some cases. Don't wait until then to get help. Every amputee needs someone to talk to, and some may need a professional counselor or therapist. You should understand that the changes an amputee goes through also affect the family, so family members may find professional counseling helpful, as well. You needn't be ashamed of that.

Family members can provide a real source of strength and support for an amputee, or they can add to the struggles, making the person psychologically, physically and emotionally dependent. Caring family members may try to do everything for the amputee, not realizing they set the stage for the person to feel like — and become — an invalid. The most important ingredient to family readjustment is communication. Take time to talk about the amputation with your loved ones; share your feelings, as well as hopes and dreams. It may help to have one or two particularly supportive members of the family involved in discussions with your doctor and prosthetist.

And what about talking to your children about your

amputation? Some parents are hesitant, but some go overboard trying to explain what has happened. It's important to remember to give children "age-appropriate" information. You don't want to scare them so that they have nightmares. On the other hand, you want to give them enough information that they aren't afraid they're going to lose you. Talk to them as you would about other things happening in your life. Answer their questions. But most importantly, don't let your amputation stop you from enjoying those special moments together.

Amputation is a life-changing experience. Some people are better equipped to deal with it than others, just as some people are better able to deal with the death of a loved one or close friend. In fact, some amputees compare the grief that you go through after an amputation with the death of a close friend or relative. It can be very traumatic, and you may experience a roller coaster of emotions.

One of the keys to getting back into life after amputation is to put things in perspective and deal with one thing at a time. There's no need to feel like you have to be perfect at every task. Again, don't be so critical of yourself. You don't have to be bigger than life to be a success just because you are an amputee. Enjoy the successes — no matter how small — and don't dwell on the setbacks. If you constantly feel you have to "prove" yourself, you'll only end up adding additional unnecessary stress to your life. And who needs that? Such an outlook on life will be frustrating and difficult for you, as well as for those around you. Remember, the goal is to make steady progress — not to do everything perfectly. It is a continuing process. You can't turn everything around in five minutes, five days or even five months. Give yourself some time.

You need to look at the amputation not as an end to life, but the beginning of a new stage in life. Sure, there will be changes, but those changes need not all be negative. Many amputees report discovery of a greater enjoyment and appreciation of life after an amputation — along with a greater appreciation for many things people take for granted. Why? Rather than focusing on the "I can'ts," they choose to embrace the possibilities of all that life has to offer.

For some people, the road to acceptance leads them on a spiritual journey that puts them much more in touch with what life is all about. I've found that amputees who are firmly grounded in a spiritual faith seem to do better and adjust more quickly. With God as a companion, they don't seem to experience that deep sense of "aloneness" that some other amputees struggle with. Their personal faith sustains and strengthens them through the toughest hours. Some amputees do not speak directly of God, but they admit their survival and success hinges on calling upon an indescribable inner strength which each person possesses. Those who call upon that inner strength, whether or not they connect it with God, tend to be highly motivated and committed to making life as an amputee happy and fulfilling. The journey of each amputee is similar, but no two are the same. Only you can ultimately decide which direction you will travel.

As an amputee, you can do most anything you did before, although you may not do it exactly the same way. There's usually no need to give up driving, working, dating, sports, hobbies, or recreational activities just because you are an amputee. Decide what you want to do and try it. Sometimes you may have to force yourself to get back into an activity. You may be self-conscious about being an amputee, especially at first. But how you approach an activity will influence how others respond to you. In other words, should you decide to live like an invalid, people will tend to treat you that way. If you decide to live with amputation as one of life's challenges, people will most likely treat you as they always did. Only you can determine when you will put self-pity aside and move ahead. To some amputees the word "depression" is only another word for "self-pity." That may sound harsh at first, but self-pity only turns you inward, thinking of "poor me," and that leads to depression. It can be a vicious cycle. You have to get out of that cycle — focus on something larger than yourself. Being depressed and feeling sorry for yourself won't change the fact that you are an amputee. But wallowing in pity will certainly cripple you for life.

"The key is that in my own mind I don't set myself apart from everyone else," says one amputee. She simply doesn't put herself in the "amputee category" but sees herself as a whole person. Developing that confidence and positive self-esteem is not something that just happens a week, a month, or even a year after an amputation. For some people, it comes quite easily, but most of us have to work at it and cultivate it. And I should note that self-confidence and a sense of wholeness is not dependent on the fact that you wear a prosthesis. Naturally, I see more people who wear artificial limbs, but some amputees choose not to — more often those who have lost arms than legs. Those people still have full, rich lives and find wholeness without limbs. What feels comfortable for one amputee may not be right for another. To many people, a prosthesis becomes like a part of the body. It's incorporated into the self-image, and the amputee doesn't want to be without it. Whatever the choice — with or without a prosthesis — it does not make an amputee any more or less whole as a human being.

As you work on confidence and feelings of self-worth, you may find valuable information and new friends through an amputee support group. Such support groups are growing across the nation. Even if there isn't one in your community, the various groups have newsletters and can give you names of other amputees to call. But your total support group need not be confined to amputees. Counselors often tell people who are having difficulty facing any life change to get involved. You can find new friends through church or community organizations. Some people have discovered volunteer work — an opportunity to help someone else — is a step toward personal healing. As they help others in need, they also help themselves to heal emotionally.

You may be hesitant to take the risk to make new acquaintances at first, especially if you are looking for a dating relationship. But again, if you can relax and be yourself, most likely, others will accept you as you are. I've talked with many amputees who are bothered by people who stare at them. How do you deal with that? I think you have to realize that people have a natural curiosity about anything or anybody that is different. They aren't necessarily staring because they find you're ugly. After all, aren't you inclined to take that second glance if you see someone who is taller, shorter, or more beautiful than the norm? If they have questions, you can provide honest answers. Why not educate them a little? You have a wealth of knowledge to share. If you feel at ease with yourself, they likely will feel at ease also.

If a relationship or friendship fails, it's not going to be just because you are an amputee. Don't take it personally... look at the fact that these things happen every day to all of us. You may meet the occasional rude character who is so biased he can't accept anyone who is different, but chalk that person up as narrow-minded — like you would if you weren't an amputee — and go on. On the other hand, don't use amputation as a scapegoat. It may be easy to blame shortcomings, whether in a relationship or at a job, on the fact you are an amputee. You'll only be cheating yourself.

So what about male/female relationships? Invariably, amputees have questions about sexual intimacy. Normally, there is no physical reason for avoiding an intimate relationship. If you are married or have been in a long-term relationship, most amputees say the answer is communication with your partner. One amputee said she struggled with the fact that she and her husband began to develop more of a brother-sister relationship, avoiding intimacy after her amputation. It was a matter of communicating. Her husband was simply afraid he might hurt her residual limb. Often for women, this is a time when they must re-establish those feelings of femininity, while men want to prove that they are still masculine.

Ivy Gunter

Amputee Ivy Gunter admits her initial reaction was to ignore her residual limb. "It took me almost a year to stand in front of a full-length mirror," she adds. Those kinds of feelings can translate into fear of what your mate or companion will feel and make you question whether you will ever again be sexually attractive.

"When I first lost my leg, it was all so new. My first thought was that my husband, Don, would leave . . . that the physical appearance of a wife with one leg would simply be too much for him and that he might leave me," says Ivy. "My presentation into the bedroom changed from the allure of slinking in dressed in a Christian Dior gown, to wheeling into the room in my wheelchair, crutching in, hopping — or even crawling in. I was determined to regain the sensuality and sexuality that I once had."

Sensuality and sexuality are sensitive subjects — and it may take some time for you to work through your feelings. Try to be honest and open with yourself, as well as with your mate.

What about children? Many female amputees are concerned about pregnancy. One may wonder if she can even get pregnant, while another has doubts about carrying a child to full term. In most cases, an amputation should have nothing to do with whether you can have children. Of course, pregnancy means additional weight and volume changes. It may necessitate prosthetic socket changes, but most women continue to wear their prostheses throughout pregnancy.

Returning to work may or may not be a traumatic experience, depending on what type of work you do. Many amputees find a whole new support group among their peers at work. If you have to find a new job, you may have feelings of self-doubt rekindled when, for the first time you have to include on a job application that you are an amputee. Don't let that deter your ambition. If you are qualified for the job, go after it.

Other than job applications, you are not obliged to announce to everyone you work with that you are an amputee. One patient said a co-worker never knew she was an amputee. He noticed she limped occasionally but thought it was just an injured knee or something. Even when people ask about your leg or arm, you are not compelled to go into a complete medical history. An elaborate explanation isn't always necessary. Again, your attitude will affect those around you and how they respond to you. If you do decide to share your story, many times people gain a new respect for you — that in spite of an amputation, you have persevered and overcome many hurdles.

I have found that amputees have had such defining experiences that their maturity levels far exceed those of able-bodied persons the same age. Having dealt with amputation has so defined their characters and broadened their perspective of themselves and others that I want to "grow" in the same way they have. I want to share time with them and be with them, and I think other people feel the same way. Amputation is not a drawback; it can be an advantage in relationships.

Regardless of what happens in our lives, I am learning that the only person you can really change is yourself. Developing a positive attitude means putting the loss of a limb in perspective — looking at it along side all the other things that are important to you. Put your life in perspective and focus on what you can do, instead of what you can't do. It's good advice for amputees, as well as the rest of us. Learning to accept our strengths and weaknesses, while cultivating a positive self-concept, is a long road for many people. But that is exactly what many of the amputees in You're Not Alone have struggled with. They have courageously shared their intimate journeys in their stories, and I hope you will take time to read each of them.

I encourage you to first select stories about people with amputations similar to yours — but don't forget to read the others for additional advice from amputees who have been through it all — the feelings, the frustrations, and the struggles mixed with success, the changes and the journey to new life. Each amputee has a special wisdom and insight to share that will help you cope, stretch, grow — become.

Ken Whitten

It's a Two-Handed World

KEN WHITTEN, 30

*He was working for a power company when a
bizarre accident sent thousands of volts of
electricity pulsating through his body. The electrocution
forced amputation of the right arm below the
elbow and left arm above the elbow. He became one of
the first to wear two myoelectric arms.*

The day was strange from the start. I was chief of the underground crew for Duncan Oklahoma Power and Light. But that October day in 1986, the company was pulling new overhead lines from one of the power substations. They asked our underground crew to help the overhead crew.

The foreman went over the details of the job. I spent much of the morning at the trailer where we unrolled the large spool of wire that was to be strung. We worked several hours and stopped for a short coffee break. Afterward, we had to splice one of the lines, but the line had to be hung so that the splice was not over the roadway. Since I had more climbing experience, I volunteered to climb the pole to pull the splice down.

I didn't know the safety guards had slipped or that the line was carrying 7,620 volts of electricity. All of the lines were supposed to be dead.

61

I grabbed the line. I don't recall feeling anything. The next thing I remember was awaking on the road as crew members went through rescue procedures. I drifted in and out of consciousness as the helicopter flew me to the hospital at Duncan.

Emergency room doctors had to cut off my work gloves. I remember looking at my hands. I didn't think they looked so bad. They packed them in ice. I talked briefly with my supervisor. The next thing I knew, I was on a chopper headed for Baptist Burn Center in Oklahoma City. I heard someone say the flight would take 30 to 40 minutes. Then, I was out.

At the burn center, they placed me on a gurney and rolled me into a room with a big bathtub. They stripped off my clothes. It was embarrassing. I asked for a towel to cover myself as 10 to 15 doctors and nurses stood looking at me.

Later, I awoke in the intensive care unit. The doctors told me I had to make a decision. They wanted to cut off my hands. They told me gangrene would set in if they didn't. "Well, take them off," I told them, as I fell back asleep. I wasn't thinking about losing my hands then, but about pulling through . . . about staying alive. I don't remember waking again until after the operation.

My wife, Alicia, had to make arrangements for the surgery. I don't know how long it was before I awoke again in ICU. I was thirsty. I reached out to grab a glass of ice water on my bedside table. I couldn't do it. My hands were gone. I couldn't even get a drink of water. It made me mad, and I started to cry.

I wasn't bitter or mad at any particular person, but I wanted to know what happened. As I asked questions about the accident, they told me my friend Carl was dead. The accident that had left me with no hands had taken Carl's life. He was only four poles away from me at the time

— at the trailer where I had been only shortly before the accident.

The doctors kept me on a high-powered pain killer. Most of the time, I only felt the pressure of the swollen limbs. I had a lot of what they told me were phantom sensations. I'd think my hands were there — I'd reach out for everything, but I couldn't grasp anything. The only real pain I remember was when they cleaned the wounds and cut away the dead skin. Then, they can't give you enough medication to take the pain away.

I was in the hospital 36 days. As the days wore on, I began to realize the number of things I could no longer do for myself . . . things I had to ask others to do for me. Little things, like dab my runny nose. Or, when I went to the bathroom, and I had to ring for the nurse to wipe me. It was humiliating. It's those little things that people don't think about that really bother you.

A psychologist visited me, wanting to talk about the accident and what I was feeling. I was stubborn. I didn't much want to talk to him. He kept asking me how I felt about losing my arms. I was upset — what did he want me to say? I had friends who came to talk with me. I didn't want to talk about the accident with a stranger.

I wasn't at all sure how my three kids were going to react. They hadn't seen me since the accident, so Alicia was going to bring them to the hospital. I didn't know what I would do or say. I just kept thinking about how my boy loved baseball. How was I going to play ball with him? How was I going to do all the things with the kids that I used to? When they arrived, I met them at the door. The three of them ran and gave me big hugs. I cried. All they cared about was that I was up and walking, and that they could see me again. They knew Carl was dead.

Of course like all kids, they were curious. My 3-year-old daughter wanted to know how long it would be until

my hands grew back. But I think by the time they left the hospital, they were satisfied that I was going to be okay.

Sometime during the second week of my hospital stay, an occupational therapist made me a cuff to go on my arm. With it, I was able to eat and brush my teeth. As I felt better, I began to feel cooped up. I worked out in the hospital weight room, using weights on my legs. The doctors weren't too keen on that idea, however.

I didn't think too much about artificial limbs. No one talked about prostheses. Frankly, as I lay there in the hospital bed, my biggest concern was that while I was there and away from my job, the bills were piling up. How was I going to pay for all this? In the meantime, a lot of my friends were researching what was available for me in the world of prosthetics. During my third week in the hospital, a prosthetist paid me a visit. We discussed the options of myoelectric arms or hooks. Few people in the United States had ever worn two myoelectric arms, and everyone kept telling me it would be too hard. They said I'd be too confused because the arm muscles make the hands work, and it would be hard to work two arms. They kept telling me I needed at least one hook.

But there really wasn't anyone around who had experienced what I was going through. No one could tell me what it was going to be like . . . how I could function without hands . . . or how I could go back to work. Few people have lost both hands. One amputee who had lost one arm came to see me, but his visits only depressed me. He had a myoelectric arm, but he wasn't very encouraging. When I got out of the hospital, I wanted to be able to do everything I'd done before. He just wanted to sit in an office and do paperwork.

The real test came when I was allowed to leave the hospital for Thanksgiving. It all hit me then. I was faced with the reality of life without my hands. All the family was gathered at our home for the holiday dinner. I had my cuff, but Alicia still had to cut my meat and help feed me. It was tough being around all the family . . . kind of embarrassing. I wanted to be back to normal and do everything I always did. There were things I wanted to get done around the house, but I couldn't. It was so frustrating. My hands had quit, but my brain hadn't stopped. I couldn't take it — I wanted to go back to the hospital.

Three or four days before I was to be permanently dismissed from the hospital, the doctors discovered the muscle in my lower left arm didn't function. For weeks, they had been finding dead tissue. They re-amputated the left arm at the elbow. Little did I know it would be the first of several surgeries, including a bone spur operation and a revision surgery that would allow room for a myoelectric elbow. I ended up with the left arm amputated above the elbow and the right arm below the elbow. I began to think the amputations would never end.

It was tough leaving the hospital. While I was there, the nurses did everything for me. I knew from my experience at Thanksgiving that things weren't going to be as easy at home. One of the first things I did when I got home was go out to the barn. In addition to my job at the power company, I farmed. I just walked and walked around the barn. I thought about all the things that needed to be done . . . all the things I couldn't do. One day I tried wearing a hook. As I gazed at my shadow against the barn door, it looked like a huge dagger. That was all for the hook.

I was determined this was not going to get the best of me. Within two weeks, I was driving the car. I'd just put my arms in the steering wheel and go. I wanted to see how people were going to react. I wanted to get back into circulation. All along, I knew I'd go back to work. I wanted to work so something like this didn't happen to anyone else.

It was July, 1987, when I got my first temporary prosthesis on my right arm, but it was February, 1988, before all the surgeries were complete and I had two working myoelectric arms. Just getting two new prosthetic arms couldn't solve all my problems though. It takes a lot of muscle control to use the arms, and it takes a lot of practice. I remember sitting for hours picking up potato chips with my new hands, or crushing soda cans. I'd have Alicia toss dimes on the table, and I'd try to pick them up. I wanted to see what I could do.

Some things I learned easily, like writing. Other things took a lot more patience . . . patience I didn't have. I remember standing in the barn several times and getting so mad I thought I was going to go crazy. I'd be trying to do something simple, like fix the lawnmower. All I needed to do was turn the screwdriver, but I couldn't do it with my immobile prosthetic wrists. Then, I'd be doing something else and a hand would break. Or, I'd fire up the chain saw and it would interfere with the battery-operated hands. One day, I got so mad I beat the arm against the barn wall. This is a two-handed world. Everything is built for the human hand.

Why . . . why did this happen to me? Why didn't I get to die? Why was I left on earth to survive with something less than I came in with? I didn't understand why it all happened to me. At the same time, I'd always preached to the kids not to give up. How could I show them not to give up? How could I live what I preached?

Then, one day I pulled into the parking lot at the doctor's office. A lady with a walker was struggling to get out of her car, so I went to help her. I was wearing a long-sleeved shirt, so it wasn't until we reached the office door that she noticed something wrong with my arms. "Oh, I see you've got problems, too," she said. I guess I realized then that I could still help someone else.

67

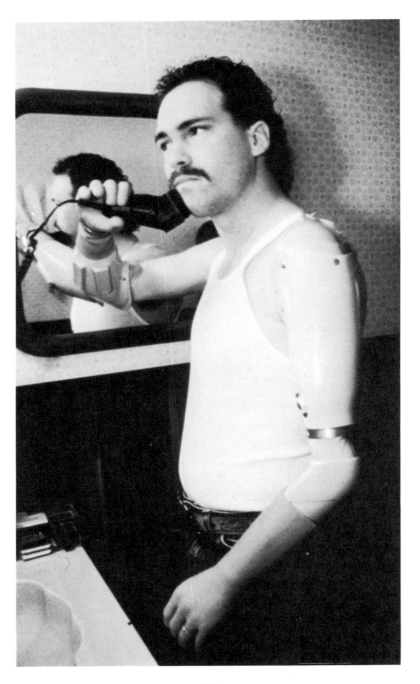

68

I may never come to grips with having someone help me do things that I used to be able to do myself. I still want to be able to do everything, and every day is a new challenge. I work with my prosthetist alot, and so far, he's been able to make changes in the arms and hands to help me do whatever I wanted to try. From the beginning, he worked very closely with my doctors on the revision surgery to make sure I'd be able to get the best use of the myoelectric arms. He recently added a ball joint at my wrist so I can scratch my ear or comb my hair. I think he likes the challenge, too, and wants to see how far he can go to improve the arms.

Even if you can do things for yourself, it doesn't stop other people from assuming you can't. I still had my job at the power company, but it was a fight to get them to let me go back to work because of the company's insurance firm. I had been classified as 100 percent disabled. First, they didn't understand why I was going back to work. When I convinced them I was going to work, they insisted on a driver's license that said I was disabled. I went to the highway patrol station to get the license changed. After driving with me, the officer wanted to know why I was even there, because I did everything correctly. The only restrictions on the new license were turn signals on the steering column and I have to wear both arms when driving.

It's those little things that degrade people who have lost limbs and keep them from going back into society to work. After the accident, I went back to work doing what I'd always done, except I didn't climb poles. Since my boss retired, I'm now foreman.

When I wear long-sleeved shirts or jackets, most people don't notice the artificial arms unless they hear the battery-operated hands move. When I wear short sleeves, people are amazed that the myoelectric arms look so real. Of course, kids ask lots of questions, especially when I coach baseball or go camping with the scouts.

What I missed most after I lost my hands was feeling my kids when I picked them up. I'd lift them up for a hug, but I couldn't feel them in my hands. I miss the softness of my little girl's skin and being able to touch my wife at night.

But my family has supported me through it all. I don't know how I would have made it without Alicia. Just after the accident, doctors told me stories about other burn patients whose wives couldn't handle their amputations and left them. I worried whether Alicia would want to stick with me, but she always has been there for me. My main regret is that I still have to depend on her for a lot of things.

It bothers me that while I'm my own person during the day when I have my arms on, I'm always dependent on my wife to help me in and out of my arms. The arms have to be pulled on with socket socks, so I can't get them on by myself.

When I'm wearing my arms, I feel like a whole person. I look in the mirror, and I look normal. But at night when I'm walking around the house without my arms, and I catch a glimpse of myself in the mirror, I always complain to Alicia how different I look. I just want to look normal.

Meet My Friend Sam

LAURA MCCLURE, 20

*It seemed like a simple sprained knee, but it didn't
get better. The diagnosis: cancer. At age 14,
her right leg was amputated above the knee, and she
suffered the dehumanizing effects of
chemotherapy. Yet out of tragedy grew not only a
desire to run, but a new passion for life.*

I 'd like you to meet Sam. We first were introduced when
I was a teenager. Sam is my artificial leg. I was 14 and a
freshman in high school in Waverly, Tennessee. I started
at a new school that year, so I had lots of new friends. I even
had a boyfriend.

I was in gym class when I fell against the bleachers and
sprained my knee. It hurt, and after two weeks, it wasn't
getting any better. My father was a physician, so he heard
all my complaints, but he didn't seem too concerned.

As time passed, my knee got worse. It began to give out
when I was walking, and I couldn't walk up steps. My dad
decided to take me to the hospital for X-rays. Not that he
was too concerned about it . . . it was more to pacify me.

He looked at the X-rays, shrugged his shoulders and
tried to convince me it didn't look like anything serious.
But that night when he called a friend of his who was an
orthopedic doctor in Nashville, I realized just how con-

71

Laura McClure

cerned he was. It was 9 p.m. on a Sunday when Dad said he wanted me to see the doctor the following morning.

Something wasn't right. I called my best friend, Mary Anne, and told her I was afraid something was really wrong with my leg. My dad didn't call friends in the middle of the night to make doctors' appointments.

The next day, I went to Nashville to the doctor. He did a few more X-rays and poked around on my knee. When he was finished, he said it was nothing to worry about. He gave it some name I could never pronounce or remember and told me it would go away with time.

But as I was getting dressed, he came back to the examining room. He asked if he could make just one more X-ray . . . maybe get another opinion from another doctor. That afternoon, he told me I might have a tumor in my leg.

I really didn't know what that meant. He said there was a 10 percent chance that the tumor might be malignant. At the time, I didn't even know what malignant meant. When I questioned him, he said there was a slight chance I had cancer. Cancer! I thought that was something only old people got. The doctor said it was a slim chance I had cancer, and he didn't seem overly concerned.

But the next day I found myself on a plane to the Mayo Clinic in Minnesota. Mayo is a 14-floor hospital, and I think I saw every floor in three days. I didn't feel comfortable there. The doctors were all strangers, and they did about a dozen more X-rays.

I ended up in a tiny waiting room . . . waiting for the diagnosis. The doctor came in . . . sat down . . . and waited several minutes before saying anything. I remember watching my father's expression. The doctor looked straight at me. "You've been diagnosed with osteogenic sarcoma, a malignant bone tumor," he said. The diagnosis would need to be confirmed by a biopsy. If it proved malignant, he wanted to amputate my leg above the knee.

73

I'd never felt like that before. I started to cry. I saw tears running down my father's face. I never would have thought the cure for cancer would be amputating your leg. I thought that was inhumane . . . something cruel. I thought people lost their legs in car accidents. This couldn't possibly be a cure for a disease. Amputation. It sounded more like a disease than a cure.

We didn't do the biopsy in Minnesota. We returned home and went to Memphis. My father decided the biopsy would be done there, and if the amputation had to be done, it would be done there also.

A couple of weeks went by. It was December 17, and my Christmas present was a biopsy the next day. As I sat in the hospital, I wondered if I'd have one or two legs the next day . . . and how many friends I'd have left. I didn't wonder . . . I was sure I wouldn't have a boyfriend anymore. My friends stopped by the hospital, but they didn't seem to know what to say to me. I think that hurt worse than anything. They weren't trying to be mean . . . but they didn't know what to say.

The next morning when I returned from surgery, I remember the orderly lifting me into bed. "I still have two legs . . . I can feel them," I thought to myself.

"They didn't amputate my leg," I told my mother. "Yes, honey . . . they did," she said. She was wrong. I didn't believe her . . . not until she pulled the covers back and let me feel. I reached down and I felt around my thigh. To my horror, as I felt further, there was nothing . . . just an empty space where my leg had been.

The following day, a very pretty lady entered my hospital room. She was pushing a wheelchair and carrying a metal pipe with a size 10 mannequin foot attached. "My God, I hope that's not my leg," I thought. I hadn't thought much about what they'd give me to replace what they took.

"This is your training leg," the lady said, smiling. She

74

explained that she was the physical therapist and was going to teach me how to walk on crutches and use the training leg. I thought she was crazy, but she finally talked me into getting into the wheelchair.

She wheeled me to the physical therapy room. "This can be very easy or very difficult . . . depending on how much work you want to do," she said. "You can feel sorry for yourself and stay in a wheelchair, or you can go on with the life you were living if you do what I say."

In a day, I learned how to stand again. She attached the metal pipe to my cast . . . I stood on the size 10 foot, and she taught me how to drag it along and walk between the parallel bars. I was excited. I was even more excited when she taught me how to walk with crutches.

A week later I left the hospital with my metal pipe, size 10 foot and crutches. I had learned how to unlock the knee, making it work like a real knee. I was in good spirits.

My friends were at my home to greet me. They still didn't know what to say, but that was all right because they were talking and happy to see me. Even my boyfriend was there. He kissed me on the cheek and told me it didn't matter . . . he liked the size 10 foot.

Christmas passed, and I thought the worst was over. But when January arrived, I went to St. Jude's Children's Research Center in Memphis. It is a hospital for children with cancer. I didn't know the doctors wanted to do anything besides amputate my leg. I thought I was cured because the part of my leg with the cancer was gone. Was I wrong!

We were in another little waiting room. I knew something bad was going to happen. The doctor said I ran the risk of still having cancer cells in my body . . . cells that wouldn't necessarily show up on an X-ray. He wanted me to begin a 44-week, experimental chemotherapy program as soon as possible. He explained the side effects of the

chemotherapy . . . nausea, diarrhea, mouth ulcers . . . none of it sounded good. Then, he mentioned I'd lose my hair. Lose my hair! No way. I fought it tooth and nail — I didn't want to take chemotherapy.

After the first treatment, my fever shot up to 104 degrees. I didn't get out of bed for four days. It felt like the double flu. Gradually, I felt better. But as I ran my hand through my hair, it fell out by the handful. I think losing my hair was the most dehumanizing thing that happened to me . . . not only did I have an artificial leg with a mannequin foot . . . now I was bald. I was beginning to feel like I was no longer a real person. Everything in the hospital was sterile. They didn't let me have flowers, and I couldn't even keep my stuffed animals with me. It only reinforced that feeling . . . that I was no longer a real person.

While I was confined to the hospital, I continued physical therapy. There were times I didn't feel like being out of bed. But there were other kids there who were amputees and had cancer. We all walked around with our I.V. poles, the chemotherapy rushing through our veins. It's hard to describe what went on . . . how we all got through it. Some people probably would think it was sick humor. We had races in the halls, pushing our I.V. poles as we went. We made bets on how many times we'd fall. We also bet on who could go the longest without throwing up from the chemotherapy.

We made it as fun as possible. Everyone's leg had a name. I named mine Sam. We were afraid to look at things from the serious side. We might not make it. We took one day at a time . . . one step at a time.

I finally made it through chemotherapy. And I had my new artificial leg with a soft, sculptured cover. From across the room, it looked really nice. I could wear skirts, and when I put on blue jeans, my leg had a shape again. It made me feel like a girl again . . . I felt feminine.

But getting a leg that fit well was a problem. It was a tedious process. They'd fix one thing, and something else would be wrong. I'd walk, and it would rub blisters. It hurt. I felt like the leg was the only thing holding me back . . . the only thing keeping me from getting on with my life. The prosthetist would work on the leg, but nothing seemed to help.

I told my parents I wasn't going to wear an artificial leg anymore. It was easier to get around on crutches. They were really upset. My father started searching for someone who might be able to fit me with a leg. He found a prosthetist in the middle of nowhere . . . Oklahoma! The prosthetist had made legs for Ted Kennedy, Jr., and a fashion model named Ivy. I decided to give it one more shot.

The fitting took a couple of weeks in Oklahoma. I still had blisters at first. There were minor problems, but I went home with a leg I could walk on. I learned how to tighten my leg muscles so I didn't limp so badly. I started wearing shorts even in the public malls. People still knew I had an artificial leg, but it looked nice. I walked with less of a limp and didn't feel as self-conscious as before. I realized when I didn't feel self-conscious, others didn't feel self-conscious about talking to me.

I'd worn the leg for a year when I told my father that I wanted to learn to run. My first prosthetist had told me to tone down my expectations . . . they were too high. He told me I'd never run, only sort of hop. But I went back to my new prosthetist for a leg that would let me run . . . a leg I could climb trees and fall off a bike with. The indestructible leg is what I wanted.

He built me one, but it wasn't very pretty . . . with a leather cover and hard foam. It had a hole in the back where you could see the three-inch knee unit. The prosthetist took me to the park as soon as it was built. He was holding my hand and walking beside me . . . walking

78

faster and faster until I could no longer keep up. He kept pulling me along. I started to fall, but I caught myself and kept on. Suddenly, I realized I wasn't walking . . . I was running. I'll never forget what it felt like to run again after more than two years.

I had met another amputee who told me about athletic competitions for persons with disabilities, so I began training. I'd never run competitively before, but I signed up for the 100-meter dash in the U.S. Amputee Nationals. I did well enough to land a spot on an international team. Being an athlete became an important part of my life. We traveled to Australia, England and Canada to compete. I usually competed with other above-the-knee amputees. Occasionally, I'd end up in a race with someone who had lost a leg below the knee, which can be pretty discouraging. Of course, an above-the-knee amputee can never run as fast or as far as a below-the-knee amputee.

I practiced and trained. I think I inspired others. And others inspired me. My goal was to learn to do everything for myself. In 1988, I was selected to go to Seoul, Korea, for the U.S. Disabled Olympics, as a sprint runner. Those 25 seconds it took to get down the track in Korea in front of 10,000 people were the biggest moments in my life. The run was also my greatest accomplishment. I ran my personal best time, but I didn't come in first. I beat a few people . . . a few beat me. But what was important was that I made it there.

After that, I knew I could do anything. My senior year in high school, I was an athletic trainer for the football team and was in lots of extracurricular activities. I did everything I think I would have done had I not lost my leg . . . and then some. Life meant more to me. I'd had to fight so hard to do everyday things . . . to be an everyday person. I knew when I graduated from high school and was accepted at college, I'd be okay. I'd battled cancer, and I'd be all right.

That doesn't mean there weren't struggles. There are still struggles. There are days when my artificial leg doesn't quite fit. When it fits, I'm on top of the world. I think the hardest thing about having an artificial leg is fear . . . fear that people won't like me or will think of me as disabled. I think because I lost my leg, I want to be more than I ever wanted to be.

As a college junior, I still have some of the same fears, but I'm learning some of them are unfounded. I used to think no guy would ever think I was pretty . . . and I'd never have a serious relationship because guys would think I'd be a burden. That simply isn't true. My boyfriend and I have a strong relationship. Without him, I don't think my confidence level would be where it is.

I met my boyfriend after track practice my freshman year. I was wearing a leg that looked a good deal like that metal pipe that so horrified me when I first had my leg amputated. It's a high-tech leg without a cover. I like it so much; I wear it everywhere.

My boyfriend tells me to this day that one of the most attractive things about me was my willingness to accept what had happened to me . . . to make it a part of my life, but not a problem in my life. He's one of the most supportive people in my life. He and my best girlfriend won't let me sit on my rear and give up on doing a task they think I can do. But my boyfriend is also there to put his arms around me when he realizes I've run into a wall . . . hit my limitations.

Yes, there are limitations, even though I choose not to focus on them. I don't have the same endurance I once did. I can't run as fast as I would with a real leg. Sometimes, I still get blisters, or I lose my balance. But I look at it from the perspective that everybody has bad days. Everyone sits down and cries once in a while. And that's okay. My bad days may be because something went wrong with my artificial leg . . . or one too many people stared at me at the mall. Those are the times when I need that friend to say,

"Hey, get back up . . . there are a lot of people in the world worse off than you." That's what my boyfriend and best girlfriend do for me.

The most frustrating part of being an amputee is having your leg worked on. You have to learn to communicate with your prosthetist. Even at that, your leg isn't always going to fit correctly . . . particularly if you lose weight like I did. Most college freshmen gain 15 pounds, but I lost 15 pounds. When I did, my leg literally fell off. It's taken time to get the leg to fit again because I lost a lot of muscle volume, changing the shape of the leg. It was like starting over. My prosthetist and I screamed at each other . . . and probably would have thrown things had something been handy. But we kept at it . . . kept trying. Eventually, things like that work out, but they don't work out on their own. You get them worked out only if you and your prosthetist are willing to work at it.

If I could take all the knowledge I've gained, all the friends I've made, all the places I've been and trade it back in for my leg . . . no, I wouldn't do it. I've gained an appreciation and love for life . . . a passion to live, to be happy and be the best I can. I often think, "What would I tell someone who is going to become an amputee?" Someone once told me to do the best I could despite the fact that I lost a leg. But I think that attitude sells you short. I believe you can do anything you want to do, keeping in mind you may have to do it a little differently or it may take a little longer. But once you learn how, it will mean more to you.

Perhaps most importantly, you have to get to know your artificial leg as a friend. Sam is a part of my life. We've developed a good relationship over the years. He's my friend. Oops . . . gotta go. Sam and I have a date!

Mike Roberts

Jerk Is a Four-Letter Word

MIKE ROBERTS, 28

Struck by a car while attempting to fix a flat tire,
both his legs were amputated above the knee. As a
21-year-old amputee, he questioned his
masculinity as he suffered severe depression. But after
grieving the loss of his limbs, he discovered that
there's something worse than being an amputee.

I t was a typical autumn day in September, 1983. Or at least so I thought. I had driven to Baltimore that weekend to visit family and was returning home to Washington, D.C. I didn't know what lay ahead on that road . . . or that I would spend the first of many nights in the hospital as I began a long road to physical and emotional recovery.

As I headed into D.C., I was about five miles from my apartment when I came upon road construction where two lanes of the interstate were being repaved. I struck an object in the road and ended up with a flat tire. I got out to change the tire. I was standing at the rear of my car with a spare tire when I was struck by another vehicle. I was crushed between the two cars, my legs partially amputated.

I don't remember the actual collision. My first recollection is of the emergency room. It was the strangest feeling I believe I've ever had. It was almost like a dream. I knew I was talking to doctors and nurses — but it never registered that since I was talking to them, I was in a hospital. The nurses asked my name, address, and phone number. Just before I slipped into unconsciousness, they asked me to move my legs. I remember trying with all my might to move my legs, but they wouldn't move no matter how hard I tried. Then I was out.

Suddenly, I was awakened by a doctor who was physically shaking me. He introduced himself and said I was at an emergency room in a hospital near Washington, D.C., because I'd been in an automobile accident. Then, he said they would have to amputate both my legs, or I'd be dead by morning.

I can remember thinking, "Wow, I don't remember what happened, but I'm in real bad shape." He shoved a consent form in front of my face, and I made a lazy attempt to sign it. I realized then that I was going to be an amputee, but it was a choice of losing my legs or my life. "Okay, let's just get this over with," I told the doctor.

I awoke the next morning in intensive care. What an experience! I was 21 and had never been in a hospital before . . . now I had every machine known to man attached to my body. It was overwhelming.

I remembered the conversation with the doctor. As I looked down toward the foot of the bed, the blood-soaked sheets were a vivid reminder that I was now an amputee. The doctors had a tough time trying to keep blood in me. It ran out about as fast as they pumped it in. As I looked to my left and then to my right, there were intravenous lines on both sides. I had all kinds of electrodes, monitors, and hoses. I drifted back to sleep.

It wasn't long until I was rudely awakened. I had accidentally disconnected a heart electrode. An alarm sent a rush of nurses bursting into my room to check me. It really scared me, because I hadn't realized my physical condition was so fragile. For the first time I remember thinking I might die.

After four days, I was moved to the orthopedic floor, to

begin what would be the toughest weeks of my life. At that point, I wasn't too worried about not having legs. I was in such intense pain that I just wanted my body to heal. The pain was so gripping that I recall lying in bed, trembling as if I had the chills. A nurse would give me a shot of pain killer, and I'd sleep for a few hours.

The doctor said I'd spend six to eight weeks in orthopedics if there were no other complications. "What was he talking about?" I thought to myself. "I've never spent one night in the hospital before. I don't know who they are talking about, but I'm not spending six to eight weeks in a hospital." As it turned out, I was released from the hospital three weeks to the day after the accident.

It was after my discharge that my feelings that I was an inadequate person began to surface. The hospital was barrier-free. I didn't have to do anything for myself. When I wanted a drink, I rang the bell. When I wanted a soda, I rang the bell. When I needed to go to the bathroom, I rang the bell. At home, the bell was the first thing to go. My mom provided the best care she could, but I wanted more. I always wondered why she had to stop at midnight. It wasn't the round-the-clock care that I had come to depend on.

Frustration seemed to spark my feelings of inadequacy. Frustration over no longer being able to spring out of bed and use the bathroom or get a drink of water. Frustration over having to use a wheelchair, and, worse still, not having legs from five inches above each knee. As I look back, I can see the distinct emotional stages I went through.

As frustration mounted my first month home, I went through denial. I thought, "This is so terrible . . . it really isn't happening." Then came the "Why me?" stage. "Out of all the people in the world, why did this happen to me?" I kept asking myself. That was a tough question and I really haven't answered it to this day. Accidents, like what happened to me, occur without any good reason.

85

What followed was depression. I could feel myself sinking deeper and deeper into depression. It was compounded by the fact that I normally wasn't a depressed person. I found myself being depressed that I was depressed, if that makes any sense. I didn't know what the hell was going on. I'd sleep for hours on end. Anyone within speaking distance was a target for one of my tongue lashings. I went through a period of not being able to do anything but cry when I awoke each morning. I always had been a bright, go-getter person. I was not used to feeling like this.

About that time, I met another bilateral, above-the-knee amputee who was about my age. I'll never forget that first meeting. He was full of positive energy and enthusiasm. He bounced down my basement steps, hopped into a chair, stuck out his hand and told me his name was Jim Leatherman. The funny thing was that he reminded me of myself . . . before the accident. I sat there in amazement.

Jim helped me see that I could still be a positive person full of energy and capable of doing things. He made me feel stupid for being so down on myself. "I've got some good news and some bad news," Jim told me. "The bad news is that your legs aren't going to grow back. The good news is that the quality of your life isn't going to be compromised just because you are an amputee." He was absolutely right.

Jim taught me the "amputee lessons." He told me I had to forget the way I used to do things because now I had to do them a little differently. Things like going up and down steps . . . and hopping up on the kitchen cabinet to grab a glass of water. Being the avid sports enthusiast that I am, Jim introduced me to wheelchair athletics. I haven't been the same since. Wheelchair athletics was my vehicle to discovering that what I can do is more important than what I cannot do.

As I have done some advocacy work with other amputees the last several years, I have tried to promote that philosophy. When a person goes through a disabling injury, he or she tends to focus on what can't be done, because that is what's most apparent. The human mind is an amazing thing — but no one ever wrote an owner's manual for it. I discovered what occupies your mind is what is most real to you. By concentrating on my abilities, rather than my disabilities, my abilities became most real in my mind. It sounds almost too simple to be true — but it is. And with that philosophy, I have experienced many successes. Most recently, I became a successful prosthetic user.

My doctor always told me that as a bilateral, above-the-knee amputee, I would never walk. In my heart, I knew that I could, if I could find a piece of equipment worth using. I did finally in May, 1989, and now I can walk without canes or crutches.

I learned many lessons during my recovery. I discovered a lot about human nature and a lot about myself. Unfortunately, I was slow to learn some lessons. My biggest regret is how I chose to deal with relationships — particularly relationships with women. At the time of the accident, I had a girlfriend who was everything anyone could want. Our relationship had cooled somewhat before the accident because she lived in Baltimore, and I had just moved to a Washington, D.C., suburb. She couldn't believe what had happened to me and still cared a great deal for me. She stuck by me through thick and thin. What did I do? I rewarded her affections with nothing but heartache.

I questioned her motives. "Did she think she might get some money out of the deal? Why would someone that attractive stay with a guy who didn't have legs?" I asked myself. It didn't dawn on me that the fact that I didn't have my legs didn't matter to her.

Once I was physically able, I set out to prove my masculinity . . . to prove that I still had what it takes to be a man. I wanted to know if women would still find me sexually attractive. It was a big concern for a 21-year-old guy whose priorities were all mixed up. As it turned out, women did find me sexually attractive, and I steadily reinforced that point for the next two years. Eventually, my girlfriend had her heart broken so many times that she told me to take a hike. It wasn't until later that I realized what I had done.

I discovered there is something much worse than being handicapped — single-syllable disabilities are much worse than multi-syllable ones. "Jerk" is a four-letter word that has more limitations than being an amputee.

A Whole New World

GEORGIE MAXFIELD, 57

*Riding a motorcycle on a mountain pass, she was
struck by a car. The accident forced amputation
of her left leg above the knee. At age 53, she began
searching for a prosthesis that was bearable
to use. She formed an amputee support group to learn
and help others experiencing similar struggles.*

I 'd been riding motorcycles since I was 15. My husband,
Don, and I had ridden and backpacked through most of
the Western United States. We had ridden to Alaska
and played in the glaciers . . . traveled the entire perimeter
of Mexico, living on beaches and climbing Mayan ruins. In
June of 1986, we were on a Sunday ride in a nearby Nevada mountain pass when I rounded a curve to find a
vehicle driving in the middle of the highway . . . headed
straight at me. The driver apparently didn't see me. With a
cliff on one side and a wall of rock on the other, the choices
weren't good. The car hit me.

On impact, my left leg was broken in seven places and
deeply severed; my right leg was broken above the knee.
My pelvis was separated, and my left arm was broken. I
must have been thrown over the top of the car. As fate
would have it, a nurse was riding in the car behind me. She
put a tourniquet on my leg . . . and saved my life.

*Georgie Maxfield and
husband Don — Round Dancing!*

Don was on his cycle ahead of me. I had dropped farther behind than usual because I had a new motorcycle and was being extra cautious. When he noticed I was no longer in sight, he turned around to locate me. He found me lying in a pool of blood in the middle of the highway with one leg over my head in an almost impossible position. It was a horror for him to face. We had lived, worked, and played together for 31 years. Now he had to hold my head, still in the helmet, and talk me into staying alive until the ambulance arrived.

The ambulance stopped at the first little town to do blood transfusions, and I was transported via helicopter to Reno. There wasn't room in the helicopter, so Don had to drive into Reno. That must have been a nightmare for him.

At the hospital, doctors told me I would lose my leg. I couldn't agree to that! I sat upright in the bed arguing with them until my son, Mike, arrived. "Baby don't let them take my leg. I can't live like that," I begged Mike. "Mom, there's nothing they can do; there is nothing left to save," he told me. I finally consented to the amputation. At that moment, I believe I gave up and fell back on the bed . . . maybe I passed out. At least that's how I remembered it, but months later I read the medical reports and no one in that condition was sitting up in bed.

They amputated my left leg above the knee. With such extensive damage, they didn't expect me to live . . . and I had no desire to live. Don, our sons, my dad, and friends came to see me, but I barely knew they were there. When I couldn't, or didn't die, doctors began piecing me back together, wheeling me in and out of the operating room day after day . . . for seven operations. I wasn't much interested in it all, but it did seem like dying was taking an awfully long time.

My first real memory is of the horrible phantom pain. I knew the leg was gone, but it felt as if someone was twisting my foot off at the ankle. I didn't know then what it was. No one told me anything about phantom pain. I just thought that I was crazy and asked for stronger pain medication. I didn't mention this insanity to anyone. Doctors and nurses should explain phantom pain to their patients.

I was in intensive care for three weeks and spent a total of three months in the hospital. My family and friends helped me make it through one day at a time. Then my dad suffered a heart attack. We were in the same hospital, one floor apart. My parents lived with us because of ill health. Mother had died the year before, and Dad was 88.

Dad died just a month after I was released from the hospital. He had a heart attack in his room at our home. I fought to give him CPR from my wheelchair while Don dialed 911. I made burial arrangements and attended his funeral in a wheelchair, all the time feeling as though my accident had contributed to his death.

Hospitals are arranged for handicapped people. Going home was the shocker. It was hard or impossible to do anything. Everything I saw reminded me of the life we had led before. Shoes in the closet made me cry. Depression lived at our house, and it felt like a great, black hole. Then, as before, I contemplated suicide. Dying looked good compared to this. I kept asking myself, "Why the hell did they save me, and how can anyone accept being in this condition? You can bleed to death in four lousy minutes, so why couldn't they just have left me alone that long?"

I can't truthfully say how, but Don's strength was there, and only the fear of hurting him more made living necessary. I do remember making one decision: "I'll give it one year. If I can't become a productive human being in a year, I'm checking out."

I met my first temporary prosthesis that October. It was a white plastic, adjustable, fits-all, fits-nobody socket with a black pipe, hinge-like knee and SACH foot. It was the ugliest thing I'd ever seen. It was cumbersome and awkward . . . and I was crushed.

Still I was thrilled to stand between the bars and totter forward. Looks fell by the wayside really fast. Walking and movement were what was important. First it was with a walker, then the trauma of using crutches, followed by a balancing act between two canes. Wow! I had the beginning stages whipped. Nobody told me I'd spend the next six months inching along like that, waiting for the stump to heal and Medicaid to approve a permanent limb. I had a million miles to go.

About that time I decided to stop thinking in terms of pain. I decided it was a sensation, a new sensation. When I thought in terms of pain, I held myself back.

I had a residual limb that was difficult to fit. The stump was 11 inches long, but there was only six inches of bone, with five inches of soft tissue on the bottom. A long and deeply recessed skin graft covered the top of the thigh. My doctor felt I needed special attention and sent me to Los Angeles for evaluation. The evaluation cost $400, and no one prepared us for that. My brother paid for it since the facility didn't take Medicaid. I quickly discovered a good leg was going to cost a lot more than we had imagined.

Once back home, I began searching for another amputee . . . someone who might have some information about prosthetics. I couldn't afford to "learn" at the going rate. I found two amputees — a lady with a hip, disarticulation and a lady who was a below-the-knee amputee. They gave me all the information they had.

Armed with new insight, I urged my doctor to send me to Denver to the prosthetist my friend recommended. The prosthetist was a delight to know. We became instant friends, and he arranged for my husband and me to attend an amputee support group. He created a special socket to protect my scar tissue. It was a hard quadrilateral socket with a hydraulic knee and Kingsley foot, all weighing just over ten pounds.

In this type of socket, the entire body weight is supported by the pelvic bone, which moves up and down on a hard shelf with each step. The hip is rather loose and migrates out to the side. My stance was very wide, and I had a severe shoulder dip. I believed I could learn to overcome all of that. Within a month, I gave up both canes. I was reasonably mobile, but the more I walked, the greater the energy output . . . and the more I would sweat, which contributed to a growing infection in my scar tissue. Revision surgery was necessary in August of 1987, after I had used the leg three months.

Revision surgery is akin to re-amputation. A plastic surgeon removed the skin graft area and shortened the stump to reduce the swinging mass of soft tissue. I spent six weeks in a wheelchair.

Interwoven during this time was the growth of the Northern Nevada Amputee Support Group, born from our original group of three. As amputees, we learned from each other and were amazed to find how few amputees had ever spoken to another amputee outside a prosthetic facility. And we came to realize that we, the prosthetic users, knew almost nothing about the products our lives revolved around. Prosthetists, the gods of this world to us, all speak a foreign language.

Getting the support group going wasn't an easy task since doctors, prosthetists, and hospitals must hold records confidential and won't give out names and addresses of patients. I practically chased amputees down the street when I saw them . . . and suddenly, I did see them. "Had they been invisible to me before?" I wondered.

Our amputee support group now numbers nearly 200. We have educational meetings and share prosthetic information through our meetings, newsletter and video library.

We make hospital visits, help with family adjustments, work with a "buddy" system, and raise funds to help with purchase and repair of prosthetic devices and wheelchairs. We've made mistakes along the way, but our community support base continues to grow.

During my recuperation after the revision surgery, I had time to study videotapes and information that made me realize there were other above-the-knee amputees who could walk circles around me. Since my quad socket would no longer fit the revised stump, my doctor sent me to a prominent West Coast medical facility . . . a prosthetic engineering department that stayed abreast of the latest in artificial limbs. With financial help from Medicaid, Vocational Rehabilitation, and Hill Burton Assistance, I was fitted with a state-of-the-art, lightweight CAT-CAM . . . a super-duper leg. It was a big deal, and Don and I were happy people.

I found alot to like about my new leg: its light weight of just six pounds, the foot, ankle, and knee. Everything was fine except the socket.

Beware... all CAT-CAM sockets are not the same. I discovered the socket is a product of each individual prosthetist. As I continued to use the socket, Don and I attended several amputee conferences and studied the different sockets worn by amputees we had seen on videotape. No matter what anyone chose to call it, the socket I had was a glorified quadrilateral with attempted pelvic containment. My rather soft thigh tissue twisted and wrenched in the inner thigh area with every step, while the pelvic bone worked its way off the edge of the socket.

Eventually, I was back to blood and blisters. My activity level was greatly reduced — no dancing, no tennis, no camping or hiking. A cyst that developed near the pelvic bone meant I finally could no longer wear the leg.

The components were still serviceable, but I had to

have a new socket. Medicaid wouldn't fund it, so we begged and borrowed from relatives to buy a new socket produced in Reno. It was another version of CAT-CAM. The prosthetist created a socket that didn't breed cysts and blisters, for which I was grateful. (He also made me a shower leg that I could even wear into the lake, making swimming a pleasure again.)

But as I wore it, the socket still twisted around the inner thigh, causing a burning, irritated mass. My hip still migrated out to the side and stayed there. I decided my problems were unsolvable and I'd have to adjust my lifestyle. Life became timed in short spurts of action. I leaned on the grocery carts to take some weight off the leg while I shopped. At home, I used the walls, halls, furniture, kitchen counter-top — anything to relieve the strain. I had no balance and bruises became a way of life.

Here I was an encyclopedia of prosthetic knowledge, none of which seemed to help me. I decided it was all a pack of lies. The videos were made of "special people," athletic stars who were paid to perform and lied through their teeth about the comfort. I felt like it compared to the quack miracle cures — all hype and no delivery. Don't misunderstand. The prosthetists I encountered gave me their best. I do not feel they took advantage of me. Each of them tried, but they were limited by their experience. Still the money was gone, Medicaid refused further payment, and I didn't have a leg I could use. If these special legs existed, they were saving them for someone else, I decided.

About that time, I attended a prosthetic convention where another amputee, Donna Kennedy, was featured. She had tissue problems with her stump that were similar to mine, but she had found success with a leg built by Oklahoma City prosthetist John Sabolich. Once I was able to contact her, I realized there was still hope. I also knew there was no more money for another leg.

With a great deal of fear and trepidation, my husband and I borrowed money against our home. It was about all we had left after all the travel, hospital, and medical expenses. It was a difficult time of life to be going into debt, but we felt it was worth the investment. My husband and I drove from Reno to Oklahoma City in our 1961 pickup, pulling our son's old camper. We lived in that trailer for a month. It was a trip filled with love and hope. "We're off to see the Wizard, the wonderful Wizard of Oz," I sang as we drove. And I prayed it was true.

The day we arrived, the prosthetist went to work and the casting and fitting of a new socket went quickly. Adjusting to the pressure of a true total pelvic containment, however, was something else. Uncomfortable as it was, it felt good because I was stable — the socket really fit. The difficulty with the pelvic pressure was slowly adjusted until I felt fine walking or standing, but I still found it uncomfortable to sit because my tailbone hurt. My prosthetist urged me to endure, explaining that too would get better. After a month or so, it did.

One day, the prosthetist was teaching four other above-the-knee amputees to run in the parking lot, so I gave it a try. I didn't run fast or well, but it was the fastest movement I had experienced in four years. Don videotaped us all. It was thrilling. Later, we went to a park to ride bikes. Some went horseback riding or played tennis to test their limbs, but Don and I went to flea markets, an amusement park and the auto races. Doesn't sound like handicapped activity, does it?

After four years, all the legs and travel expenses came to well over $40,000 — but I finally had a leg that looked good, let me walk, and be the person I wanted to be. The mental, physical and emotional wear and tear are beyond evaluation. I wanted to share my story in hopes that someone will be spared the strain of learning everything the hard way, as I did. Don and I thought long and hard about advice we would attempt to offer (because all advice can be dangerous), but we feel these points deserve attention when you choose a person and place to make an artificial limb.

1. Beware of the term CAT-CAM because anyone can use it. There are as many variations of the socket as there are prosthetic facilities.

2. Observe the personality and disposition of the prosthetist you select. Volatile temperament is not a desirable trait. Cool, calm, and collected people get the job done.

3. Ask to meet and talk privately with some of the prosthetist's patients, people with your type of amputation who are using the components you are interested in.

4. Learn to speak the prosthetic language. It isn't difficult. Your prosthetist can teach you if you let him know you don't understand.

5. Establish and maintain communication. Remember, no one can feel what is happening to your body except you. Guess work hurts both parties.

Today, I have a good, strong prosthesis that is improving my life. My activity level is approaching normal. I feel better about my existence and future.

In September, 1990, Don and I returned to round dancing . . . our first time on the dance floor since the accident. Round dancing is a stylized version of ballroom dancing, done by couples moving around the room in a circular motion. It's the Fred Astaire and Ginger Rogers stuff. We love it. We'd been dancing for 25 years before the accident and even taught round dancing.

We're starting over with a class, re-learning not just the steps and maneuvers, but the body mechanics. And we're making adjustments for a few movements I can't do. It is challenging, but it's wonderful to accomplish something personally important to us as a couple. We're dancing, laughing, talking and enjoying the company of our friends.

There are people who still find it difficult to be comfortable in my presence because of the amputation. Whether they can overcome that remains to be seen. But I no longer waste my emotional stamina trying to make myself acceptable. A hunk of flesh is gone, but I'm still a mind, soul and being to be considered and acknowledged. If Don and I can recover from the amputation, surely other people can, too. Thank God the bothered souls are few and our loved ones are many.

The amputee support group continues to grow, keeping me busy. Don is one of the most vital forces in it. We have met and enjoyed many phenomenal people. I was proud to be elected to the board of directors of the Amputee Coalition of America and hope to serve a useful purpose in the national organization. I urge every amputee to reach out and contact a support group or other amputees. The benefits are many. After all, life is learning and sharing . . . and even amputation is just another learning experience.

Riley Bradford

Oh, My Beautiful Baby

RILEY BRADFORD, INFANT
(AS TOLD BY HIS MOTHER, TAMMI)
*There's nothing more exciting than a new baby, and
Tammi and Kyle Bradford looked forward to
the birth of their second child. But after Riley's arrival,
they confronted an issue they never expected to
face — whether his severely deformed right
foot should be amputated.*

"There's the head and a full head of black hair. It
may be a girl," the doctor said, as he encouraged
me to push. I rejoiced as I heard a cry loud
enough to let everyone know our second child was making
an entrance into the world. But my joy and excitement
turned to shock as the doctor laid Riley on my stomach.

Riley's right foot was severely deformed. He had only
two toes and the entire foot was pulled toward the back of
his calf muscle. My husband hadn't noticed yet that there
was a problem. "There's something wrong with his foot,"
was all I could manage to mumble, as tears streamed down
my face.

My husband, Kyle, immediately turned to the nurse
who then was holding Riley and found he also had problems with the other foot. His left foot had only four toes, all
curved toward the inside of his foot.

Here was a precious baby boy — our second son. We

had looked forward to the birth with such anticipation. But now we didn't know what the future would hold for Riley or our family.

Later, X-rays told part of the story. Riley's right foot did not have enough bone mass to develop into a workable foot, and he was missing the fibula bone from the knee to the foot. Halfway down the front of the leg, the tibia bone was bowed slightly back and to one side. X-rays also revealed only three bones in his left foot. The big toe bone was very wide, and doctors suggested two bones may have fused together.

I was pretty much in a state of shock after the delivery. "Don't worry. He'll be okay," a nurse told me. "He's such a beautiful baby." As I gazed at him, she was right. He was a beautiful baby (and still is). Kyle stayed with Riley in the nursery for quite some time, and then took our other son, Zachary, home. Zachary had been there with his grandfather when Kyle came out of the delivery room and explained there were problems. So Zach knew from the beginning there was something wrong with his little brother's feet, but that didn't stop him from loving him.

Lots of friends and family came to visit while Riley and I were in the hospital. One of my best friends stayed with me for a long time. She told me to go ahead and cry to get those feelings out, or they would be buried inside forever. So I just let the tears flow, all the time asking why God had let this happen. No matter how many times I asked the question, I always came up with the same answer: "You will love him like no one else can."

It was more difficult for some friends who came to visit us during the hospital stay. Some asked questions, but others didn't know what to say. Kyle and I discovered it was easier if we brought up the subject. On my last night in the hospital, a nurse named Ruby stopped by to see me. She had a granddaughter who was born with a deformed hand. I always will be grateful to Ruby and her daughter, Amy, who shared so many things with me and gave me strength to deal with Riley's problem.

"It will get better every day," Ruby told me. "There will come a time when you find yourself forgetting that there is anything wrong with your baby."

Kyle was my strength while I was hospitalized. He did everything — ran here and there and talked to doctors about Riley's condition. The reality didn't hit him until Riley and I were home from the hospital. I guess after we were safely home, the fatigue finally caught up with him, and he had time to sit back and realize what a big mountain we had in front of us. He was quiet for a couple of days, then we began to really talk about what we had to do.

We discussed how people might relate to Riley — how it was up to us to make others feel comfortable. We agreed we couldn't baby him because we wanted him to grow up as normal a child as possible. Kyle and I also faced the financial realities and agreed we'd even sell the house if that became necessary. We fortunately had a lot of family support and that made dealing with it easier.

As Riley grew, we took him to several doctors, including specialists at Shriners' Hospital in St. Louis. The opinions were all the same. Riley's right foot would have to be amputated above the ankle, and he would need to wear a prosthesis. Somehow, I guess I thought the foot could be fixed. We struggled with the thought of amputation. We questioned what new miracles might be available when he was 18. Would doctors have the skills to remake his foot then? Maybe they would be able to; maybe not. How would he cope with it until then?

Ultimately, we had to put our own selfish feelings aside. We had to think of what would be best for Riley. We came to realize we had to look past the "what ifs" and all the wishful thinking and go with what he had. He would have a workable foot with a prosthesis. Amputation was the only choice. After we'd made the decision to go ahead with the amputation, the hardest part was waiting. I wanted his foot fixed right then. But we had to wait until he was a little older before we could do anything to help him.

I had good days and bad days. I'd be shopping at the grocery store and catch myself looking at other children. I'd think, "I wish Riley could have had feet like that," and I'd wonder what it would be like for him as he grew and how he would cope. I had to make myself put those thoughts out of my mind. I had to concentrate on what he would be able to do, not on what he wouldn't be able to do.

Riley's surgery was scheduled for April 9, 1990, when he was seven months old. It had to be postponed until April 23 because Riley developed a runny nose and congestion. That may have been a blessing in disguise. Kyle and I were nervous and apprehensive about the surgery. The extra two weeks gave us more time to gather the inner strength we needed to help Riley get through the ordeal.

The surgery took a little more than an hour. Riley came through without any problem — probably better than Kyle and me. The hardest part was watching him in the recovery room. He was so disoriented and confused. He was on pain medication every four hours, but his little body thrashed back and forth until the pain medication took effect. Once the anesthesia wore off, Riley was crawling around in his bed with a bright smile on his face. He stayed in the hospital only one night, and we checked out early the next morning.

The doctor showed us how to change his bandages. He wanted to see Riley again in two weeks to remove the stitches. Those two weeks passed rapidly, and Riley didn't seem to notice anything had happened to him. We kept his leg wrapped at all times until he was fitted with a prosthesis.

A month after the amputation, we took Riley for his first prosthetic fitting. After a week and some minor adjustments, he had his new temporary leg. Weighing only two ounces, it's the lightest artificial leg made. Riley is adjusting well, pulling up on the furniture and learning to walk like any other baby.

His older brother Zach was explaining to his cousins all about Riley's new leg the other day. He told them since Riley had his surgery, he had a new little artificial foot that was going to help him walk. Zach always had accepted Riley as he was, and he told other people that Riley's foot just didn't work, so the doctor was going to give him a new one. That's what we had told him.

As the older brother, Zach is bound to leave some big footsteps for Riley to follow — but I know he'll manage nicely. I suspect Riley will even add a few footsteps of his own along the way.

We know now we will get through it. The entire ordeal brought us closer as a family. It also brought us back to the church, where we found the inner strength we needed to deal with the problem and help Riley. I know Riley will face lots of obstacles in the future, but I also know he will have the strength to deal with whatever comes along. As a family, it is up to us to make sure he is treated like any normal, healthy child.

Our early fears that Riley would never walk now grow smaller each day. It's still hard. Some days I wonder what I'm going to tell Riley when he asks in a few years "Why did we have to do this?" and "Why don't I have regular feet like other kids?" That's just a bridge we'll have to cross when we come to it.

Jacqueline Ann Taylor

Rubber Bands and Paper Clips

JACQUELINE ANN TAYLOR, 28

*Doctors don't know what caused her to be born
without arms or legs. Many babies with such
severe birth defects are institutionalized, but her family
took her home, loved her, and treated her like
their other children. She hasn't let the lack of limbs
deter her from pursuing a career in law.*

T he snow and ice that covered the ground in Oklahoma City on February 28, 1962, were only the
first of many challenges my parents would face that
day. By some miracle, my mom made it to the hospital in
time to deliver me, her fourth child. It was apparent from
the beginning, however, that I was not like the other
children in my family.

After my mom regained consciousness from the anesthesia, the doctor came in to tell her that her new baby girl had
been born without limbs. Worse yet, no one knew why. The
next few days must have seemed like a lifetime for my parents,
who, with the help of the doctors, had to decide what to do.

The doctors, of course, had to advise my parents of the
full list of options. These ranged from giving me up for
adoption to institutionalization. Finally, one doctor told
them, "Just take her home and love her — she will be fine."
Fortunately for me, they did.

While my childhood was often lonely and difficult, it had some wonderful bright spots woven through it as well. My siblings, Jerry, Doug, and Kay, were all quite a bit older than me, but Kay and Doug played with me often and taught me to sit up and climb stairs on my own. Other tricks that Doug taught me were not so constructive in my parents' view.

One spring day, when I was about three, Doug climbed out of his second-story bedroom window to sun himself on the roof — with me in tow. He had me yell for Mom until she came out in the backyard to see where I was. When she looked up and saw us on the roof, she nearly had a heart attack! Doug and I laughed hysterically. That was a great moment.

Almost two years later, in January of 1967, Doug severely and permanently injured his midbrain when a car hit the motorcycle he was riding. He had gotten the motorcycle less than a month before, on his 16th birthday. Doug existed in a nursing home, in a persistent vegetative state, for the next 18 years. His loss is but another example of the hardships our family has faced over the years.

Next to my mom and my siblings, my maternal grandparents probably did the most to shape who I am today. My grandma Viola was the kindest and wisest woman I ever knew. None of her grandchildren will forget the love she gave to everyone around her.

Granddad Evert was the perfect contrast to Grandma. Although loving, he was feisty and liked to tell his grandkids tall tales about anything that came into his mind. He was also a retired school teacher and a garage inventor. One early "adaptive device" he made for me was an extended crayon holder, which he made by wrapping rubber bands around the crayons and placing them in the ends of spent Roman Candle firecrackers. His motto was, "If you can't put it together with rubber bands and paper clips, you don't need it."

My grandad taught me to read and write before I entered kindergarten. That advantage helped me gain confidence in my abilities, which I would need growing up with a severe disability. Grandma and Granddad also made me feel loved and accepted by taking me wherever they went, proudly introducing me to all of their friends. In their own way, they greatly reduced the attitudinal barriers about disability, at least among the people they knew.

When I reached school age, my parents had the financial resources to send me to private school. This was fortunate, because at that time the Oklahoma City Public Schools did not mainstream students with disabilities with able-bodied students. In fact, I would have been placed in a classroom with profoundly mentally disabled children. Although it would have been easier and cheaper to place me in public school, my family knew that a good education was my only chance for future independence.

Despite the wonderful learning environment I had in elementary school, I was often sad and lonely because I had few friends. Kids are very physical at that age, and they don't understand how to relate to a peer who cannot be physical with them. I did have a couple of very close friends growing up, however. One girl in particular is still a friend today. We have shared so much that whenever we see one another, no matter how long we have been apart, we can talk as if we had never been separated.

While my disability alienated me from many of the kids at school, I met other childhood friends because of my disability. These were kids who, like me, went to rehabilitation hospitals for prostheses and/or therapy. But because the field of children's prosthetics was still developing in the early 1960s, only certain centers in the United States were specializing in child amputees. Unfortunately, Oklahoma did not have such a center, so I had to travel out of state.

My first significant encounter with prosthetics came at

age four when I traveled to Grand Rapids, Michigan, to the Amputee Clinic at Mary Free Bed Hospital. At the time, it was one of the most innovative centers in the country for children's prosthetics. Although my mom took me to Michigan, she had to leave me there for several weeks while I was fitted with prosthetic arms. That was my first time away from home without my family, and I think it was much harder on them than it was on me.

Much to everyone's surprise, I contracted chicken pox from another patient at the hospital and had to stay in quarantine for over a week. That was the pits! Once the mini-epidemic was over, however, I began to learn how to use what would be my first pair of arms.

Because I have only shoulders and no residual arms, the prosthetic arms were held on by plastic caps, which were molded from a plaster cast to fit over my upper body. These early arms were unusual in that their movements were powered by carbon dioxide stored in miniature tanks on the back of the plastic caps. The gas travelled to the motors of the arms via a system of plastic tubing, and aside from the irritating noise it made as it moved through the tubes, it was quite effective. Later arms that I used, powered by cadmium batteries, never worked efficiently.

I could make the arms go up, or make the hook open by pressing small switches inside the caps with my shoulders. Although there were three switches for each arm, I quickly mastered them and was able to write, feed myself with a spoon, and grasp some objects. Before I got the arms, I relied on someone else to feed me, and I wrote with a pencil held in my mouth or between my shoulder and chin.

When I started school, the arms were a conversation piece for several days. The kids were interested in how they worked compared to their own arms and hands. Soon everyone, including me, realized there was no comparison, and they became commonplace tools that simply changed the way I performed some tasks. Nevertheless, I made two pilgrimages per year to Mary Free Bed from the time I was four until I turned 13.

Because of the severity of my congenital disability, the doctors and prosthetists used me to try out the latest technology in artificial arms. I later decided to try my own experiment with walking on prosthetic legs, despite the protests of the doctors that this was unsafe because I could fall too easily. But as usual, I was determined and stubborn. This time the doctors were right, and I decided that I would stick to power wheelchairs or scooting around on the floor at home for mobility.

Even though at age 13 I abandoned all prosthetics except the legs, which I wore (and still wear) for cosmetic purposes only, the trips to Michigan were certainly not wasted. There, I finally realized that many other children had been born without limbs or had lost them in accidents at an early age. That realization was important, because I knew that I was not alone. We all learned so much from each other. I hope that some of us can meet again through a Mary Free Bed reunion.

The other childhood experience that gave me a sense of being part of a group was attending the Easter Seal Handicamp in Idaho Springs, Colorado, for eight summers. Kids from Colorado and several surrounding states came to the camp each year for adapted activities, such as swimming, horseback riding, archery, and fishing. We also came for friendship, in a place that was designed for us. For me, Colorado is still a magical place.

When I entered high school, I began to make many new friends. The impenetrable cliques of elementary school still existed, but many other students were open and friendly. Because I was happier socially, my grades improved, and I eventually graduated with honors.

Like all teenagers, I tested the boundaries of acceptable behavior, which meant I got into trouble on a fairly regular basis. While I now know what grief I must have put my parents through, I am not sorry for the experience I gained. In fact, the period I went through in high school helped me to mellow and mature somewhat faster than many of my peers.

My college years were also quite fulfilling. I attended Scripps College in Claremont, California, where I majored in international relations. I elected to go away to school because I knew it was time for me to have my own identity, apart from my family. Scripps, a small women's college specializing in humanities, was the ideal place to learn independence while still feeling part of a closely-knit academic community.

Part of the independence that I had to learn was how to train and manage a personal assistant. My mom had undergone serious surgery about one month before I left for college, so my dad took me to California. Upon our arrival, Carolyn, the young woman who would be my personal assistant throughout my years at Scripps, met my father and me at the airport. She was a nurse's aide that my parents had arranged for through a southern California nurses' registry, before my departure from Oklahoma.

Carolyn was truly a gift. We became fast friends, and she also became good friends with Nancy, my best friend at college. As my personal assistant, Carolyn lived in the room adjoining mine in the dorm. She attended classes, ate the often deplorable cafeteria food, and went to the crowded parties with me. In my opinion, she deserves an honorary degree.

The most incredible part of my Scripps experience was my junior year abroad. As an international relations major, I had to choose a language in which to minor. I selected French because I had studied it for four years in high

school. Eventually, I fought for, and won, the opportunity to attend the Scripps Year Abroad in Paris. Upon my arrival in France, I would soon discover why the professors were so reluctant to allow me to go.

The summer before I left, my mom and a friend of hers went to Paris to locate an accessible apartment for me. They succeeded in finding a new building that only had one step into the front door, and a small elevator to reach the apartment. It was situated in the Montparnasse section of the city, where Sartre and Hemingway once practiced their arts. Believe it or not, that building was the most accessible one we ever saw in Paris.

A good friend of mine from Oklahoma City, who also knew French, went with me to Paris to be my roommate and personal assistant. Paris was beautiful, but very difficult to negotiate in a wheelchair. The curbs were enormous and did not have curb ramps, so most of the time we travelled through the city by asking strangers to help us climb or descend several flights of stairs at the Metro subway station.

Throughout my stay, I wondered why I never saw one other person who used a wheelchair, or anyone with a disability for that matter. I later discovered that at least some of the disabled people in France live in totally accessible suburbs outside of Paris. There, doors unlocked and opened, and lights turned on and off, all with the push of a button. These towns were wonderful, but the residents were completely segregated from the rest of French society. The French government may pick up the tab for all of the physical needs of its citizens with disabilities, but the trade-off of segregation does not seem worth it to me.

During my year abroad, I took French classes with French students and my California classmates. I also spent time in cafes, museums, and travelling around the French countryside. When I returned, I could speak French fluently. The experience would not have been possible,

115

however, without the help of the woman who ran the Year Abroad program in Paris and our landlady, who took us under their wings and allowed us to try everything, even if they feared we would fail.

Because the professors and staff made Scripps such a perfect environment in which to learn, I excelled academically. But after graduation, I discovered that I still didn't know what I wanted to be when I grew up, so I came back home to think it over. When the Independent Living Project in Norman offered me a job providing independent living services to others with disabilities, I jumped at the chance.

There, I became much more aware of the political issues faced by people with disabilities, such as funding for accessibility projects and Social Security disability payments, upon which a number of people depend. I worked at the project for two years, and saw a lot of turmoil and change occur within it. Although the work was often stressful, it was also rewarding. I learned more through that job than I could ever give in return.

It's odd, but I actually don't remember why I eventually elected to go to law school. The world certainly has enough lawyers! But I wanted to give back to the disability community at least some of what it had given me. I wanted to be an advocate for groups and/or causes that I believed were worthwhile.

Three years later, I reached my goal. I graduated from the University of Oklahoma College of Law in May, 1990, passed the Oklahoma Bar Examination, and currently work for United States District Judge Wayne E. Alley in Oklahoma City. The judge arranged for the federal government to employ a full-time assistant at work for me. Fortunately, a good friend of mine, who is a paralegal and had already worked for me during law school, is now my assistant. We both really enjoy the work because we can observe other attorneys and research many different types of cases, without having to work with clients.

Other areas of my life are coming together, too. I recently bought a used van with a wheelchair lift, so I can now transport my power wheelchair. Also, a wonderful man and his wife from Dallas, Bill and Joyce Baughn, are helping me to become more independent by building inexpensive, practical adaptive equipment. And through their contacts, we have arranged for some engineers with General Dynamics and Bell Helicopter in Texas to build a customized power chair. This chair will do all of the things that a regular power chair will do, plus the seat will go up and down so that I can look people in the eye, instead of in a much more familiar, yet uncomfortable place.

My sister Kay, who is now a cinematographer, and I are continuing to work on a film about my life, and about disability issues in general, that we started in 1982. If we can raise some grant money, we hope to have the film ready for distribution in two years. Finally, I am planning to get a service dog that will perform such tasks as retrieving dropped items, opening doors and pushing elevator buttons. I look forward to having my dog as soon as possible.

Knowing my love for travel, I expect to take another bar exam before my two-year tenure with the judge ends, so that I can be ready to move to a new state, to see what new adventures await me there. No matter what else can be said about my life, it is rarely ever dull.

Swept Into Another Life

MONA PARTHUM, 33
Caught in a tornado, she clung to a tree for dear life.
Flying debris was embedded in her body,
leading to infection that forced amputation of one leg
above the knee and the other below the knee.
She wore two prostheses with relative comfort until after
her pregnancy, when she thought she'd never find
artificial limbs that fit properly.

I was on my way to a cake decorating class in Wichita Falls, Texas, when the wind began to blow. Debris began to batter my car. I'd seen pictures of a funnel cloud, and suddenly, at age 22, I was facing one, less than 100 yards in front of me. The sky turned a strange greenish-black. I got out of my car, but I got no farther than the median where I lay on the ground and held on to a small tree to keep from being swept away.

I slipped in and out of consciousness as the storm swirled around me and debris pelted my body. When it was over, I found myself sitting on the curb. A 2-by-4 had blown into my right leg, leaving my leg hanging by the skin.

I screamed to a passing truck . . . at least I thought I was screaming. At first the driver didn't see me. Then he backed up, loaded me in his truck and took me to the hospital. I was the first of many casualties to arrive at the emergency room in the wake of the tornado. I guess the good Lord was looking after me. I was alive.

I kept telling the emergency room personnel my name, but they didn't understand. I thought I was saying my name, but somehow it wasn't coming out of my mouth right. I'd lost so much blood, the doctors weren't sure I'd live, and they still weren't sure who I was. As I lay on a gurney, they tagged my left foot: "Mona Rake (the name they thought I was saying), near death."

It was a few days later when I was told my right leg had been amputated below the knee. I don't remember my parents telling me. I was so heavily sedated that I only vaguely remember an amputee coming to my room to see me.

I was hospitalized two weeks in Wichita Falls. Then, because the debris embedded in my skin caused so much infection, I was flown to Medical City in Dallas, where I remained for nearly six months. My memory is foggy of those first two months because of the pain I was in and the medication I was given. But my general daily routine included scraping the infected tissue from my left leg. The doctors just couldn't get enough of the infection out of my system, and my fever remained high. I ended up back in intensive care and later — on the operating table. To save my life, they amputated my left leg above the knee.

I wasn't aware of what was happening. My parents had to make the decision to amputate. I didn't know until a couple of days after the surgery when I asked my dad to scratch my knee. "Which knee?" he asked. "My left knee," I told him. "Honey, you don't have a left knee," he replied softly. As we talked about that conversation years later, my dad said it was all he could do to keep from bursting into tears.

The doctors continued to prescribe morphine, along with Demerol, for the extreme pain during the dressing changes. The Demerol depressed me, and I cried a lot. My mother knew that because of my depression I was unable to put up the kind of fight for life she knew I wanted to. Mother knew I didn't want to be sad and depressed all the time, so she asked the doctor to take me off Demerol. He was very reluctant because of the amount of pain I was in, particularly when they changed my dressings.

"It's going to be okay," my mother said as she looked at me. "When you scream, I'll scream. When you cry, I'll cry. We'll get through it together." And we did. When they changed my dressings, my mother and I screamed and cried into my pillow. I squeezed her hand, and she squeezed mine. My parents knew what I would want...they made the decisions when I couldn't.

But after one dressing change without Demerol, and after the doctor explained to my mom how nerves were being exposed each time they changed the dressing, she consented for medication to be used as long as it was something other than Demerol. And that was fine.

By August, I had undergone more than 30 operations. I was taken each day to a huge whirlpool of medicated water, designed to kill the infection. Normally, they lowered and raised me from a stretcher, but then the day came when I was to sit up in a wheelchair after my whirlpool treatment. It was the first time I really had taken a look at myself. I remember looking at my legs for the first time. It was the ugliest sight I had ever seen. I broke down and tears streamed down my face. But the physical therapist knew exactly what to say and helped me through what was the biggest hurdle I can remember.

For the first time, I started talking with my doctors about my amputations . . . asking questions about what my limitations would be . . . and if I would walk again. Also, for the first time, I began to think that no man would ever want to look at me again. No one was ever going to think I was pretty.

But my doctors pushed me along. "You'll do whatever you want to do. The sky is the limit," they said. We started talking about artificial limbs, and the doctors sent a lady who was an above-the-knee amputee to visit me. She made me realize that this was not the end of my life. I knew then I would walk and be independent again. I was fortunate that I had a lot of support from my family and friends. In my heart, I knew this had happened for a reason. I may not have known why yet, but God had a plan.

I was fitted with my first prostheses in August while I was still in the hospital. They were wonderful at the time. After all, they enabled me to walk and drive, two things some people thought I'd never do again. I remained in the Dallas area, living with an aunt and uncle for a month after I left the hospital, and I continued physical therapy three times each week. That November, I went back to my hometown of Henrietta, Texas, returned to work, and bought a new car. I never looked back.

I still was walking with canes or crutches. I'd only walk alone around the office or home. But after six months, I put the canes and crutches in the closet.

I lived with my parents for 10 months, and I think my mother thought it was like having her teenager home again. She did almost everything for me because I was still so weak. At the time, I couldn't have cared less about dating. As long as I had my friends and family, I was fine. Besides, driving 20 miles to and from work after a long day really did me in. I usually crashed at night.

The following November, I moved out on my own and got an apartment. I met a guy in my apartment complex — we went out once and then became really good friends. We'd watch television together, play cards, just everything. He introduced me to a friend of his, whom I dated off and on. Dating never really was a problem. It was just that split second when I first met a guy that was somewhat uncomfortable. But if we talked for very long, I knew I could put him at ease. I decided if someone didn't like me, that was their problem.

At work, we listened to a disc jockey named J.D. Stone

on our favorite radio station. I decided to call him one day to tell him what a blast it was listening to him. It turned out he banked in the same building where I worked, so he said he'd stop and see me sometime. I doubted it, but I'll never forget Friday the 13th in February, 1981. He came into our office, and we hit it off right from the beginning. He asked me to the movies the following weekend. When he came to my apartment that night, I told him I had something I thought I should share with him. I explained that I had two artificial limbs. He couldn't believe it, but it didn't matter. John and I were married that December. Like the rest of my family, he's always been supportive and encourages me in anything I want to attempt.

In March, 1982, I was fitted with what was supposed to be an above-the-knee CAT-CAM prosthesis on my left leg. It was lighter, but it was still a hard quad socket that felt like I was sitting on a rock. My right leg still had a strap that held the prosthesis on at the knee. The prostheses were definitely more comfortable than my original pair, and I had no major problems wearing them until I became pregnant in April, 1985. That August, we learned we were expecting not one, but two babies. I started retaining fluid during my fifth month and couldn't wear my above-the-knee prosthesis at all. I began using a wheelchair. I could still do most everything. I could have walked with crutches, but I was more comfortable with the wheelchair, partly because I didn't want to take a chance of endangering the babies by falling. My doctor prescribed strict bed rest in October to prolong my pregnancy so the twins wouldn't arrive too early. Having children wasn't something I (or my doctor) was sure I would ever be able to do. And after so many surgeries, my doctor wasn't sure if I could withstand a normal delivery or if I would need a Caesarean. To everyone's surprise, I delivered two small, but healthy girls, Stephanie and Marissa, normally on November 6, 1985.

After losing the majority of the 45 pounds I gained during

pregnancy, I made an appointment the following August to be fitted with new prostheses. I once again was fitted with a hard quad above-the-knee socket on my left leg and had a strap across my right knee that held on my below-the-knee prosthesis. These prostheses were horrible. Even people at work said my below-the-knee prosthesis looked like a tree stump. Both sockets fit so poorly that I had more sores in the year that followed than I had had the entire time I had been an amputee. I could walk on the artificial legs, but I couldn't wait to rip them off as soon as I got home from work.

The prosthetist kept blaming it on my pregnancy. How could that be . . . he wasn't trying to remake my old legs . . . these were new legs. I had a second below-the-knee leg made, but it didn't help.

My husband recalled the name of the prosthetist who developed the CAT-CAM prosthesis, and I called to talk with him. I went through a hassle with the insurance company and the Texas Rehabilitation Commission concerning payment for the new limbs before I made an appointment with the prosthetist. I had my permanent legs by September. I was fitted with a light-weight, comfortable CAT-CAM above-the-knee prosthesis on my left leg. And my below-the-knee prosthesis was no longer held on by a strap, but with a rubber sleeve. The new flexible feet allow more stability when walking, especially up inclines and stairs.

I'm now proud of the way I look and walk. I do things that I've been unable to do since 1979 . . . like mow the yard, ride a bicycle, and keep up with two very active little girls. The only problem I have is an occasional breakdown of scar tissue during the hot summer months.

I know how much it helped me to talk with other amputees, because only they really know what you are going through. I've talked with several amputees in the hospitals in Dallas since 1979, and John and I have gone as a couple to talk with some. One lady with a below-the-knee

123

amputation was particularly concerned that her husband would never want to touch her again and her kids wouldn't love her. John told her that her husband should love her for what she was on the inside. We stayed in touch with the family for months. Helping others is such a good feeling.

In April, 1979, when I was nearly swept away by that tornado, I felt alone. I felt like no one knew what I was going through. Now I know I'm not alone. I'm a strong person and will grow stronger with the help of God, my family, and friends.

Bubby's "Canacal"

JEREMIAH MAXEY, 6
(AS TOLD BY HIS MOTHER, EVELYN)
*She and her husband looked forward to the birth
of twins, but her joy turned to sadness when
their baby boy had medical complications that threatened
to end his short life. Miraculously, he survived,
but there were problems with his arms. Doctors said
amputation of the right arm below the elbow and
part of the left hand was the only answer.*

The twins were born in Casper, Wyoming, on July 20, 1984. They arrived a month early by Caesarean section. The doctor and I had suspected for some time that something might be wrong with baby "B."

I awoke in the recovery room a few hours after surgery. It was apparent from the look on my husband Glenn's face that something was wrong with one of the babies. "Did baby "B" make it?" I asked. In a shaky voice, he said: "We have a boy and a girl . . . and the little boy has some problems."

I fell apart. I asked him what was wrong. "The doctors don't know what it is, but he has some problems with his arms and a mass on his left side." The doctors had contacted Children's Hospital in Denver, and a medical team was being flown in to get the baby.

I wanted to see Jeremiah, as we had decided to call him. He was on life support, so I had to go to the nursery to see

125

Jeremiah Maxey and his twin sister Danelle
double-up on the slide.

him. Dragging my I.V. and still half-sedated, I made my way to the nursery. There he was . . . so tiny and beautiful. With both arms covered, tubes running into his small body and his face covered with an oxygen mask, he was still precious. I just knew he had to make it. At that moment, my only thoughts were on him, leaving my baby girl — small, but perfect — without the attention a beautiful newborn deserves.

The Denver medical team arrived, and I saw what I feared might be the last glimpse of my son as they rushed him to a small jet. My husband went with Jeremiah, while I stayed in the hospital with Danelle.

When Danelle and I were released, we went to Denver. We stayed at the Ronald McDonald House and spent most of our time at Jeremiah's bedside in the intensive care unit. The doctors discovered he had too many platelets in his blood, and his whole system had clotted. The worst clotting was in his arms and kidneys. They put him on Heprin to thin the blood, but doctors offered little hope that Jeremiah would survive. They feared a clot could move to his heart, lungs or brain...but that didn't happen. It was our first miracle.

The days passed, and Jeremiah was getting better. Weeks passed, and his general health continued to improve. At the same time, his arms were getting worse. His right arm was turning black, along with his left index finger and forearm. I had a very hard time seeing what I did not want to see. We had come so far, and every day was a big step. He was still on oxygen and had to be fed through a tube, but he was getting better. I just couldn't face the fact that blood to his arms, especially the right one, had been cut off too long, and that they were not going to get better.

I had taken Danelle with me to the hospital cafeteria one day. As I returned, the mother of the child in the crib next to Jeremiah's crib said the doctors had brought an orthopedic surgeon to see him. "I heard about Jeremiah's arm, and I'm so sorry!" she said. "What do you mean?" I replied, in shock. She started to cry and went to get the nurse.

"We were waiting for your husband to come from Wyoming this evening to tell you," the nurse explained. And I knew what I had tried to deny was about to happen. I just couldn't deal with it. The nurse said Jeremiah was scheduled for surgery at 7 a.m. Monday to amputate his right arm below the elbow and part of his badly damaged left hand.

Jeremiah hadn't even reached five pounds yet, and I couldn't believe this was happening. The doctors said the gangrene was so bad that it was becoming a threat to his recovery. I prayed: "God, please don't let this happen; please take my arms, my legs, my life . . . but not my baby's." We had come so close to losing him six weeks earlier, and now I was losing a part of him.

"Mrs. Maxey, it's all the better that if it has to happen, it happen now," the doctors said, trying to comfort me. "He will never suffer the mental anguish or worry. You and your husband will do that for him. And all his energy will be spent on recovery."

But I still wanted to change this . . . it just couldn't be happening. I was an emotional mess. The hospital staff psychologist talked with my husband and me. She was used to dealing with "why my child" parents. She gave us the best advice anyone could offer at the time. "Go ahead and cry, throw a fit, be mad and grieve," she told us. "When he comes out of that operating room, his arm will be gone. As in death, it's final, gone forever. The only way to heal is to grieve, mourn. Then, you come to accept your loss and start to recover."

I cried and questioned "why?" and I worked through all the normal things you do when faced with a loss. Monday came, and all I could think of was "Please God, let him live through this surgery . . . he's so small and has been through so much . . . please, please, let him live!"

Five hours later, the doctors came out of surgery and said Jeremiah was on the way to the recovery room. We could see him in a little while. I was so happy to have my twins . . . both of them. I put the loss of his right arm and part of his left hand in perspective for the first time since it had all started.

Soon after he recovered from surgery, our lives started getting back to normal, or what would become normal from then on. After not having any children for ten years, and now having twins, "normal" took on a whole new meaning. Jeremiah returned to Denver Children's Hospital every other week for the first year. It was a five-hour drive from our Wyoming home. He went through four surgeries on his left hand and had a cast for six months, as doctors tried to stretch tendons and straighten the damaged fingers.

Jeremiah was fitted first with a passive mitt at 6 months and wore a hook for four years. His hand specialist started talking about myoelectrics to replace the hook, in part because the fingers on the left hand had been so badly damaged. Jeremiah was fitted with his myoelectric hand at age 5, and it's the best thing that's ever happened to him. He adapted to using the myoelectric hand fairly quickly, although he had to re-learn some of the things he had been doing with the hook. He's able to do so much more, and it helped improve his self-image as he started school and began dealing with other children.

Jeremiah and his sister are quite a team. Danelle is a real defender when it comes to her brother. They are very close. They were playing outside at a friend's house one day. Some neighborhood kids told Jeremiah his arm looked stupid, so he went inside to play Nintendo. But Danelle would not let it drop. She told the kids they were very rude and that Bubby's "canacal" (what she calls his myoelectric hand) was not stupid! She came home very upset, telling her dad and me about the incident.

"That's okay, Sissy," Jeremiah said. "Those kids just don't know some people have two arms and some don't. But it's really okay because we're all different."

Out of the mouths of babes . . . there's nothing like a reminder that everything really is okay.

Don't Listen to Anyone

PETER THOMAS, 27

*At age 10, both of his legs were severed below the
knees in a car accident. Snow skiing gave him
a renewed sense of freedom, independence and pride.
He excelled in college and went on to law school.
Now he is an advocate for the disabled on Capitol Hill
and has a world of practical advice on how to
make the most of a physical challenge.*

I was in intensive care three to four days after both of my
legs were amputated below the knees. A man who had
read about my automobile accident came to visit me.

As we talked, the man unbuttoned his pants and,
literally, jumped out of them and up on to the bed beside
me. I was shocked. I hadn't even realized that he was an
amputee. "I'm a great golfer, have a family and everything!"
he said. "If I can do it, so can you."

It's a moment that I'll never forget. It was a turning
point in my life. He made me understand that I didn't have
to look or act like an amputee. What I did or became was
entirely up to me.

After 17 years of living with two artificial legs, the best
advice I can give to anyone with a physical challenge is very
simple: don't listen to anyone except yourself. You are
limited only by your attitude and determination, not by
your particular physical situation and certainly not by what

131

Peter Thomas

someone else thinks you can or cannot accomplish. The visit by the stranger was proof of that.

Having said that you are not limited by your physical circumstances, I must say the loss of both my legs below the knees at age 10 was a relatively minor handicap when compared with other disabilities. I was young and adapted to my amputations rather quickly. I still had mobility in my knees, and my stumps (or paws, as my girlfriend calls them) were in good condition. When I think of the tremendous accomplishments of people who have lost their knees or arms, are paralyzed or blind, I realize I have it pretty easy.

Lest you think dealing with two artificial legs day after day is a cake walk, I must say there were times when I'd rather sit and stare at the wall than endure the pain of getting up to turn on the television. When you think about it, I walk on stilts, suspended a foot above the ground. Regardless of how well they fit, there is going to be some degree of pain at some point. When there's pain, think of how fortunate you are to be mobile — then, see a good prosthetist. In the early days after my amputations, I encountered pain frequently, but it seemed to fade once I encountered some success with my physical challenge.

Some people who genuinely love and care for you are so careful not to get your hopes up that they wind up telling you all the things you "can't" do. These good-hearted people will wait on you, comfort you, and not encourage you to challenge yourself — all in an attempt to ease your pain. What they don't realize is that the loss of a limb can soon become a handicap, or disability, rather than a physical challenge in an amputee's mind. And the difference is more than semantic; it is attitudinal. A "physical challenge" is an obstacle to be positively challenged and overcome. A "handicap" immediately assumes an inferiority to the rest, while a "disability" emphasizes an inability to do something. Once your amputation becomes a handicap or disability, the psychological effects of the loss can be devastating.

I was fortunate to have two positive and supportive parents and a close-knit family that didn't cater to my physical limitations. My father used to secretly walk behind me at the shopping mall and then say, "You're limping to the left." I hated it at the time, but I developed a very straight gait.

I also became immersed in a quality group of friends who constantly treated me like "one of the boys." If there was an activity that I felt was physically prohibitive, I was never left out, nor was the activity cancelled. Instead, my friends found some way to incorporate me into the activity. In time, people begin to see you as a friend or family member — not as a disabled friend or family member. I can think of no greater compliment than when an old friend seriously asks me if my new shoes are too tight or if my feet are cold. When you and your artificial limb become one in your mind and in the minds of others, in a sense you become whole again.

While I believe it would be inappropriate, perhaps even unhealthy, to refuse to accept your amputation — try not to let it consume and encompass your existence. There are millions of factors that make you what you are. Put your physical challenge in perspective and move on with your life. If you negatively take advantage of your disability, you eventually will be liked by few and resented by many. That type of behavior reinforces handicap stereotypes and prompts people to treat the physically-challenged population with pity, instead of respect and encouragement. However, please don't confuse exploiting one's handicap with capitalizing upon your physical challenge.

By capitalizing upon your physical challenge, you adapt your daily life to your physical limitations and opportunities will inevitably come your way. I have capitalized on my physical challenge, and my life has been richer and more exciting than I could have imagined. Before my amputation in fifth grade, I was only interested in one thing: soccer. As I struggled through my first few years with artificial limbs, I learned to walk well, occasionally played contact sports with friends, and constantly rode my bicycle. But as organized sports began to take most of the time of my junior high friends, I knew I had to adapt to and capitalize upon my physical circumstances.

At the time, the technological inadequacy of my limbs prevented me from running fast enough to keep up with any junior high athletic team. I became the football manager, but I had a real desire to be more active. I auditioned for and landed leading roles in school plays. Because few people in the audience knew of my disability, I was applauded for my performance as Mr. Bumble in the play "Oliver," and not for being a handicapped performer. This was a triumph. But in the words of Tom Cruise in the movie "Top Gun," I felt the "need for speed."

Bill Denby, now widely recognized as the Vietnam veteran basketball player in the DuPont commercial, taught me how to snow ski when I was 14. Skiing turned out to be my conduit to a new way of life. I raced in slalom, giant slalom, downhill and cross country competitions. I won 11 gold and silver medals over a four-year period in the National Handicap Ski Championships held in Winter Park, Colorado. With travel expenses paid for by local civic organizations and my equipment donated by manufacturers, there was nothing to keep me from whizzing past my able-bodied friends with wind whipping through my hair. Skiing provided an unparalleled feeling of freedom, independence and pride that began to encompass every facet of my life.

I began to excel in my high school studies and, as a senior, was elected class president. Because of my physical circumstances, I took high school seriously and looked toward a good college to help land a career with a decent wage, but without strenuous physical demands. I received a settlement for my accident which assured that I could attend college. I set my sights on Boston College and was accepted by early decision. I know that my physical challenge positively affected the college's decision to admit me — not because they wanted to give the handicapped kid a chance, but because I had accomplished a significant amount during my adolescence despite my handicap. I had, in effect, capitalized on my physical challenge and turned it to my advantage.

I'll let you in on a little secret: If you are unassuming and humble . . . if you disregard your physical limitations and carry a good attitude, living life the way a good-spirited able-bodied person would . . . people are in awe of you even if you have done nothing spectacular. It's like Helen Hayes says: "At my age, people admire you for just being alive." The same is true of someone who seems to get along as well as, if not better than, everyone else but who has a physical challenge most would consider insurmountable. People admire you for just being "normal" and will extend themselves more acutely than they usually would. This is when opportunities arise that would not, if not for your physical challenge. Capitalize on these opportunities with a positive attitude, and your life will be enhanced by your physical challenge.

I learned the most about being physically challenged during my years at Boston College. I rejected the "handi-capped room" and opted for unadulterated dorm life. Initially, I received some pretty uncomfortable looks in the common showers when 6-foot-5-inch football players would walk in and see me on my knees at 4-foot-5-inches. My ice-breaking line was always the same: "Just call me Neil." It seemed to relax them long enough for them to realize that I was approachable and just like any other freshman. My roommates quickly adapted and took full advantage of my car privileges for late-night pizza runs. And for the first time, I experienced being with a woman and not being treated differently when my artificial legs were off for the night. I realized a woman could be attracted to me and consider my artificial legs as an interesting, even positive, attribute instead of an impediment to a meaningful relationship. Through all of this, I learned the value of having very good friends and the support generated from those relationships.

In addition to graduating cum laude from Boston College, I served first as chairman of the student senate and later as president of the student body. I represented the 8,500 students on the University Board of Trustees and was selected to represent Boston College as the One Millionth Graduate from an American Jesuit College or University. As chairman of the handicapped committee, I conceived and organized the first Handicap Awareness Day. Subtitled "Sensitivity '86," students simulated a handicap for a day to personally experience accessibility obstacles. The highlight of the day was a speech given by Teddy Kennedy, Jr., who is physically challenged and an accomplished amputee athlete.

It was then that Georgetown University Law School ignored my rather mediocre standardized test scores and accepted me to law school. I had entitled my application essay: "Adversity, Adjustment, Action, Achievement." I surprised the director of admissions by striding into his office to ask whether I had been admitted. Once he realized the rather brash person in his office was a double amputee, I suspect that he made his decision on the spot. It was not because I had artificial legs that I was accepted to law school. Again, it was because my accomplishments were on a par with other applicants who had not encountered a physical challenge. Two artificial legs were just the icing on the cake — or, in his words, "a great gimmick."

I moved to Washington, D.C., rented a two-bedroom apartment and began looking for a roommate. I wanted a person who pulls into first day classes at law school with no apartment and no plan. I found two such drifters and developed a fantastic group of friends who were every bit as understanding and supportive as my college buddies and my hometown friends. I struck up a relationship with a beautiful woman who could not have been more accepting of my physical challenge.

Some amputees speak of prejudice and discrimination that they encounter, but I have personally experienced little of that except when I've been wheelchair-bound after an occasional revision surgery. I have noticed a major difference in how people treat me when I'm in a wheelchair versus when I'm on my limbs. They want to cater to your needs and coddle you. They don't mind inconveniencing everyone else if it is better for the guy or gal in the wheelchair. To me, this seems like an unhealthy attitude that only reinforces handicap stereotypes.

It was in law school that I became involved in a nonprofit, disability advocacy organization called the American State of the Art Prosthetic Association, which has an office in Washington, D.C. The group, comprised of prosthetists, orthotists, and consumers, strives to benefit amputees and disabled individuals by technologically advancing the state of prosthetic and orthotic devices. I became consumer vice-president and lobbied on Capitol Hill for legislation to benefit amputees and the disabled. The legislation was signed into law in November of 1990.

As a result of the legislation, a National Center for Medical Rehabilitation Research will be established at the National Institutes of Health, to coordinate, conduct and support research on medical rehabilitation, including research on the development of orthotic and prosthetic devices.

I became involved in the organization because I felt many

amputees were not satisfied with their artificial limbs, and I felt I was in a position to help. I encourage you to get involved, too. The support of all amputees and consumers of orthotic and prosthetic devices is needed to assure continued progress in these fields. But if amputee advocacy organizations are not for you, I encourage you to get involved in sports, clubs or organizations that interest you. In the words of NIKE, "Just Do It!" The worst thing you can do is to sit on the sidelines and let everyone else have all the fun.

I've had 11 sets of artificial limbs in 17 years and have experimented with just about every type of limb on the market. I have seen my 10-pound leather and rawhide, stiff-ankled, thigh-corsetted leg become a two-and-a-half pound, carbon fiber, multi-axial limb, complete with soft "skin" and toes to match. There have been many technological advances in the past decade that have benefitted amputees. But there remains a vast gap between what is available from different prosthetists and orthotists. Some have led the way to new fitting techniques and material application, but others continue to produce and fit the same old devices.

A new amputee or orthotic user needs to understand there are choices. Ask questions. Talk to more than one prosthetist and even other amputees. Tell the prosthetist about your activities and goals, and place the burden on him to come up with a device that meets your needs. If he can't or won't, the answer is simple: go to someone who will. There are very few amputees who cannot be fitted with prosthetic devices. Make sure you exhaust your options before deciding not to obtain a prosthesis.

But even if you can't wear a prosthesis or choose not to, your life can be as fulfilling as anyone else's life. All it takes is a positive attitude and a lot of determination, because these are your only two limits. I can say unequivocally that, were it not for my capitalizing upon my physical challenge,

I would not have lived my life to its fullest. I choose to listen only to myself and to words of encouragement from family and friends.

And so I say to you, when someone says that you can't do something — be it a task, a sport or whatever — flash them a grin and then proceed to conquer your physical challenge. Don't listen to them — because they are wrong. Don't listen to anyone except yourself!

Facing Life with Confidence

JOYCE BAUGHN, 52

*At age six, her arms were amputated below the
elbows when she was run over by a train. She used
prosthetic hooks until a control cable broke.
Then she discovered she could do everything
without prostheses. She and her husband, Bill, launched
the first amputee support group in North Texas.*

I was born and grew up in and around Sweetwater, a
small West Texas town divided by several sets of railroad tracks. This geographical fact had a lasting impact
on my life.

One beautiful day in May, as I was on my way home from
my grandmother's house where I had been playing after
school, I found a train stopped across the street. It never
occurred to me to walk the block or so necessary to go around
the train. I was only 6 years old, and this was the only route I
knew. I soon became impatient with waiting, and a solution
occurred to me. If I crawled under the train and out the other
side, I could be on my way. The idea frightened me, but as I
continued to wait, its appeal increased.

After looking around to make sure I was unobserved, I
crawled under the train. Just then I heard the jerking sound
that boxcars make when they start to move, and I knew I
was trapped. I lay very still and waited for the train to pass,

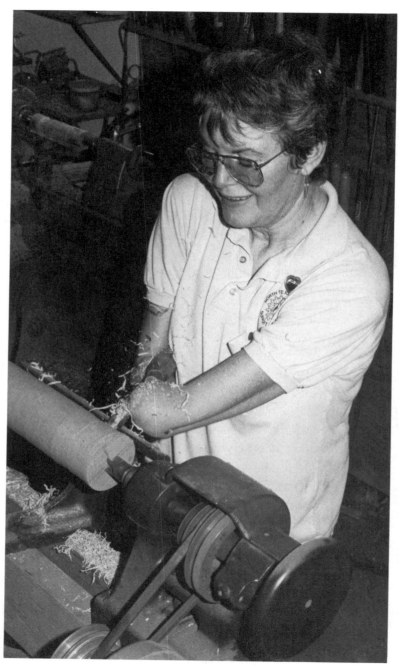

Joyce Baughn

not realizing my hands were across the rail. Only after it had passed over me did I realize that I had lost both my arms below the elbows.

Fortunately, two soldiers, who were waiting in their car for the train to pass, saw me under the train and were ready to use their belts as tourniquets as soon as the train passed over me. They rushed me to the local hospital where our family doctor did the necessary surgery in the emergency room. He really did a fantastic job — I've never needed further surgery, nor have I experienced phantom sensation. I was in the hospital 11 days.

After my arms healed, I was taken to McCloskey Hospital in Temple, Texas. At that time, as World War II neared the end, it was being used by the military for combat veterans. There, I was fitted with prostheses that had child-size split hooks. After they were built, they were shipped to my home and arrived early in August, in time for my seventh birthday.

With only a month until school started, I had to work hard to learn to use the new prostheses. I have very loving parents, but my mother is also a very disciplined lady. She was told that I had to learn to use hooks, so she did her part to see that I did. Each morning I was dressed for the day, and this included putting on the hooks. They only came off when it was time to get ready for bed. I went back to school that fall with the rest of my classmates. I could print, eat and do the few things required of a second-grader.

In the summer between third and fourth grade, one of my control cables broke. Replacing it was not easy because there were no prosthetic facilities in Sweetwater in the late 1940s — there probably still aren't. And society was not so mobile then. Besides, there was no real urgency since I wasn't in school.

As I went without prostheses, I used my arms to do things. By using both arms, I could grasp and manipulate things. It quickly became apparent to my parents that I was learning to do everything that I had been doing with hooks,

143

plus things I hadn't been able to do with them. Using my arms was easier for me. It required less energy, and it was certainly more comfortable. The biggest advantage to using my arms instead of hooks was that I retained my sense of touch . . . I was no longer totally removed from everything around me. The control cable never did get fixed.

Looking back, I wonder what my schoolmates thought. The last day of first grade, I had hands. When I started second grade, I had hooks. The last day of third grade, I was using hooks, and when I started fourth grade, I was using my arms. Some of them must have been confused, but I don't ever remember being made to feel different or unwelcome.

Life continued for me much as it did for my friends. I learned new skills about the same time as others my age — with a few exceptions. The things I wanted to do, such as drive, I learned to do. Things I really wasn't motivated to do, I postponed learning — such as ironing and becoming functionally independent. I only learned to dress and take care of myself when I left home to go to college. Accepting help at home from family was one thing. Needing help from others was something else.

One area in which I was slow to develop was socially. I do not blame this on my lack of hands. I was, and still am, shy. The difference is that today I work at overcoming this tendency. I was more interested in reading a book than being with people. I dated some, but I wasn't very comfortable with men, so I decided they were more trouble than they were worth.

My love of reading influenced my career choice. I recognized that I needed to prepare myself to make a living . . . I would make a lousy waitress! I had worked in the library in high school and college, so I decided to become a librarian. After getting a bachelor's degree in English, with a minor in psychology, I received a master's degree in library science. For several years, I worked as a cataloger in various college and public libraries in Illinois, Massachusetts, Oklahoma,

Texas and Florida. I liked to travel, and this seemed like a good way to do it.

I enjoyed living alone. I had an apartment, a car, my job and friends. I could be alone or not — as I chose. I didn't think things could be better . . . then I met Bill Baughn. He is so totally different from anyone I have ever met. That is one of the reasons he fascinates me, and perhaps what has enabled me to view life from a different perspective. I do know my growth curve took off like a rocket when we met. He is truly my other half.

Bill is a theatrical technician and was active in that field until recently. We travelled a lot with his work, and I "retired" for a while. Being retired enabled me to pursue some untried interests. I become interested in genealogy, made some redwood burl clocks, learned to do needlepoint, and stained glass using the copper foil method. I enjoyed retirement, but it was time to move on and "grow" some more.

We moved to Dallas to be near my family and, more or less, settled down. I went back to work, but didn't go back to library science . . . I had "done" that and was ready to try something different. I went to work for a parts distributor where I have worked in several positions from pricing invoices to back orders and expediting accounts receivable and accounts payable. I discovered I am very good at payables and enjoy it — in spite of the fact that I barely passed math in school.

Bill is a skilled woodworker. He had just gotten his first lathe, and we decided to do some arts and crafts shows — though we both had some reservations about how I would react to it. I had never worked with the public before. Our reservations were totally groundless. Not only did people accept me as a saleslady, but they were ready to believe I had done the work! That was an ego boost, and it encouraged my interest in learning to work the lathe. We acquired a second lathe, and Bill taught me woodturning. There is

real satisfaction in producing a piece that someone is willing to buy.

A friend got us started going to the PALS group, an organization for parents of limb-deficient children. Most of the children have birth defects and are being treated at Scottish Rite Hospital. I feel that by being there with my husband, I can encourage by example, even when the questions aren't asked. And I am always open to questions at the meetings.

The amputee support movement had started, but there was no organization in Dallas. There was talk, but no action. Bill and I decided the time had come, and the only way to get something going was to jump into it. We called a meeting for anyone interested, and the North Texas Amputee Support Group was born. We have been involved with it ever since and feel a real commitment to helping other amputees adjust to their new lifestyles, and in some cases, come up with methods of adapting.

I have been asked the secret to my successful adjustment to life as an amputee. I believe it was the way my parents raised me. At the time of my accident, they wished the train had killed me — not because they didn't love me, but because they did. They couldn't imagine how I would be able to do anything and didn't want a life of helplessness and dependency for me.

Since I didn't die, they took me home to love and do whatever was necessary . . . for however long it was needed. Fortunately, it wasn't long before they saw they were wrong in their initial assumptions. They allowed me to grow and develop at my own pace, and they treated me the same as they treated my two sisters. There was never any question in my mind about their love and acceptance of me. Because of this, I grew up with a feeling of self-worth that enabled me to face life with confidence.

Teddy Alvis

A Brief Detour

TEDDY ALVIS, 21

*A week after high school graduation, he was
looking forward to college life. A head-on crash
took the lives of two friends and left him a bilateral
amputee. Although he walks with two prostheses,
he has renewed his self-confidence playing
wheelchair basketball.*

My spirits were high. I was 18 years old and had just graduated from Murphy High School in Mobile, Alabama. Two friends and I were on our way to take a look at the University of Alabama campus, where we thought we might spend our college years. I was planning a career in broadcasting and wanted to be a disc jockey.

It was a rainy June day in 1987. We were on a two-lane highway when a tractor-trailer rig came speeding right toward us. It hit us head-on.

I was taken to a hospital in Birmingham, where I later learned that both my friends had been killed. I was badly burned, especially my legs, and my left thigh was broken. For three days, the doctor worked to save my legs. But there was nothing that could be done. The doctor talked to my folks and me about amputation. I signed the papers for the surgery and told the doctor to do the best he could. My left leg was amputated above the knee and my right leg below the knee.

I can't say that I was angry about the amputations. It's difficult to remember all the emotions I felt. At the time, I was more devastated by the loss of my friends than the loss of my legs.

I was in the hospital 47 days. During that time, several amputees visited me. They encouraged me, even though the doctor told me it would be at least a year before I'd be able to walk again.

During my hospitalization, I began physical therapy, which I continued as an outpatient at the rehabilitation center even after I went home. I'll never forget that first time I was in the swimming pool for therapy. There, in the water, I felt like I was standing again. For the first time since the accident, I felt like I was on two feet. It was a wonderful feeling.

I kept up my therapy two to three times each week. Because of my burns, it was a long healing process. I wasn't fitted with my first artificial legs until February, 1988. I had another friend who had lost his legs during the Vietnam War. He took a look at my legs and said they looked just like the wartime design.

They were conventional, old-style prostheses with metal side joints. Strings laced up the leg. I had so much scar tissue that the prosthetist wanted to take as much pressure as possible off the ends of my legs. That meant I wore moderately heavy straps and a waist belt. I started out with big wool socks over my stumps and leather sockets that fit high over the hip area.

It took me about two months to learn how to walk with my prostheses. I began walking between the parallel bars, progressed to crutches and then to a cane. I took one step at a time and didn't rush because every step was painful. The scar tissue and skin grafts continued to cause me

problems . . . I had to be very careful how I walked to keep
the skin from breaking down. I learned how to use the legs
fairly well.

It wasn't long after my amputations that a friend introduced me to wheelchair basketball. That was probably one of
the keys to my recovery. I had played basketball all my life
and was on the high school baseball and golf teams. I just
loved sports. The basketball court is where I regained a lot of
my self-confidence. I realized my life would go on . . . and I
could still play basketball. My first time on the court was a
powerful, emotional experience. Playing from a wheelchair is
different, but overall it was an excellent experience. Now,
our team plays November through February against teams
from all across the southern part of the United States.

I began college during the fall of 1988 at the University
of South Alabama. I'd walk on my prostheses, but after a
time my scar tissue would break down again, and I'd end
up back in a wheelchair.

Going back to school wasn't a tough decision since I
knew my life was headed toward a career in the radio
industry. College students are probably more accepting of
the disabled than some other people, although there is still
a lot to be done to make campus buildings more accessible
for the handicapped. Of course, some people do stare.
You've just got to say "the hell with them" and go on. If
they are going to stare, they are going to stare, and you just
have to get over that. And there are some busy-bodies who
have all kinds of questions. I sometimes tell them I was in a
shark attack or something else. That usually leaves them a
little stunned, but they don't ask any more questions!

A college friend told me about a prosthetist who was
making legs that helped amputees run. I saw a video tape
of all the things other amputees could do and got on a
plane to see if I could be fitted with better prostheses. I was
excited about the possibilities.

151

I still had a rod in my left thigh, which the doctor wanted to remove. I had it taken out, but then I re-broke the thigh. It meant my leg went back into a cast, and I spent nine more months in a wheelchair, so the legs had to wait awhile. There are no words to describe being confined to a wheelchair. I don't think you really appreciate all that people in wheelchairs go through until you've been there.

It was February, 1990, before I got my new legs. Now I have silicone socket inserts that protect the areas that were burned on my legs. I can walk longer without the skin breaking apart.

The most exciting things about my new legs are the hydraulic knees. I knew the minute I stood up with the new knees how much less effort it was going to take to walk. Now I can stand up straight and am better supported so I don't fall. With suction sockets on my prostheses, I don't have to mess with the belts, so it's easier to put on my legs.

The new legs have made me a lot more mobile. I was able to walk to class every day last semester. I just don't have the problems when I walk like I did before. I still have episodes of phantom pain, but in a way, I like the phantom pain because I can still sense the feeling in my feet. Sometimes a twinge of pain wakes me up at night, so I squeeze the leg to try to cut off the circulation and stop the pain.

Occasionally, I have a down day, but I won't let myself wallow in self-pity. I believe all things happen for a reason and events in our lives are pre-determined. I never blame God for that. God gave me, and I still have, a brain and a heart. I believe you have to do the best with what you've got. I guess I could say "the hell with everything" and give up, but that would be self-destructive.

I enjoy playing wheelchair basketball, and with my new legs, I can now stand to play golf. Also, I continue to play the drums whenever I can. I used to be in a band, and I still enjoy sitting in at the drums to play a little blues or rock and roll. There are some things I can't do, but for the most part, things haven't changed all that much since I became an amputee.

I know different people react to things differently. Other amputees have told me that their girlfriends left them because they lost their legs. That's just a part of it. If someone doesn't like you for who you are, then you can't be close to them anyway. I've seen alot of people who are alot worse off than I am. I just thank God that I am alive. I think getting to know other amputees has helped me realize we're not so different from anyone else.

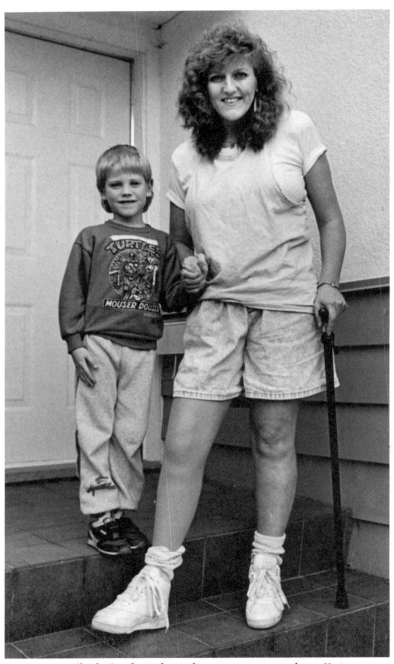

Glenda Standeven, hemipelvectomy amputee, and son, Kevin.
Photo by Jean Konda-Witte — Chilliwack Times

To Prove the Doctor Wrong

GLENDA STANDEVEN, 35

*The pain in her right hip awakened her at night.
Following surgery to remove a tumor, she was
told there was no malignancy. But a lump that appeared
later led her back to the doctor. It was cancer.
Doctors removed her leg, hip and pelvis.
One doctor told her she'd never walk.*

My first clue that something was wrong with my
hip came innocently enough. I was having
trouble sleeping on my right side. I'd awaken
during the night with a nagging pain deep inside my hip.
The pain would subside during the day only to return at
night when I slept on my right side. I tried exercise and took
up jogging, which only seemed to aggravate the problem.

My family physician began to treat me for bursitis in my
hip, but the pain grew worse. I went to a chiropractor who,
on my third visit, insisted I go for X-rays. He said there was
something very wrong with my hip — it wasn't bursitis or
anything he could fix.

I was an active 31-year-old, so I was relieved when the
X-rays revealed it was only a small bone fragment that had
broken away from the head of the femur, causing the
irritation I felt. But my relief was short-lived. The femur
head had deteriorated because a tumor had destroyed

almost the entire hip joint.

My first biopsy was in May, 1987. I was stunned and numb when they told me it was cancer. People die from cancer. The surgeon reassured me that it was not a virulent type of cancer. I would be given a replacement hip, a portion of my pelvis would be removed, and a bone transplant done. The healing process would be long, but I was young and healthy.

The day of my surgery, I was optimistic, but scared. The only other time I had spent the night in a hospital was to have my baby. I opened my eyes after surgery to find my husband holding my hand. "You've still got your own hip. They didn't have to do the surgery," he told me. I couldn't believe my ears!

They hadn't found what they expected based on the CAT scan and X-rays. The tumor had spread deep into my pelvis and resembled grains of rice. The pathologist diagnosed the new tumor as malignant, but the surgeon said it was benign. So, they did the only thing they could. They removed as much of the tumor as was visible, hollowed out the femur head and reattached my thigh muscle to the bone with a metal screw while they sent the tumor off for further evaluation.

It was more than a week before the biopsy report came back. They sent it to labs in Canada and across the U.S. The strange new tumor was benign. We were sure it was some sort of a miracle! We didn't stop to question the results, but we were grateful I wouldn't need hip replacement surgery.

Months later, after going for physical therapy twice a week to strengthen my leg, I noticed a small lump on the site of the original biopsy. "Just scar tissue," I was told. But the lump seemed to be growing. I was determined not to let my worries overwhelm me, but I went to my specialist for one more CAT scan before my husband and I began trying to have another baby. When the scan results came back, my surgeon was concerned. There was definitely a growth there. Another biopsy was scheduled.

The biopsy was done in December, 1987. It was a malignant growth that would not respond to chemotherapy or radiation. My only option was surgery. At first I thought the doctor meant he would just remove the tumor. As he explained the surgery in detail, I went into shock. He said my leg would have to be removed. "This can't be happening," I thought. "It's only a small, egg-size lump on my hip. How could I lose my whole leg? And not just my leg. They want to take the hip and pelvis on my right side, too."

The doctor said time was critical. The cancer could spread to my lungs. I didn't understand how a tumor on my hip could affect my lungs. Christmas was only days away, but he wanted me in the hospital immediately. I had a 3-year-old son, and I didn't want to spend Christmas in the hospital without a leg. That was no gift to a small child. I told my doctor I wanted Christmas and New Year's with my family. My three married sisters, my parents, and our family always celebrated Christmas together. The doctor wasn't making any guarantees that even with surgery tomorrow that I'd be there next year. I figured two weeks with my family to prepare and pray was not asking too much. I'm glad I took the time. It brought me spiritual peace and strength. And it brought our family even closer.

On January 6, 1988, after a 10-month struggle, I lost my leg, hip and pelvis to cancer. The surgical name for it was a right hemi-pelvectomy.

The night before my surgery, I lay in my hospital bed stroking my sick leg and saying my good-byes. Losing my leg wasn't a hard decision to make. I had a son and wonderful husband who loved me very much. Losing a leg would be a small price to pay to stay alive and be with my family. My favorite nurse came into the room. She started to cry when I told her I felt I should throw a farewell party for my leg. The surgery seemed to affect people who were close to me more than it did me. I think my faith in God and my family's

157

support gave me incredible strength and determination.

I awoke to pain after surgery — incredible, unbearable pain. I'd given birth to a 9 pound 2 ounce child, but this pain was consuming and unending. I was totally unprepared for it. They gave me morphine, but that was horrible, too. After the third day of floating in and out of pain and not being able to think or see clearly, I had them reduce the dosage. It was a wise decision because I've since learned how drug dependency becomes a problem for many amputees.

Nobody had warned me about the pain. If I had been able to talk to another amputee, maybe I would have been more prepared. I had assumed once my sick leg was gone, the pain would be gone. Was I wrong! The phantom pain was worse than the ache my leg caused before it was amputated. I kept a journal the first four months after the surgery. My entry from January 28, 1988, reads:

> *The phantom pain is like electric shocks zapping you out of nowhere, and you never know where they'll hit. Mostly, they seem to be around my foot for some reason. That's where the "popcorn" pain is, too. The popcorn pain is like popcorn popping inside my skin and trying to pop out. It feels really gross! The electric shocks . . . run up and down my leg with such force I want to scream . . . It starts off slow, then builds to a zinging climax . . . and there's a vise pain . . . like my foot is being crushed by a vise . . . Then there are the cramps. How do you get rid of a muscle cramp when there's no muscle to rub? When you stand up, the blood rushes to the stump, so it pounds like crazy. When you lie down, the blood rushes away, and the electric shocks zoom in . . . When I say the pain never goes away, that's sort of a lie because for five or ten seconds, the pain will stop, and it's*

like a beacon in the dark showing me the way it's
going to be someday. Someday soon, God willing!

That was written only two weeks after the surgery.
Honestly, that incredible phantom pain is nothing more than
a vague memory now. I've found most amputees continue to
suffer occasional "zingers," but nothing like the first few
weeks after surgery. Patience is the best medicine. That and
lots of hugs from family and friends. I found prayer, meditation, visualization and relaxation helped me get through it
one day at a time. No doctor can prepare an amputee for
those "zingers." But it's not just in the head. It's real pain. I
thank God for the rehabilitation center that taught me how
to deal with the pain other than by taking drugs.

After my surgery, a doctor came into my room to examine me. I'd never seen him before. I wasn't particularly
impressed by his bedside manner, but I was trying to be
cooperative. He informed me that I shouldn't get any "funny
ideas" about ever walking again because it just wasn't possible for someone with an amputation to my extent. If I did
walk, it would be with such a horrible, lurching gait that I
would be embarrassed wherever I went, he said. At this, he
stood up and imitated what my walk would look like. I
wanted to die. But he made me so angry that I stuck out my
chin and said, "Maybe you would walk that way, but I
certainly would not!" I waited until he was out of the room
before I collapsed in tears in my husband's arms. Until then,
I had no doubts about getting an artificial limb and walking.
I desperately wanted to prove him wrong.

About a month after my surgery, I was sent to a rehabilitation center in Vancouver. The center was like a life
preserver to a drowning person. There, they taught me how
to use an artificial leg. More than that, they taught me to
have confidence in myself. I was not handicapped. I became "physically challenged."

159

I threw away all the pain killers and sleeping pills. I had a rough weekend of withdrawal symptoms, but my family put up with my crankiness and irritability. Everyone knew how much I hated being dependent on drugs, so I had a lot of support when I decided to quit taking them. I found the more I exercised, the less the pain bothered me. By bedtime, I was so tired, I didn't need the pills to sleep. A special relaxation class taught me to escape the pain, and I could use those techniques when I needed them.

My husband and I enrolled in a three-day seminar at the HOPE cancer center in Vancouver. We discovered my fears about dying and feeling helpless against my cancer were quite normal. They showed me how to fight back against my disease through meditation and visualization. I was armed and ready to get well. Nothing would stand in my way. I was exercising more than I ever had in my life. My weight dropped to 109 pounds, too thin for my 5 foot 9 inch height, but when I returned home to my own good cooking, I soon regained the weight. I looked and felt better than I had in years.

After three months at the rehab center, I was sent home to begin my life as an amputee wife and mother. I never dreamed doing all those ordinary tasks again would feel so rewarding and fulfilling. My husband, Rick, and I started a cancer support group to teach other cancer survivors to fight back with meditation, relaxation and visualization techniques. The group also was wonderful therapy for me as an amputee.

My phantom pain was slowly disappearing until it seemed that one morning I awoke, and the pain was gone. It was wonderful to be free of pain. But one thing still bothered me — my prosthesis. My new leg just wasn't living up to my expectations. It rubbed me raw and was terribly uncomfortable. I needed crutches even when I was wearing the leg. I didn't know an artificial leg could be comfortable and functional. I just assumed the discomfort was to be expected.

Back then, I didn't know better.

It wasn't long before I discovered that I could go faster on my crutches without my leg. So Peggy, as we affectionately called my prosthesis, spent more and more time parked in the closet. I became more and more comfortable going places without her.

One day my son, Kevin, and I went to a water park. I crutched into the washroom with him at my side. It was filled with a busload of foreign tourists. As I entered the room, there was silence. They stood open-mouthed, wide-eyed, staring at me. I was uncomfortable, to say the least. For my son's sake I decided to hold my head high. As I washed my hands and fixed my hair, Kevin was getting anxious to go. "Mom, everyone is staring," he said. I replied, "Yes, honey, I noticed that. What do you think they are looking at?" He looked up at me with such innocence and love and said, "Beats me. Let's get out of here!" That's how all my family treated me. I'm still Glenda on the inside. Only my outside packaging has changed.

Through it all, I discovered maintaining a sense of humor is a must for an amputee. When my leg squeaks a little, I quip, "Hmmm. Must be a quart low." One above-the-knee amputee friend was getting out of the lake when some kids asked her what had happened to her leg. She never missed a beat. "Sharks," she said. With a smile and a joke, you can set the tone for how others will accept you. If you let it become a burden or an embarrassment to you, others will sense your discomfort and be uncomfortable around you.

I gradually forgot about wearing a prosthesis. I wore my leg only to church (and prayed the sermons were short), weddings and social functions. The pain wasn't worth the cosmetic appeal. But it bothered me so because I wanted to prove that certain doctor wrong.

I refused to let the loss of the leg slow me down much. Skiing was a sport I enjoyed before the amputation, and I found I enjoyed it even more on one leg. The sense of freedom . . . of gliding . . . of going fast like you're running . . . is almost overwhelming. I was frightened at first, but the instructors soon had me skiing better on one leg than I ever had on two. I even won two silver medals in the 1990 British Columbia Winter Games.

I also met a wonderful girl, Louise Henrioulle, who had been an above-the-knee amputee for 13 years. We both loved to ski and became fast friends. She spent many weekends at our house. Together, we tried "amputee racquetball" and devised our own set of rules. Then, we bought toe clips for our bikes. Without our prostheses, we went bike riding around the neighborhood. There were alot of double-takes, but I think we inspired alot of able-bodied neighbors to get out and enjoy life. When we went to the beach, Louise and I hopped down to the water, and we got more than our share of strange looks. I like to think people admired our courage and determination. Maybe, just maybe, they're a little more grateful for all they have taken for granted.

About a year ago, a friend saw a television program about a prosthetic center in Oklahoma. She contacted my sister, who sent for information. A video showed a girl with the same type of surgery I had who was walking with a cane. The smile on her face made me determined to get a prosthesis like she wore.

My Vancouver prosthetist checked into it, but said he couldn't duplicate the design. However, he was willing to learn new techniques. If I arranged coverage for the cost of a new leg, he would accompany me to learn how the special silicone socket was made. Our local medical program was not willing to spend that kind of money on a new limb, but after six long months of red tape, I was given permission to get the leg. Insurance covered 80 percent of the cost of the leg, and the Canadian Cancer Society gave me $1,200 to help with airfare and hotel costs. My parents gave me

$1,000, and I was set to go. What made the trip even more urgent was that I was two months pregnant and a prosthesis was available that could be adapted to fit my growing shape. I arrived at the prosthetist's office looking for a miracle. The news media covered my story on province-wide television. I was determined not to let my family and friends down. I was going to go home with my crutches in a bag . . . no matter how hard I had to try. As it was, I didn't have to try too hard. My new leg was ready in just under three weeks. When I boarded the plane for home, I walked with just a cane. My family was there to meet me at the airport. We all cried as my little boy ran up to meet me, and I was able to bend over and pick him up for the first time in almost three years. I didn't have to drop my crutches or settle for a hug around the leg any more. As the media and others watched, I even waltzed with my father. My husband and I walked out of the airport arm in arm, also something we hadn't done in nearly three years. It was the miracle we had prayed for. I had proven that doctor wrong.

Now, when I go shopping, people don't stare or ask rude questions. They just think I have a sore leg. They couldn't be more wrong. My leg doesn't hurt at all. I'm fortunate I'm able to wear my prosthesis even though I'm six months pregnant. The only drawback is that my torso is contained inside the silicone socket, so I'm the only one who can feel the baby kicking. The baby will be here soon. And who knows . . . I may walk into the delivery room and fulfill another dream. All I know for sure is that with faith and determination, all things really are possible.

Editor's note: Glenda did walk into the hospital wearing her prosthesis, and on November 8, 1990, gave birth naturally to a 7 pound 14 ounce baby boy. Mother and son are doing great!

You Can Still Have Fun

BRADLEY ANTHONY, 12
(AND HIS MOTHER, MARY ANN)
When Bradley was born with a severely deformed left
leg and problems with both hands, his mother
wondered why her baby boy wasn't allowed to come into
this world perfect. His leg had to be amputated
below the knee when he was 2 days old. His parents
struggled for years to find the right prosthesis
that would let their son grow and enjoy life.

From Bradley:
It's hard living with one leg. You don't get to do everything you would normally do. Sometimes I feel sorry for myself, but I realize I'm better off than some people. Even though I have just one leg, I still play sports like football, baseball and basketball.

My friends help me feel good about myself. It's not so good sometimes when people call you names and make fun of you. It really makes you feel bad, and it puts you down. Just because you are an amputee doesn't mean you're disabled or anything like that. You can still do things and have fun. I think that anybody with a disability should give their all and never give up. I don't think I'll give up. I think my life will get better and better.

I have hobbies just like other people. I collect baseball cards, and I play sports. Sometimes, I bowl and play golf. I hope to play professional baseball someday because it's my favorite sport. Fishing is another thing I do. So having one leg isn't so bad after all. I can even do things without a leg, like play sports, and I can hop everywhere.

I love getting to do things with a good (artificial) leg and such good people like Bill Ethridge who make them. Not many people have friends like him. I also hope I get to do more things as I get older. Everytime I get a new leg, it's always better, and I can do more things with it. Like this time, I got a new foot that springs and helps me run faster. I also got a new covering. So, I hope whoever is reading this does all they can do to make life a lot happier. I know I do.

I also have idols. My favorite one is Jim Abbot. He is a pitcher for the California Angels. I like him because he was born without a right hand. He is a very good pitcher.

From his mother:

The day my husband, Wayne, and I discovered I was going to have a baby was the happiest day of my life. We had been married seven years and had all but given up hope of ever becoming parents.

Our son, Bradley, was born May 8, 1978. I remember that day vividly. It was the best day of my life . . . and the worst.

As the day approached, my doctor commented that I had had such an ideal pregnancy. I was never plagued with morning sickness, water retention or any of the usual curses that go along with pregnancy. I continued to work. In fact, I was at work when my labor pains began. I drove home, met my husband and proceeded to the hospital. It was an hour away, and we hadn't counted on my pains beginning three minutes apart. We arrived at the hospital with no time to spare.

While I was in the delivery room I prayed, "It doesn't matter if it's a boy or girl; all that matters is that the baby is healthy." But that was not meant to be.

Bradley was born with a severely deformed left leg and problems with the fingers on both hands.

"This can't be happening to me," I thought. "It's so unfair. Why me? All the abortions that are performed each year . . . all the babies given up for adoption . . . perfectly formed babies that aren't wanted. Why me?"

Drug addicts give birth to healthy babies everyday. I wouldn't even take an aspirin without consulting my doctor. Was asking for one healthy baby too much? I had lost friends and family members to death, but I'd never experienced such intense hurt or despair. I simply wanted to close my eyes and not have to wake up again. When I realized I would live, I thought maybe this less-than-perfect child would die. I never prayed for Bradley to die, but then I would have preferred that he did. That way, I wouldn't have to face the terrible pain.

The doctors agreed Bradley's leg needed to be amputated. When he was 2 days old they operated, removing the leg approximately two inches below the knee. They also separated some of his fingers. Bradley's condition was rare, and there was no known cause. Sometime during the eighth week of my pregnancy, there was a rupture in the placenta. It caused sticky bands of amniotic fluid to form and attach to his outer limbs. The bones in the lower left leg never developed, and the toes on his right foot were smaller than normal. The bands attached to both hands, leaving his left hand with short fingers, but a normal-sized thumb. Only two fingers on the right hand were affected. The doctors were confident Bradley would live after the surgery.

I was an emotional wreck. I thought of giving up Bradley for adoption. I tried to visualize him with other parents loving and caring for him. I soon realized I could not just give him away. During my week long hospital stay, all kinds of thoughts raced through my mind. "Maybe he needed an artificial limb to walk, but so what? Did that

Bradley Anthony

make him need love or his parents any less? Could I live with myself knowing that I gave him away simply because I couldn't accept his disabilities? If someone else could love him, his mother should most certainly love him. He may not be perfect, but who is?"

I only was allowed to hold Bradley once before he was taken to another hospital. Wayne had to travel from one hospital to another just to see his family. He had a hysterical wife in one hospital and a 2-day-old son with medical complications in the other. I honestly don't know how I would have survived without Wayne. He was strong and understanding. He was hurting on the inside, but all I could see was love and courage.

Twelve years later, we have all survived. Even now, I still feel I was cheated out of one of life's most wonderful experiences. Every new mother wants to bring home that precious, perfect baby from the hospital . . . to be proud to have everyone brag on the child. I always will have a touch of jealousy where that is concerned. But I try to focus on the positive and not dwell on the negative. We have a lot for which to be thankful. And when Bradley puts his arms around my neck and says, "I love you, Mom," all my heartaches vanish. Being his mother is the greatest joy of all.

The first years were the hardest. Learning to accept the disability and the amputation is hard. But without acceptance, there is no hope. Understanding this is one thing, but accomplishing it is another . . . especially when your infant is being whispered about and stared at. In general, I don't believe people intend to be cruel. They just aren't aware of their reactions. Looking back, Wayne and I probably could have used some professional counseling. The trauma of giving birth to a handicapped child is devastating, and learning to cope is a struggle. No one offered counseling. We were totally alone . . . isolated . . . with no one to turn to for understanding.

When Bradley was 11 months old, he was fitted with his first prosthesis. We went to a hospital especially for crippled children. The experience was not good. Hospital policy mandated he be hospitalized. There was no consideration of the well-being of the child. He was there 10 days, during which time the doctors kept insisting we allow them to amputate his leg above the knee. Supposedly, removing his knee would make it easier to fit him with a prosthesis. We went to the hospital for an artificial leg, and they wanted to operate again! We fought over the issue.

I had lots of questions. "What would best benefit my child's quality of life? Could he better function with or without his knee?" Sometimes the easiest way isn't always the best. I tried to emphasize to the doctors that Bradley was a human being . . . not merely case number 3223.

"If Bradley were your son, which course would you take?" I asked the doctors. Ultimately, we decided there would be no further amputation at that time. It could come later, if needed. I never have been sorry for that decision. Bradley has been active with a below-the-knee prosthesis. I learned doctors are human and make mistakes, too.

The first prosthesis was a nightmare. Some 30 minutes before we were to be dismissed from the hospital, we received the leg and a crash course in how to put it on Bradley. It didn't fit well and wouldn't stay on his leg. He had gone through hell for nothing.

Our search for a prosthesis continued. When Bradley was 16 months old, we traveled to a prosthetist 1,500 miles from home. We were there three weeks but went home empty-handed. He was too young to benefit from the type of prosthesis made there. We saw another prosthetist in Dallas. He fitted Bradley with a leg that allowed him to walk but didn't allow any knee movement. He walked stiff-legged. He wore that prosthesis for three years before he was fitted with a bent-knee prosthesis. His leg functioned fairly well, but he had no control of his knee because it stayed bent all the time. It relied on metal hinges to duplicate knee action. The general opinion of the prosthetists was that Bradley's stump was too short to properly accommodate a below-the-knee prosthesis.

At age 3, Bradley developed a condition termed "bony overgrowth." Doctors told us it was common in child amputees during their growth years. The bone outgrows the skin and tissue and may even pierce the skin. It is painful and can only be treated by surgery. We researched the options and decided to go to North Carolina for the surgery. A doctor there was willing to separate Bradley's fingers at the same time. Although doing both at the same time was complicated, we felt it was better than facing additional surgeries on his fingers later. After the operation, Bradley looked pitiful, with casts on both arms from the elbow down and a cast on his left stump that extended up to his groin. He was totally immobile, unable to do anything for himself. When the casts were removed, the operation was deemed a success. Only one finger had not been separated due to circulation problems. An additional operation was performed the following year to correct that problem.

By the time Bradley was 5 years old, the bony overgrowth problem was recurring. He hadn't been able to walk for several months. We made an appointment with a doctor in Los Angeles. He told us of a doctor in West Germany who had perfected a stump-capping procedure, surgery that was not yet performed in the United States. If successful, the operation would eliminate the bony overgrowth. We decided it was worth the gamble and went to West Germany. But a continuing infection meant Bradley needed another type of surgery. After four weeks, we returned to the States. The stump capping would have to wait. Once his leg was healed, Bradley was again fitted with a bent-knee prosthesis.

Bradley was becoming more and more active. He was a determined child. He never gave up even when he could not walk for weeks because of blisters or sores on his stump. When that happened, he just used crutches.

Then we heard of an Oklahoma City prosthetic facility where they might be able to really fit Bradley. We had been told over and over that Bradley could not be fitted with a below-the-knee prosthesis. But the new team of prosthetists had a different opinion. And they were right! We felt like we'd finally reached our goal after nine years of what seemed like a "witch hunt" to find the right prosthesis.

At age 12, Bradley recently was fitted with his second below-the-knee prosthesis, after undergoing another surgery for bony overgrowth. The prosthetist also added an experimental foot that should allow him more freedom of movement. Tears ran down my face as I watched him take his first step after months of pain on crutches following the surgery. It made me realize how much we all take for granted. I watched the transformation from a sad little boy into a happy one, eager to toss the ball with his dad in the front yard.

Bradley missed this summer's baseball league, but I'm confident he'll be ready when next summer rolls around. Until then, we'll have our own family baseball games.

I don't claim to have all the answers. I only can relate how we tried to cope for the last 12 years. Today I know that with love and understanding, child amputees can grow to have wonderful, successful lives. They may have to compensate in the way things are done, but they can do it. Please never tell them they can't.

Being a good parent is a constant struggle, but it is also most rewarding. Every parent makes his or her share of mistakes, but we learn together through our mistakes. I've adopted the philosophy, "Do your best and then pray alot."

I still have an occasional pity session when I need time

alone to cry. After that, it helps to have someone to share your burden with . . . someone who understands. Wayne and I have grown closer over the years as we learned to deal with Bradley's condition. We've come a long way.

Now, I'm like any mom. I'm dreading those teen years. Bradley already has said he's "in love with some fine-looking girls." It must be true because our phone is ringing constantly. Isn't it wonderful! I am a worried mother, and Bradley is just like any other 12-year-old boy. Guess that means we're normal!

Oops, an Alligator Got Me!

SARAH EAST, 11
(AND HER MOTHER, BRENDA)

*Born without her left leg, her parents worried
what the future would hold . . . would she be accepted
by other children? Once she had a prosthesis,
nothing could stop her. In fact, her dreams of
running led to improvements in artificial
limbs that helped other amputees run.*

From Sarah:
I've never had two legs. Sometimes that's hard, but most of the time I don't think about it. I still play softball and run with my brothers and sisters.

One thing I don't like is that my parents won't let me play basketball. I can't go swimming with both legs, and in the summer, only one leg gets tan.

Sometimes kids make fun of me or stare, and I want to beat them up. Sometimes I just tell them, "Why don't you take a picture . . . it lasts longer." Little kids are curious about my leg. I tell them I got it stuck in a blender or an alligator ate it. They get funny looks on their faces.

From her mother:
Sarah was our third child. Like any mother, I was praying for a healthy baby. I had no reason to suspect my baby would be anything but perfect. I'd had a healthy

Sarah East

pregnancy, with no complaints other than the usual nausea and aches that go along with it.

My labor pains were already five minutes apart when my husband, Carl, and I started for the hospital at 2 a.m. on July 6, 1979. In a few hours, Sarah was born. As I lay in the delivery room, I heard a healthy cry. The doctor told me that I had a girl. I should have known something was wrong when he didn't let me see the baby. It wasn't the normal routine. As they gave me a pain killer that knocked me out, I went to sleep thinking I had a perfect little baby girl.

When I awoke four hours later, my room was crowded with people . . . my parents, brother, Carl, and Carl's mother. Carl's mother never had visited me at the hospital before. I should have found that strange. Our pediatrician came into my hospital room.

"You know there is a problem with the baby," he said. His words shocked me. "What problem? What's wrong?" I gasped. No one had told me anything was wrong; he just assumed I already knew. The doctor explained that Sarah had been born without her left leg but otherwise was a healthy baby. He asked if I wanted to see her.

"No, I don't want to see her at all," I sobbed. I didn't think I could bear it. The pediatrician assured me there was no retardation and that with an artificial limb my baby Sarah would live a normal life. After a few minutes, I gave in. I wanted to see my baby.

They brought her from the nursery . . . screaming her head off. But the moment the nurse placed her in my arms, her crying ceased. I cried harder.

I continued to cry . . . not understanding why this had happened to my baby. The doctor had no answer either. I later discovered that other children like Sarah were born to mothers who had taken the same medication I had for morning sickness. But we had no clue when she first was born. Sarah had her left leg down to the knee, where a tiny three-toed foot was attached. I cried so much those three days in the hospital that the doctor threatened to give me medication that would knock me out unless I stopped. There was no one else who could tell me what it was like to have a child with one leg and that it would be okay. Fear . . . anger . . . and guilt. I experienced them all at once as I sat in my hospital bed gazing at Sarah.

"What will her life be like?" "Will other people accept her and what will she do?" I kept wondering. I was afraid how others would respond when they saw her. Some people really are afraid of handicapped people. I remember stopping at a friend's house on the way home from the hospital. I pulled back the blanket so my friend could see Sarah's leg.

"Brenda, that's not so bad," she said. She didn't faint or drop dead or anything. No one has ever looked at Sarah and been disgusted.

My husband told our two older children that Sarah had been born without a leg. They cried. They were really scared. It was hard for all of us those first few weeks. Carl felt guilty and was fearful, too. We just kind of closed ourselves off, not talking much about it. But Carl and I did agree that whatever Sarah needed, she would have . . . even if it meant sacrificing other things. We also agreed we couldn't baby her. We had to treat her just like our other children.

One of our first trips into public was to church. The people there were great. Of course, they expressed their sorrow, but none of them were horrified. Some of the older ladies wanted to know what we were going to do. I simply told them, "She's all right now and she is healthy. When she's older, we will take care of it." One funny incident occurred when we took 6-week-old Sarah to a photographer. He was making such a fuss over what a beautiful baby she was. He kept wanting to uncover her legs. His mouth dropped open in shock when he pulled back the blanket. I don't think he knew what to say.

As we adjusted, I still had days when I looked at Sarah and just cried. (Sometimes, I still do.) I just didn't know what she was going to do. But as time went by and I looked at other amputees, I realized they had gone on with their lives, so I knew there was hope. Sometimes, I just have to stop and give myself a little pep talk.

Our older kids, Daniel and Chandra, were so excited about their new sister. They loved her so much and wagged her around like a little puppy. They were, and still are, very protective of her.

The doctors had told us Sarah could be fitted for a prosthesis as soon as she started pulling up. She crawled earlier than most babies and was pulling up at 4 months of age. It was nearly Thanksgiving, and we were ready for an appointment with the orthopedist. We were referred to Children's Hospital in Oklahoma City, but we couldn't get an appointment until February. The waiting was frustrating. I wanted to do something to help her right then.

We started going to children's clinics that February. It was both helpful and hurtful. I was able to talk to other parents who had similar experiences, and that helped. But the clinics involved a bunch of doctors standing around arguing about what should be done with my child. It seemed so impersonal. That was not only frustrating — it hurt.

We saw the prosthetist the same day we first visited the orthopedist. He fitted Sarah with a leg that utilized the little foot to hold it on, but he cautioned that she probably wouldn't be able to walk right away. She surprised us all when they put the leg on and she took her first steps. Carl and I were encouraged.

But my joy turned to tears the next day when I put the leg on her. She'd crawl, and it would fall off. I must have put it back on six times in a 15-minute period. I called the prosthetist, and we went back to have it fixed. It was all new to him, too. Sarah was the first little one with whom he had worked.

Sarah walked by herself at 15 months. She walked stiff-legged, but she really got around. Believe me, she could go.

The following July, doctors wanted to operate to remove the little foot that was attached to Sarah's leg. It would allow for better fitting of a prosthesis. But the doctor wanted me to put her in the hospital on her birthday. It had waited this long; it could wait a few more weeks. The hospital was no place to spend your second birthday.

I was still leery of the surgery, but the pediatrician had examined Sarah and thought she could handle it both physically and emotionally. We decided to go ahead with the operation while she was young. She would heal quickly. We tried to tell her what was going to happen . . . that it would hurt . . . but mommy and daddy would be there with her.

The doctor removed the foot and a bone that was growing out of the side of her leg. They gave her pain medication, but only the first day after the surgery. She had a big, bulky bandage on her leg. She cried, but it was hard to pick her up to comfort her without causing her more pain. I guess she finally got accustomed to the pain. Carl would take her for rides in the little red wagons that were used to transport children around the hospital. She'd try to kick the nurses as she went by. We couldn't figure it out, so we asked her why she did that. "They hurt me," she answered. Sarah thought the nurses had caused her all the pain.

The doctor put the leg in a cast before we left the hospital. But it fell off as soon as we were home. I took her back to the doctor, who showed me how to wrap it. I became really good at wrapping the leg. Two to three months later she got her first bent-knee prosthesis.

Even though Sarah was doing well, I still wondered what

it would be like when she started school. Kids can be so cruel. When she was not yet 2 years old, Daniel wanted to take her to kindergarten as his "show and tell." We went, and the kids were fascinated. Sarah was the only amputee in our small town. I think being around her has helped other children to be more accepting of people with handicaps.

Sarah was only 3 years old when she told prosthetist John Sabolich that she wanted to run. He looked at her and said, "But Sarah, you are an amputee. Amputees don't normally run." She was undaunted. "If you would make me something better, I could run. I could run fast," she told him. He videotaped her trying to run with her old prosthesis and discovered she was trying to run step-over-step. That was something above-the-knee amputees just didn't do.

To help her, Sabolich developed the OKC running cable. Sarah loved it. It made the knee snap out faster, so her leg was there when she was ready to take her next running step. Sarah just took off! She was the first above-the-knee amputee to run, normally, step-over-step. She could keep up with her friends. She raced her brothers and sisters, played ball and jumped off the porch. It was great to watch her. I knew then nothing was going to hold her back . . . nothing was going to stop her. I think the running really gave her a lot more confidence. It brought her out into the world and made her feel like she could accomplish anything.

As Sarah has grown, Carl and I have tried to stick with our pledge to treat her like our other children. Sometimes it's hard to let her do things when we think she might get hurt. She learned to ride a bike in first grade. At first, she refused to wear her prosthesis because she could pedal with one leg. After awhile, she learned to ride with an artificial leg like other kids ride with both legs. It was a scary experience for Carl and me. We live at the top of a hill. There were a lot of rocks and gravel at the bottom of the hill, and we were afraid for her. Despite our cautioning, she took off down the hill . . . like any other kid. She landed face down in the gravel. She looked like she'd been beaten, and she missed a few days of school. But within a few days, she was back on her bike. She still falls, but she gets right up and goes again. That's the way we have raised her all her life.

Probably one of the hardest moments for me came when Sarah was in second or third grade. We'd weathered a lot of the bumps and gotten through most everything . . . or so I thought. One day, Sarah looked up at me and asked, "What does it feel like to have two legs?" I wanted to burst into tears. For Sarah's sake, I knew I couldn't. I wasn't sure what to tell her. "You know what it feels like on your right leg?" I asked her. "Well, just imagine your left leg feeling the same way. That's what it feels like." The answer seemed to satisfy her, and she has never asked that question again.

When Sarah was 6, there was another addition to our family. But this time, it was a set of two. The twins were born perfectly healthy. They grew up playing with Sarah, never thinking about her leg. It wasn't until almost three years later, when she was standing in a doorway, that one of them noticed she didn't have a leg. "Sissy, where's the rest of your leg?" Zachary said. He just stood there feeling her stump, with wonder in his eyes.

Sarah is a little upset with her dad and me now because we won't let her play basketball or soccer. We just don't think she could keep up with soccer. We know she can play basketball, but we are afraid she might damage her good knee playing competitive basketball. She always has done everything the other children did in physical education classes. Other than those two things, we've tried to let her do whatever she wanted to try. We had to modify what we said to her when she was little. If we said, "You can't do that," she'd set out to prove she could. We had to learn to say, "We don't want you to do that."

Now, she helps with chores, just like the other children. If she wants to get out of work, she may complain about her leg hurting. It's like any child who feigns illness to get out of work. We try to be fair with all our children. But from time to time, there is some jealousy among the older children who may feel Sarah is getting away with something because she has one leg. I know there are times when we're overly protective of Sarah, but by the same token, if she needs a spanking, she gets one.

Sarah's growth spurts are our biggest problems right now. It is impossible to keep her comfortably fitted in a prosthesis. She will wear a leg for a few weeks, and then it's too short or too tight. We've always tried to get by for 18 months before we replaced a leg. The prosthetist has worked to make little adjustments that allow her to wear it longer. In fourth grade, Sarah refused to go get a new leg fitted until school was out for the summer. She often misses school when she is having a leg fitted, but that year, she wanted to get the perfect attendance award at school.

I think whenever you have a special child, you always worry . . . about the future . . . about what kind of job she will be able to get . . . if any man will ever love her and marry her . . . and if she'll be able to have a family. I've grown with Sarah over the years. But it doesn't mean that I've stopped worrying about her. She still weighs heavy on my heart, but the logical part of me says she'll be able to do anything she wants. And she'll probably do it better than other people. She's just more determined.

The Lord Lifted My Pain

BISHOP WILLIAM J. FIZAR, 84

*He'd been preaching the gospel for more than
50 years. On the way home from church one
evening, he had car trouble. In the roadway flagging
motorists to go around, he was struck by a car.
The impact crushed his legs, which were later
amputated at the knee.*

T he choir had finished Wednesday evening rehearsal
at my northeast Oklahoma City church on that
December day in 1977. I'd been having trouble with
my car, so I asked one of the brothers from the church to
follow me home.

As I pulled into a left turn lane, my car died. For some
reason, my church member was not immediately behind
me, so he couldn't pull in to block traffic behind me. I got
out to flag other drivers around my car. As I went to open
the trunk, I heard the Spirit of the Lord tell me, "Watch out
for that car." But I had other things on my mind. I turned
my head and a few seconds later, the car struck me. The
impact threw me into the open trunk and left my legs
hanging on by only a threadlike tissue.

My church brother rushed to my car, picked me up out
of the trunk and placed me in the street to wait for the
ambulance. It was slow in coming, and I laid there in a pool

of blood for a long time. I was awake, but I felt no pain. I believe the Lord lifted the pain. There was no earthly reason that I shouldn't have been in extreme pain.

I was taken to St. Anthony Hospital. My wife, Alsie, didn't want to sign the forms to give the doctor permission to amputate. I asked the doctor to raise me up so I could see my legs and decide for myself. I saw that the legs were mashed and crushed at the knee. I knew they were gone already. I told the doctor to go ahead, and I signed for the amputations. The doctor did knee disarticulations on both my legs.

I awoke in intensive care. I don't remember alot about that time. I had phantom pain, but it wasn't horrible. I still have phantom pain . . . that's just part of it. I'll be sitting up and feel like my toe or my heel is hurting when neither foot is even there.

I was never angry over losing my legs. I felt like I was hit because I did not listen to the voice of the Lord. I heard the voice that told me to watch out for the other car, but I had alot things on my mind and failed to obey. It was something that just happened. I just prayed and went on.

My assistant bishop was subbing in the pulpit for me while I was in the hospital. But as soon as the doctor would okay it, I preached to my congregation from my hospital bed. I have a Sunday morning radio worship service, and I was able to speak to my congregation via telephone and do the radio service at the same time. I celebrated my 71st birthday in the hospital that January.

I went home in a wheelchair months later. My church members built a long ramp with a grab rod in front of my house to make it easier for me to get to and from the house. When I went to church, the brothers would take me — wheelchair and all — up to the pulpit. So, I preached without legs for a time. Alot of people felt sorry for me, and some would cry. But I was very composed, and my reaction helped them. I never was a person to give up.

Upon my hospital release, the doctor gave me a prescription for short artificial legs that would have fit over my knees — stubbies they were called. But I didn't want those. I wanted to stand at or near my normal height. I wanted to be able to stand in my pulpit and preach.

So, I went to the phone book and found the name of a prosthetist. When I visited with him, he said, "No, Bishop Fizar. We don't want you walking around down there like that. We're going to make you some real legs." I really appreciated that.

My first legs were made out of wood, but the second ones were out of a heavy plastic. Since the legs were heavy, I started out using a walker. It took a long time to get accustomed to the balance. In recent years, I was fitted with lightweight legs which are more comfortable and make it easier to get around. But I always have been determined to do whatever I needed to do, regardless of my legs.

Even when someone tossed a Molotov cocktail into the church window and burned a portion of the building, I was determined to help rebuild the sanctuary. At one time, I had owned a construction company, so I knew what needed to be done. The church only had a small amount of insurance money and couldn't afford to hire someone to do the work. So, two church brothers and I went to work cleaning up the damage and repairing the roof.

I also put an addition on my house. I'd pull the rope to raise the rafters. I hired a carpenter to do some finish work, but I painted the entire inside from my wheelchair. Now, we're putting in two restrooms at the church. The hardest thing is getting down on my knees to look under things.

I've adapted certain things — like my desk — to make it easier to work at home and do the things I want to do. I cut off the back of a high chair, put casters on the legs and a plywood top on it, so I could roll my typewriter around where I needed it. My hobby is working on radios and televisions. When I'm not at the church, I like to fix things like that.

I feel blessed to be able to drive my car out of town when I need to travel, and sometimes I'm on the road quite a bit. I've never let what happened to my legs stop me from going or doing what I wanted to do. Amputation changes your lifestyle, but you just have to adopt a method of taking care of that.

Helping Others Helped Me

PRESTON CROSS, 36

*A 27-year-old diabetic, he underwent a simple
operation on a broken nose. An overdose
of anesthesia set in motion a series of medical
maladies, one of which resulted in the
amputation of both legs below his knees. He took up
a career he had once abandoned,
counseling others in crisis.*

As I rounded second base that game, I could see the play at third was going to be close. I would have to slide to keep from being put out. As I slid, the third baseman made the tag — right in the middle of my face. The blow broke my nose.

Doctors suggested rhinoplasty, a 30-minute operation, to clear up the breathing and sinus problems that resulted from the accident. No problem. Except for being diabetic, I was a healthy 27 year old.

But something went wrong during the operation. I received too much anesthetic. Doctors noticed protein spilling into my urine, and my blood pressure shot up to the stroke level. They weren't sure why I'd received too much anesthetic, but after the operation they told me there was kidney damage. In three to five years, I would need a kidney transplant or dialysis. It was only three months later that my kidneys failed. I began dialysis and felt fortunate

Preston Cross

when doctors found a kidney donor after a few months.

The transplant was successful, and I was back to work at my sales job with General Foods within six weeks. What I didn't know was that I had contracted a deadly virus through the donated kidney that would send me back to the hospital. CMV, as it is called, kills 85 percent of the people who contract it. I was in a coma for 14 days, paralyzed from the neck down. My weight dropped from 155 to 105 pounds in two weeks. At one point, doctors gave me less than a one percent chance of seeing the next sunrise.

Fortunately, God was with me and I survived. After a lot of physical therapy, I was back on my feet. But the high-powered antibiotics I was being treated with were experimental. They led to a reduction in both the size of the arteries and amount of blood flowing to my extremities. A year after I left the hospital, I was recuperating from the virus when I was told my right leg would have to be amputated below the knee because of gangrene.

When I awoke from the amputation, I kept thinking that maybe the doctors had been able to do something during surgery . . . maybe my foot was still there. But as I looked down the bed to where your foot normally causes a peak in the sheet, the sheet was flat. I knew it was gone. I cried. I went through all the stages of grief.

The phantom pain was unbelievable. It was the same pain I had felt before the the surgery. Normally, diabetics experience numbness in their limbs, but I already had gone through excruciating pain in my foot. Now the foot was gone, but the pain was still there. I was eating pain killers like M & Ms.

The worst time was at night . . . 2 a.m., when everything was quiet at the hospital. There was no one around. No one to talk to. I didn't want to call someone at that hour and bother them, but I just wanted to hear someone's voice. I was desperately lonely, and I cried "why me?" to God.

I went through physical therapy and got a prosthesis that let me walk. I was doing well with the new artificial leg . . . and even played softball eventually. When I first got the leg, however, I relied on my crutches. I didn't think that little leg could possibly hold me up. But one day the phone rang, and instinctively, I got up to answer it. As I turned back around, I discovered I had left my crutches behind me. I could walk on the leg.

I think it takes different amputees different amounts of time to "turn the corner," so to speak . . . to realize that there is life after amputation. It was a couple of months after the amputation that I really came to realize that even though I'd lost a leg, the real Preston wasn't gone. I had refused to be seen in shorts publicly up to that time, but one day I wore shorts to the store. I got a lot of stares, but it didn't bother me. I knew I was coming to grips with being an amputee.

Just as I was learning what it meant to have lost one limb, my left leg turned bad. Doctors told me it would have to be removed. My wife, Patti, and my mother were with me when the doctors told me the second amputation was needed to remove the leg below the knee. I was devastated. I think it was easier physically to deal with the second amputation because I knew what to expect. But emotionally, it was harder. I was ready to give up. Every time I saw a doctor, I was told something else had to be removed. I was seeing parts of my body erased inch by inch. My life was nothing but a series of operations. I pictured myself sitting in a wheelchair for the rest of my life. I was in my early 30s . . . a time when life is really supposed to be kicking off.

I believe losing a limb is harder than losing a friend or relative to death. It's like a part of you is dead and being taken away. I thought of suicide, as I did several times over the course of all my surgeries. But I decided that was the easy way out. I'd been through alot, and I'd make it through this. Life was too important.

I wasn't through yet at the hospital. Medication I was taking to maintain the kidney transplant led to different ailments and infections. I suffered a heart attack and had to have open heart surgery a year later. Later, I made two more trips to the operating room to remove fingers from both hands because of vascular disease brought about by the diabetes. I felt like my life was out of control. Everyone likes to have some control over life . . . to be able to say "no." But I couldn't stop what was happening. It still is tough to visualize myself as whole sometimes. But I keep a good outlook — it's all I've got. I don't have my body, but what I have to offer people are my thoughts and personality.

I had begun volunteer work as a counselor at a local hospital shortly after my kidney transplant. I majored in social work in college, but I never pursued a counseling career because at the time it just didn't pay enough money. Being at the hospital, however, I saw people who were much worse than I and who were suffering a lot more. After my amputations, I began to visit with other amputees at the hospital and at a prosthetic firm. Helping them ended up helping me also. As I shared what I had gone through . . . how I'd made it, it helped them. But as I shared my story, I found new strength by being able to talk to someone about my feelings and emotions. Communicating . . . sharing what's bothering you with friends, family and especially your spouse — that's one of the hardest things to do, but one of the most vital.

The amputations and all the physical problems kept my family in a state of turmoil. I have two daughters, Alicia and Kelli, who never really have known their daddy when he was healthy. They'd have a big day in their lives, and I'd be off to the hospital. My wife, Patti, and I have spent half our married lives dealing with my medical problems. We endured great emotional and financial burdens. It almost wrecked our marriage. We even filed for divorce, but we decided we'd been through so much, we'd try to get through this.

I know it sounds chauvinistic, but it was hard to reverse roles with my wife. Suddenly, she was the breadwinner. I was at home with the cleaning and the cooking. It just wasn't the way we had planned it. I was supposed to be working to support my family, while she wanted to stay home with the girls. Of course, I wondered why my wife would even want to stay with me because of my physical appearance.

Through it all, my faith in God sustained me. As I've talked to other amputees, they repeatedly share an overriding sense of a spiritual being that's helped them through their traumas. Family and friends are great support, but sometimes you are by yourself. You need to cry. You're searching for answers to your questions. God has given me strength and purpose. He was there at those 2 a.m. hours when I was lonely.

It seems people are always in a hurry. There's that old adage about stopping to "smell the roses," but few actually do. When you endure such physical infirmities, you have to slow down. You've got time to think about things. I discovered how many times I blew it . . . how many things I took for granted. I realized that fighting for money, job or status isn't what is important. I think I have come to understand why we are really here.

Editor's note: Despite continuing critical health problems, Preston rarely felt sorry for himself, and he always went out of his way to help other amputees find meaning in their lives. He felt strongly about sharing his story in this book but never had the opportunity to see it in print. Complications from advanced diabetes ultimately led to a heart attack which took Preston from us in January, 1991. He was an inspiration to all who knew him, and he will be greatly missed.

Finding the Right Leg

BILL NIENABER, 65

A telephone company marketing manager for a
five-state area, he led an active life. He and his
wife were avid snow and water skiers.
At age 63, a malignant tumor was found behind his left
knee. He refused to let the amputation of his
leg at the hip sideline him from the life he loved.

M y wife and I were skiing Vail in late winter, 1987. I was looking forward to hitting the slopes at the top of the mountain. But as I sat down on the lift that morning, my left leg felt as if I were sitting on my fist. There was a hard knot behind my knee.

I waited until we returned home to St. Louis to consult a doctor. On the way to the hospital for a biopsy, I remember thinking, "So I've got a lump in my leg; I'll just have it taken out." The biopsy showed I had a malignant tumor. It was way up inside the leg, and there was no telling how long it had been there. The doctor, who was a friend and neighbor, looked me squarely in the eye and said, "Bill, we take the leg off for this type of thing." I was in shock.

My wife, June, was at work. I waited until she came home that evening to break the news. I sat her down on the couch and told her what the doctor said. We sat and cried. It was several days before we began to overcome the shock.

It was hard to accept that I might lose my leg, but I was glad the doctor told me up front what was likely to happen. We thought about it for a month, trying to decide what we should do. I don't know what I would have done without my wife.

Then, the doctor began pushing me to get treatment. He said we shouldn't fool around with the cancer any longer. I checked into the hospital for a very aggressive program of chemotherapy. They put a tube into an artery under my left arm and ran it all the way down my side to the tumor in my leg. I underwent chemotherapy for three days. As the treatments continued, I felt awful. Nasty is the only word to describe chemotherapy. I couldn't eat — the food just wouldn't go down.

The third night I awoke screaming. I had a chemo burn on my groin. The chemicals were burning from the inside out. The pain was so intense, they gave me four shots of morphine. Nothing phased it. They stopped the chemotherapy.

I went home after a few days but returned to the hospital every day for radiation treatments. The radiation continued for 25 days as the doctors hoped to shrink the tumor, but a follow-up MRI scan revealed that the treatments had failed. It was then that the oncologist and surgeon recommended amputation. But I wasn't ready to have the leg off just because they said so. I got opinions from two other doctors.

I was told that the back of my leg could be removed and the tumor taken out. I'd have to wear a brace, and the leg wouldn't be worth much, but I would be able to walk on it. But if they removed the leg, there would be enough flesh to make a good stump for a prosthesis.

In addition, the doctors were concerned that by not removing the entire leg, there was a risk the tumor would grow back. If that happened after the back of the leg had been removed and it had to be amputated later, it would mean grafting skin from my back to close up the stump. I told them I'd sleep on it.

Two days later, I told them to take the leg off. I wanted to be done with it and get on with my life. But it took a month to get the radiation out of my system so they could operate.

While I was waiting, I wanted to talk to someone about a prosthesis. I didn't want to wait until the leg was gone. That's the way I am. When I'm building a house or working on a project, I'm always thinking about the next step. I was involved in volunteer work through my job, and I was familiar with the Shriners' Children's Hospital in St. Louis. I figured if anyone knew about artificial limbs, they would. No one had offered me information on a prosthesis.

I asked a friend at work who was a Shriner to help me. He introduced me to a prosthetist who had been in the business 35 years and who also was an amputee. I figured he must know what he's doing. I told him I was going to lose my leg and asked him to make me a prosthesis.

It was summer, 1988. I wanted to go to the lake to ski one last time with two legs. We belong to a group of water skiers that gets together every summer at Norfork Lake in Arkansas. I always had done trick water skiing, and my wife and I even did acrobatics in which she stood on my shoulders while I was skiing. I was still under the phone company's insurance program, and the insurance company didn't want me to leave the city with my pending surgery. My doctor said that was ridiculous and wrote the insurance company a letter asking them to give me a break since I was going to lose my leg.

I still was weak from the radiation and my hair was thin, but I was determined to go. I skied barefoot and slalom, and also swam. It wasn't as hard to get through it physically as it was mentally and emotionally. I love water skiing. As I tried to enjoy the trip, I kept thinking, "I may not be able to do this ever again."

But I was surrounded by friends and family who were hoping only for the best for me. Everyone was teary-eyed as my wife and I prepared to leave. It even broke up my one really macho buddy, who thought he could never cry.

I returned to St. Louis where I checked into the hospital. The next day, they took my leg off. They did a hip disarticulation, removing the leg at the hip socket. They were afraid that leaving any of the thigh would increase the risk the cancer might return.

I awoke from the operation in good spirits. It was over then, and I was ready to regroup and get my body going again. By the second day I had a trapeze over my bed, and I was doing chin-ups. I didn't have a great deal of pain from the surgery, but I had intense phantom pain. Even when I went home, those sensations in my leg that wasn't there kept me awake at night. I'd lay in bed watching television into the wee hours of the morning until I was so exhausted that I'd finally fall asleep.

When my leg was sufficiently healed, I went to the prosthetist for my first fitting of my artificial leg. He did the casting, and about two weeks later, I got my leg. He worked with me and showed me how to throw my hip out to make my leg kick out. I did it as soon as he put the leg on me, but it was uncomfortable and awkward. And I hated the way my walk looked. He told me I would just have to get used to it.

That was impossible. The socket was like a hard bucket, always pressing in on me. I was constantly in misery. I'd wear the leg when I had to . . . to a party or special function, and when I went back to work. At work, I was running an office of about 70 people, so I was on my feet all day. It really was uncomfortable trying to walk on the leg. After about three weeks, I thought: "Why am I doing this? It's not worth it. I'll just retire. I've got 42 years in."

Later, my brother was reading *National Geographic*. He said, "Hey, you've got to read this." There was a picture of a guy who weighs about 200 pounds running with two artificial legs. Of course, he had his upper legs. I knew that made fitting the prostheses easier. The guy had lightweight legs of space-age material and energy-storing feet. I figured I had to talk to the prosthetist who was able to do that.

I talked to the insurance company. They had paid for the total cost of my first leg but would cover only 80 percent if I wanted another leg. I decided it was worth it. I traveled to Oklahoma City to the Sabolich Center, the same place Ted Kennedy, Jr., had been fitted. I figured as a Kennedy, he could go anywhere, so I'd give this place a try.

The new socket is alot softer. I am no longer tormented by the socket burning around my hip bone. With a special spring on my leg, I don't have to throw my hip out any more to get my leg to kick out. When I put my weight down on my foot, that loads the spring. When I relax, my foot steps up. I no longer look weird walking down the street. If I'd had this prosthesis before, I might not have retired.

I still do everything I want. I've rigged things to compensate. Before I lost my leg, I welded a handle on my three-wheeler and my tractor so I could shift gears by hand instead of with my foot. I wanted all that done before I lost my leg so I wouldn't have to call someone to do it. I drive a four-wheel Bronco and an all-terrain vehicle. I maintain five acres, and I mow the grass . . . I can do almost anything. I have given up my mountain bike. I could put a strap on the pedal and ride with my artificial leg, but I'm used to riding pretty fast. I don't want to tear up my good leg.

Last winter was my first time on snow skis with one leg. I took lessons from an instructor who had worked with other amputees, and by the third day I was skiing from the top of the mountain. I raced a course I'd raced before. I used to do it in 28 seconds, but it took me 58 seconds. They still gave me a gold medal . . . for courage.

I want to stay active in sports. I've been back up on one water ski, too. I taught myself to ski barefoot once before, and now I'm going to try that on one foot. I know it can be done. I plan to use a boom on the side of the boat, instead of a ski rope.

I decided from the start that it doesn't do any good to sit around and cry once your leg is gone. You just go downhill, and your body wastes away. Then, there's no place to go but down. People gave me books about cancer and amputees that talked about being down and depressed, but I never really was. I'm starting a support group now, but not necessarily for those who are down. It's to help people find the right kind of prostheses from the very start. I want to share what I went through and what I learned. I want to tell them to look around to find what works for them. It's important if you want to get your body going again and get on with your life.

Marija Topalovic

A Prayer For Peace

MARIJA TOPALOVIC, 14

*Trapped in a war of aggression in Bosnia, a
single mortar shell explosion blew off both her
legs above the knee and killed her father. A
U.S. missionary found her in the midst of
countless injured Croatians and sought to
make her wish to walk again come true.*

My life in Bosnia was much like any teenager's—
that is, before the war. My hometown of Vitez
was a lovely city. I was in seventh grade when
the Serbian aggressors came.

There is no comparing war torn Bosnia today and the
Bosnia I knew before the war. When the fighting began,
the schools were shut down. Sometimes when the bombing stopped, we would return to classes. When I stopped
going to school, it was like I wasn't living any more. We
had no contact with the outside world. Our lives centered
around "who got killed today" and "whose funeral was
yesterday."

It was two days before Christmas, 1993, when my
father and I left the house where we were living to
return to our family home that was then in ruins. Our
home was one of many left in shambles after repeated
bombings, but the basement, where we had stored some
baking pans and other Christmas things, was still there.

We thought keeping some of the holiday traditions would ease the pain of the war.

Because of the continued sniper fire, we only dared to go out when it was foggy or at night. With the cover of darkness, my father and I set out on the 15-minute walk to the house, by then very near the front line of the fighting. I was going to gather the things from the basement, and my father wanted to drop off some food for my brother and some of the soldiers. One of our neighbors yelled to us that we had better get out of there because the shelling was starting again. We heard explosions and ran toward a barn for shelter.

Suddenly, a strange twinge-like electricity shot through my body as I went flying up into the air. Back on the ground, I could only feel a gritty sand in my mouth. I started screaming to my father, "Help me, Father, help me!" It seemed like I was yelling for five minutes or more. There was no answer. I could only hear him breathing heavily. My brother had seen the blast and heard my screams, so he came running. I remember he kept slapping me. I guess I fainted or was in shock. Then, a few feet away, my brother lifted my father's head and held him. My father murmured painfully "Goodbye", and then he was dead.

I felt like it was all a dream. Some soldiers were carrying me. I asked them where my legs were. "It's okay. Another soldier is carrying them." There was too much shelling to safely bring a car for me, so the soldiers carried me across town to a Catholic church that had been converted to a hospital.

It was dark in the hospital. There was no electricity, so the doctors and nurses had to do everything by candlelight. I looked down at my left leg; I still had a knee, but the crushed bone was sticking out. The church was not equipped to be a hospital, so all the patients were in one large room The beds were made of wood and very uncomfortable. I could not believe this was happening. I screamed out when the medicine no longer eased the pain.

Of course, my mother didn't know what had happened. My uncle went to get her. He told her I had been critically wounded, but he didn't tell her that I had lost both legs until she arrived at the hospital. I knew in my heart that the hospital situation was not good in Bosnia, and I was sure I'd never walk again. One of the doctors was very encouraging though. "Sure, you'll get some legs, and you will walk again," he told me. I really wasn't convinced, but I had to hope.

An American who was visiting the hospital one day stopped to talk with me. All I really knew was that he was in Bosnia to bring food and relief supplies for our people. We knew we were getting help, but we really didn't know where the food was coming from. The man turned out to be Larry Jones, the president of Feed The Children, a charity devoted to serving children in need around the world. When he promised he would help me, I didn't realize he meant I would be flying half way around the world to the United States.

After some days passed, I was taken to a hospital in Split, Italy, for further treatment. Larry Jones saw me on a news program as I was being transported to the hospital. After that, things began to happen quickly. Another man from Feed The Children contacted my family and made arrangements for my mother, three of my sisters, and me to be brought to the United States. I had no idea traveling to America would take so long. I wasn't sure exactly what was going to happen, but the trip and the kindness of the people turned out to be more than I even wished for.

When we arrived in New York, there were many re-porters and television cameras. I could not believe I was getting all this attention. They all had so many questions. There were still more reporters and more questions on our stop in Dallas and later in Oklahoma City. They wanted to know if I felt America should become more involved in the war in Bosnia. Yes, I wanted America to help my country. "Food is nice, but somebody needs to do something about the fighting," I told them.

In Oklahoma City, I was scared—scared the fitting of my artificial legs would be painful. I still had doubts about walking. Arrangements had been made for me to be fitted with new legs at the Sabolich Prosthetic and Research Center. It was there I saw a picture of a model who had lost one of her legs. Her leg was beautiful. That's what I wanted—pretty legs.

I began a series of physical therapy workouts, and there were measurements and castings for my legs. The pain I had feared didn't happen. I watched videos of other amputees and met some girls who had been born without legs. The visit with the girls was the first time I thought that I might really walk again, and that there would be a life after having my legs blown off. I wanted to get my pretty legs and wear a mini skirt—or maybe a super mini!

It wasn't long until the first phase of my legs was complete. Once again, the cameras and the people were there to see me walk. I was excited and scared at the same time. I looked down at two pink tennis shoes on my artificial feet. The temporary legs weren't really pretty, but I couldn't wait to feel something underneath me when I stood up and to walk again. The prosthetist helped to steady me as I took my first steps holding the railings on either side. It was amazing—I was walking, and I felt like I had been reborn! I was so excited that I let go of the railings, turned and raised my hands over my head in celebration. I reached out to hug the prosthetist as tears ran down my face, and I realized that something good had come out of something so very horrifying.

I was relieved. I'd seen others who had lost legs in the

war in Bosnia, and they will never walk again. I knew I was the lucky one. Even as I was taking my first steps, I thought of others left behind in my homeland, including some of my family. I continue to pray every night that somehow peace will come to Bosnia. I pray there will be no more children who lose their legs or their fathers—no more who suffer as I did.

Editors Note: Marija has remained in the United States to complete her education. Her mother and sisters returned to Bosnia while Marija lives with a guardian family. Her future plans depend on the war in Bosnia.

For Love of Country
And Vietnam Veterans

BOB CONETTA, 47

*A Vietnam veteran who came home from an
unpopular war minus a leg, an eye and hearing in one ear, he
struggled for years with a painful leg prosthesis.
What started as an effort to secure a better artificial limb
for himself turned into a crusade to get adequate health
benefits for all who had served, as he took on the Veterans
Administration for love of country.*

The Vietnam era. It was a painful time in our
country's history. For many Vietnam veterans, it
remains more than something to read about in a
dusty history book. It is a personal war which continues
even now in the '90s, more than two decades later.

Those of us who came home missing a leg or an arm,
paralyzed, or just haunted by wartime horrors thought that
the Veterans Administration would take care of us. We
were the ones who risked our lives for our country, and the
fact that we haven't been cared for is a pain even more
agonizing.

For my service in Vietnam, I was rewarded with two
bronze stars, a purple heart, a modest disability pension
and a lifelong battle with the VA, trying to get what I more
than earned by serving my country. And I am not alone.

Some people are still angry that 59,000 Americans were
killed in Vietnam, but what they don't realize is that another

60,000 veterans who came home from Southeast Asia have committed suicide since the war. I had a buddy who was hit by a rocket; it didn't go off, but it shattered his spine. He killed himself three years ago because he couldn't endure the pain and suffering anymore. And the VA was basically ignoring him. They just weren't providing him the health benefits he needed and deserved.

I was drafted at age 18, and I went willingly to serve my country in Vietnam. I was part of the First Air Cavalry Division—Custer's ol' outfit that I had read about as a kid. In the short time that I was in Vietnam, I saw combat in the Battle of Kason and the TET Offensive.

It was July, 1968, and my unit was on a search and destroy mission along a heavily wooded trail when the explosions from the mortar round rang out—they were everywhere. Two of my buddies were killed; another injured. My left leg took a main hit, and shrapnel lodged in my face, hands and eyes. Before I was found and could be transported from the jungle, gangrene had developed in my left leg. There was no option other than amputation. I also lost an eye and a good deal of my hearing.

My preliminary medical evaluation and amputation took place on a hospital ship. It was a knee disarticulation. From the ship, I was transported to a military hospital in Camp Zama, Japan, and by August, I was back in the states at Walter Reed Hospital where I was fitted with my first leg prosthesis. The leg was good in a way—I was standing and walking, which I hadn't been able to do for months since my leg had been amputated. But as far as being comfortable, it never was. The leg was made of a rigid plastic with a wooden frame, and it weighed like an old anchor. I had alot of pain, and blisters developed particularly when I wore the leg all day. I honestly thought that was the price I had to pay to be able to walk. I wanted to be up and able to get around and return to work. I wanted to be just like everyone else. I thought I just had to learn to live with it.

Then, one day a few years ago, I saw a newspaper article that talked about high-tech artificial limbs and how amputees were running, not just walking. I couldn't believe it. I began research to find a new leg that would be so comfortable that I might consider running. I saw a video that showed people who hadn't been able to walk but now could run on the new prosthetic limbs. This was beyond my wildest dreams. I wondered what it might be like to work my regular dawn to dusk hours and be really comfortable for a change. I also thought how wonderful it would be to be more active with my family—to run or ride a bike with my children. Maybe after a long day's work, I would be able to sit on the couch with my wife, instead of having to deal with the pain of a throbbing residual limb.

But new technology does not come cheaply. When I had decided on a prosthetic facility, gotten a prescription from my doctor, and talked to other amputees about their success on the new artificial legs, I went to the VA to see if they would cover the cost. My request was met with a resounding "NO", based solely on the cost, with no real interest in how the new leg would dramatically improve my quality of life. The new leg was estimated to cost between $18,000 and $22,000—but the VA would spend no more than $6,000 on a new prosthesis. I was quite familiar with the quality of prosthesis that amount would buy; it also buys sores on the stump, constant pain, and a reduction in physical activities. As I began to talk with other veterans around the country, I discovered that one guy in Kansas had received $12,000 for a leg; another in the President's home state of Arkansas had received funds for a high-tech leg. It became apparent to me that the VA was not consistent in what it paid for artificial limbs or offered to do for different veterans. For some reason, there were vets like me in New York receiving less coverage than vets in other states.

Only in a few cases were Vets getting what they deserved for giving up a limb for their country.

After passage of the Americans with Disabilities Act (ADA), I thought vets might be better off—maybe more attention would be given to the special needs of amputees. Over the last 20 years since Vietnam vets came home, the VA has been very good at telling you what you couldn't get, but they didn't tell you what you deserved. Often times, benefits that were available were never publicized. I have spent more time fighting the VA for what I clearly deserve than I spent fighting in Vietnam. And I know there are other veterans just like me.

In 1993, I attended the first ADA conference, where President Bill Clinton spoke. He told the disabled that if they wanted their rights, they would have to fight for them. What he didn't tell me was that I would be fighting the government for my rights as a disabled veteran. I was at the conference wearing several hats—including financial secretary of Local 1-2 Utility Workers Union of America, AFL-CIO, as well as president of the Utility Workers Vietnam Veterans Association. Following the conference, I sent a letter to the President sharing my frustration as a veteran who had fallen through the cracks in attempting to obtain health benefits. Here are excerpts from my letter:

"...While I lost a leg, an eye, and a tremendous amount of hearing in an explosion in Vietnam, I have always held a good job which provided adequate benefits. However, these benefits do not extend to my service-connected disabilities. Herein lies the problem.

I strongly feel that when a person is permanently injured in his country's service, he deserves the best rehab available, not the least expensive. I have worked hard to get where I am today. I often ignore hours of grueling pain to accomplish what needs to be done in the course of the day. I have never been known to shy away from a challenge either before my injury or after. However, as I age, I find the pain induced by my artificial leg increases. I have long accepted this as a fact of life...

What bothers me the most is that the VA does not meet the needs of the veteran with service-connected disabilities as well as it should. The ADA is designed to insure that the disabled person will live the most fulfilling and productive life possible. The VA was denying me this by refusing to give me the best prosthesis available for my needs..."

What is ironic is that had I lost my leg any other way, my private health plan would pick up the cost of the new prosthesis. Had I not taken the time to write the President and talk with other politicians, I would not have gotten any further help with the VA. But the war still isn't over—they have agreed to up the ante from $6,000 to $11,000, but that still will not cover the cost of one leg. And based on what research I've done into veteran's benefits, I am entitled to two legs—not just one. With the VA, it continues to be only a budget question—they do not put a premium on a veteran's pain and suffering.

Based on the hope that additional funds will be forthcoming from the VA, I obtained a new contoured, flexible socket and leg in February, 1994. I am amazed at the difference. I've been an amputee for more than 20 years and for the first time, I have a leg that is almost painless to wear—and for the first time, I can run! No more blisters, no more rashes, no more pain making me want to pull the leg off.

The director at the VA really raps my new leg as being too expensive and continues to tell me I could get the same leg cheaper somewhere else. But I asked him how that could be. I've tried wearing the cheaper legs that the VA would have me wear, and over the years since I first lost my leg, they have improved, but there is a world of difference between those legs and what I wear today. The VA continues to say they offer the best possible treatment for vets. I think they truly believe that, and in some cases, they may be right—but in my case and many others, they are not. I don't look at it in dollars and cents; I look at it as what I think is the best for me as an individual.

As I closed my letter to President Clinton, I again reminded him that Vietnam veterans served their country well, and in turn, our country needs to give them the benefits they deserve:

"I must say that if I had to do it all over again and I knew the outcome, I would still choose to answer my country's call. In closing, I leave you with an old military saying:

> *It wasn't always easy,*
> *And it wasn't always fair,*
> *But when duty called we answered,*
> *We were there.*
> *Commander, who is there when the veteran calls?..."*

Elaine Naismith

Still Flying High

ELAINE NAISMITH, 44

At age 30, she'd been a flight attendant for almost 10 years when she lost her right leg above the knee as a result of a motorcycle accident. She vowed to continue her active lifestyle, as well as her career, and became the first flight attendant with a major disability to return to work in the skies.

There are events that occur in your life that you can never really prepare for. Accidents happen . . . and sometimes in the space of a few hours, all your future plans and dreams can lie like shattered fragments upon the pavement.

I was working for United Airlines, based in New York. When I boarded Flight 711 from New York to Las Vegas on March 24, 1976, I hadn't a clue that the following morning I would be in a Las Vegas hospital.

We had a layover in Las Vegas, so several members of our crew met for dinner. It all happened so suddenly. I was a passenger on a motorcycle as we returned from dinner. A car struck the motorcycle, throwing me across five lanes of traffic. I was conscious as I lay in the gutter with a mangled right leg.

The paramedics rushed me to Sunrise Hospital, expecting that I would be dead on arrival. I didn't know until much later that I had been given transfusions equal to three-quarters of the blood in my body. In the emergency room, I looked down at my foot and leg. The foot was white and blue. I knew it was bad . . . it was not a pretty picture! The doctor examined me, sticking my foot and leg with a pin and various instruments, asking if I could feel it. I was tempted to fib and say I did have feeling — I didn't want them to do anything rash.

"You'll most likely lose your leg," the doctor said after looking at my limb. "What if I don't?" I questioned. "You'll probably die," he told me bluntly.

I told him I had to phone my husband first. Ian was back home in New Jersey. After a discussion with the doctor that I couldn't overhear, Ian gave me a convincing talk . . . and encouraged me to do whatever needed to be done. I consented to the surgery, and I put my trust in the doctor.

The doctor did a mid-knee amputation, explaining that ultimately I would be an above-the-knee amputee. By amputating lower, he said I would end up with a longer residual limb in case there was infection. I would need a second skin graft operation and later, a revision surgery. Revision sounded like such a little thing. I didn't know then it would be the worst of all the operations.

When I awoke in intensive care about 2 a.m., I was covered with sheets. I couldn't see my leg. "I did lose my leg, didn't I?" I asked the nurse. She confirmed that I had. It was odd because I could feel my leg as though it was still there.

I didn't think much more about the amputation then. My mind clicked over to thoughts of my job. "I have to call the airline to tell them I won't be able to make my flight," I told the nurse. "And could you get in touch with my flying partners at the hotel and have them pack my luggage?" It didn't cross my mind at that point that I might not be continuing my career as a flight attendant.

My parents and husband were by my side the next day. I kept asking my parents to bring me a mirror. It wasn't until I was out of the hospital that they explained my face was so bruised and swollen they didn't think I should see it.

I was in incredible pain. Doctors ordered Demerol injections, but the shots only took the edge off the pain for about 15 minutes at a time. I couldn't sleep. To guard against any infection, the doctors had drainage tubes in the leg. The day they took the tubes out, they couldn't have given me enough pain medicine.

I had so much support from family, friends, and people I didn't even know at the airline. They phoned, they stopped by, and even brought picnic lunches and suppers to my hospital room. A constant stream of flowers and cards helped brighten my days. I couldn't have asked for more.

As I went through the surgeries and got better, I began to ask lots of questions. I made a list to discuss with the doctor. For one, I wanted to know, not if I could walk, but if I could play tennis. One doctor, who was filling in for my regular doctor, scoffed at the very idea. "What? You? You're 30 years old and a female. No way," he said. Maybe I was just feisty or stubborn. I took that "no" as a challenge. I resolved that my amputation would not interfere with my sports activity.

After six weeks in the Las Vegas hospital, I headed home. I refused a wheelchair and boarded the aircraft on crutches. Once home, I continued physical therapy to strengthen my body and prepared for being fitted with a prosthesis. In addition to working with a therapist, my husband and family helped me exercise at home. I wanted to get back into shape.

I went through some down days . . . some "why me?" times, but not so much while I was hospitalized. The worst "downer" I can remember was the June day I went to be fitted with my first artificial leg. It was just frustrating and depressing seeing that mechanical, foreign object that was going to be a part of me. It was very unfeminine. I called it

213

my ten-pound clunker. It had nuts and bolts on the side and was held on by a leather belt. They had to pad the belt because I was so thin. It felt like something you'd put on a horse. The head of the therapy unit told me to use a cane for a month while I got used to the leg, but I didn't need it. I had no problem with balance. I was on the tennis court the next week.

My first attempt at tennis wasn't really fun. I had just taken up the game the year before. Now, I discovered I had to really anticipate shots. It was frustrating not to be able to dash across court or get those overhead shots. "Nice shot" got to be the name of my game. Sometimes opposing players would say they were sorry for hitting balls that I couldn't return. "Nice shot," I'd say.

After my first time on the court, my father must have spotted a tear in my eye, or perhaps I in his. "Why are you putting yourself through all this?" he asked. "Because I'm going to do better," I replied.

Probably one of the funniest incidents occurred on a tennis court in Arizona. The prosthetist had made me a suction socket but had me wearing belts and buckles for more stability. I was in the middle of the match when the belt literally rotted off. I finished playing the point. Then I got rid of the belt for good. The prosthetist had said there'd come a time I would no longer need it. I guess that was it.

I really worked on perfecting my walk. I had my husband install mirrors at each end of the hall. I practiced everyday. I knew if I was going to go back to flying, I had to have good balance and total confidence.

As soon as I had my prosthesis, I started to prepare to qualify for flying duties. I crawled out of the windows of our small car . . . I carried my mother from room to room as if she were an injured passenger . . . I balanced trays of china and crystal as I walked across the carpet. When I felt ready, I went to the inflight services manager at United

Airlines to ask for my job back. He thought I wanted to return to work on the ground. "No, I want to be back up in the air," I told him.

It had never been done before. I had to have approval of both the airline and the Federal Aviation Administration. They agreed I could resume my flight attendant duties if I could pass a two-day emergency training test. The first day was a one-on-one with FAA and airline representatives. The second day I spent with a class of flight attendants. I was confident. Within 14 months of my amputation, I once again was a crew member aboard a DC-10 coast-to-coast flight.

I may do some things a little differently because of my handicap. But my wish is that people would look at me, and others with handicaps, and see what we have rather than what is missing . . . what is there rather than what is not. In addition to continuing my career, I resolved to emphasize my femininity . . . to appear as sexually attractive as I had before the accident. I was determined to wear skirts and dresses. I bought fake fingernails, painted them and glued them on my prosthesis so I could wear sandals or open-toed shoes. I dyed my thigh-high prosthetic stocking to match the various shades of tan of my real leg.

When I was first home from the hospital, I worried about my relationship with my husband. He never touched me. We had fallen into a brother/sister relationship. After we discussed it, I understood why. I slept with pillows all around my leg at first, and it was painful whenever I moved. My husband was afraid he was going to hurt me and didn't want to cause me any more pain. Things got back to normal after we took that time to share our thoughts.

I still have pain from time to time . . . phantom pain. Only twice has it kept me from my job. Once I was flying when the pain hit. I had to go home on crutches. The other time, I was home and spent five days in bed. I had the flu, and it attacked my weakest spot, my residual limb. I also

get what I call "big owies," often in the summer. Those are boils or friction sores on my leg. The "owies" and the phantom pain are some of the frustrations and inconveniences resulting from the loss of my leg, but neither of them are insurmountable. I'm still the same person I was before the accident.

Of course, that doesn't stop people from staring, particularly when I go swimming. I was on a beach in Hawaii. "You mean she's going to the same beach we are . . . she's going to swim here," I overheard people saying. It was as if they thought I had a contagious disease. Sometimes on down days, particularly if I'm on crutches, I get annoyed with people who stare. But I just keep a "stiff upper lip" and go on with what I'm doing. I refuse to let their stares keep me from what I enjoy. I've always been an active person, and I see no reason to change now.

I continue to play tennis, and my husband and I have won some doubles tournaments. I also still play paddle tennis and have learned to ski. For three years, I skied competitively. Now, I ski for recreation.

In recent years, there have been great improvements in prosthetics . . . both in function and cosmetics. My newest prosthesis is more comfortable and has greater flexibility, which allows me to better compete on the ground or in the air. But it is important to me to have an artificial limb that is also cosmetically pleasing. Now, that is a reality too.

I've shared my story on national television and through a variety of publications. As a result of the media exposure, I discovered a whole new world . . . a world of people with handicaps like mine, people looking for advice (physical, emotional and sexual) and encouragement. Many have written to me, and I try to keep up with the correspondence despite my hectic flying schedule. In addition, I became the New Jersey representative for the American Amputee Foundation and one time, served on the board of directors of the New Jersey Easter Seals Chapter.

It's become a priority for me to encourage people, especially those with handicaps, to make the most of what they have and try to overcome any disability. Sometimes I speak to groups of doctors, nurses, amputees and their families, or school children. My message is always the same: we are real people with real abilities.

Our plans may change unexpectedly, but we must build on what we have . . . not be preoccupied with what we have lost. I've come a long way since that awful night in Las Vegas, and I intend to keep reaching and challenging myself. I want people to know there is reason to live, not just exist, after an amputation. Even with one leg, I still get a kick out life!

On My Last Leg

PAT SHAUGHNESSY, 50

*At age 34, he was bound for a preaching mission in
South Korea when a bomb exploded at the
Los Angeles Airport. His right leg was blown off above
the knee and the left leg severely injured. His
unwavering faith in God gave him strength to deal
with the amputation. He returned to his pulpit
four months later and has since traveled worldwide.*

It was August 6, 1974. I had left Phoenix the day before
and was killing time in the Los Angeles Airport, waiting
to board my flight to Seoul, Korea. I was looking
forward to the 30 days I'd spend preaching in three Korean
cities. It was an honor for a young preacher.

I was standing near the Pan Am ticket counter, reading an international travel schedule. I had no idea that less
than 25 feet away was a baggage locker loaded with
plastic explosives.

It was 8:10 a.m. The locker exploded! One second I
was standing. The next I was on my left side on the floor
. . . lying in a pool of blood . . . fighting for my life. Pain
shot through my body.

The ensuing scene is one that remains graphically
painted on the canvas of my mind. People and debris
everywhere. My friend and traveling companion, Won
Yong Koh, had stepped into the men's room and was

spared from the blast. His wife and children also were uninjured. But around me were 33 injured bystanders and nearest to me . . . two people lay dead from the explosion.

I had been blown 29 feet from where I originally had stood. I looked down toward my feet. My pant legs were gone. I could see the left leg. Not a pretty sight. It looked as if someone had placed a couple of pounds of raw hamburger meat on the inside of my left knee. I couldn't see my right leg. There was no flesh below the mid-thigh. It had been blown off.

Two thoughts flashed through my mind as I lay waiting for help. First, I worried about my family in Phoenix. I was afraid someone might knock on the door and tell my wife that her husband had been blown up. Secondly, I knew that God had allowed this to happen for a reason . . . and he would take care of me.

Don't misunderstand . . . I hurt . . . and groaned under the piercing pain. I wasn't sure that I might not be ushered into the presence of God at any moment. But there was a strength . . . an inner strength that sustained me. Someone said that we react to stimuli of life based on what we believe. I believe the Bible is uniquely inspired by God . . . absolutely trustworthy, authoritative and relevant. My reaction to the incredible pain was based upon my beliefs.

I believe the Bible teaches us that with God there are no accidents . . . only incidents. This was only an incident. I felt a sense of security because I knew God was in control. In Romans 8:28, the Bible tells us: "We know that in all things God works for the good of those who love him, who have been called according to his purpose."

It was time for a mid-term exam in my life. At age 34, I was pastoring a growing church in Phoenix. I was in the best physical condition of my life. God was asking me if I really, really believed that part about "all things." I did. And it was that confidence in God that gave me strength beyond myself.

I was taken to Hawthorne Community Hospital, where doctors gave me only a 40 percent chance of surviving before they took me to surgery. They upgraded my condition, giving me a 50 percent survival chance after operating on my legs. I was young, athletic and strong. My right leg was amputated about 10 inches below the hip. I had four fractures in the left leg and two in the ankle. I awoke in intensive care. I looked down at the sheet . . . now a flat sheet . . . where my right leg used to be. Funny how we take so many things for granted. But when you lose something, somehow what you have left seems to take on a more valuable role in your life.

Since my body had suffered such shock and trauma, the doctors expected me to be in the intensive care unit for a week. I was there little more than a day. Hospital officials told the press my recovery was "miraculous." I later learned that I was the closest person to the bomb who survived.

My family flew in from Phoenix. They were very supportive. But my 2-year-old daughter was a bit confused about where my right leg had gone. Once she thought she had found it under the bed. "It" was the sand bags used to put my left leg in traction.

I spent a couple of months in the Los Angeles hospital before I was transferred to a hospital in Phoenix. There, I got my first glimpse of the world of prosthetics. What a scary experience. A prosthetist came to my room, saying he was going to take me to the prosthetic center to fit me with an artificial limb. As he rolled me into the center, I thought I was in a house of horrors. "Surely this must be where Frankenstein lives," I thought. Hands, feet and legs were hanging all over. It was a psychological thing that I had to get over. I think it's a psychological hurdle all amputees have to overcome.

Even before I got my finished leg, I had my first public outing as an amputee. A friend of mine coached the Phoenix hockey team and gave me tickets to a game. The doctors made me a foam leg to fill out my pant leg. They attached a shoe. I went to the hockey game in a wheelchair . . . and sat in the handicapped section for the first time. I didn't feel very secure. After all, I had one foam leg, and the other one was broken in six places.

It wasn't long until I was fitted with a quadrilateral socket and artificial leg. It had a steel brace that came up around the hip with a belt to hold it on. Every time I bent over, the metal brace dug into my body. The leg weighed about 17 pounds, but I was up and walking. I walked with a cane for about a month until I felt stable. I went back to church to preach the Sunday after I left the hospital . . . new leg, cane and all.

I guess the hardest thing to change is your attitude about other people helping you. Becoming an amputee takes away some of your pride. When I first came home from the hospital, I had to learn to depend on my wife for some things I'd always done for myself in the past. Finally, I swallowed my pride, realizing that people who really loved me really did want to help.

Although I was walking, I wasn't walking well. It seemed like the leg was too long or too short each time it was worked on. Eventually, I had another leg built by a different prosthetist. The new leg was better, although the hard socket was always uncomfortable and I still had pain in my stump. It's a chronic pain that remains with me, but like a toothache, I've gotten used to it.

I've had several legs since 1974. Each one has made it possible for me to continue a fairly normal life. I've been to Korea three times since the day the bomb exploded and have traveled to 30 countries to preach the gospel. I've stood in my own Phoenix pulpit three times on a Sunday morning and again in the evening to preach.

I always got around on the hard socket, but it hurt. I

couldn't wait to get home and take it off. It was painful to walk and painful to sit. It wasn't until 1989 that I discovered there was something better . . . a lighter leg that wasn't painful to wear. Now, I can even jog with it! I can wear my leg from the time I get up in the morning until I go to bed. After all these years, it is hard to believe such a thing exists.

I am grateful for each day on my new leg. I thank God for life and healing . . . and that someone has taken the time to learn to make artificial limbs that make life more enjoyable for people like me . . . people who are on their last leg.

Dancing to a Different Tune

HOLLEY HOWARD, 32
*At age 21, she was an attractive, vivacious young
adult looking forward to a dance career.
A freak boating accident resulted in amputation of
her left leg below the knee. After years of pain
and life on crutches, she had revision surgery to remove
her knee, but still encountered setbacks and struggled
to find an artificial leg she could wear.*

The summer of 1981 was great in Tyler, Texas. My lifelong dream of becoming a dance instructor was about to come true. I was to get my big break teaching dance and was enrolled at a dance camp for instructors, beginning the week after July 4th. Everything seemed to be going my way.

A friend and I were celebrating the Fourth of July weekend in typical fashion at the lake. Some people laugh when I say I was practically raised in the water, but I'd been swimming since I was a toddler and water skiing since age 8. I felt at home on the water, especially at Lake Tyler. I had no idea that a nightmare was about to unfold that would change the rest of my life.

Sarah and I were out cruising in my family's boat. I was driving when suddenly something caused the boat to pitch. The impact was incredible, and Sarah was tossed across the boat into me. Before either of us could react, we were

Holley Howard

thrown from the boat into the water. Maybe one of us hit the steering wheel as we struggled to stay in the boat — or maybe it was just the force that sent the boat into a spin. We don't know exactly what happened. But as the boat spun out-of-control, it ran over us repeatedly.

As we lay side-by-side in the water, it was as if Jaws was in the lake with us. We could only scream for help and fight for our lives. Somehow we got away from the prop. Sarah eventually passed out — I held on to her and just kept treading water. But I knew in my gut that I couldn't tread water much longer.

It's strange how at such a terrifying moment you can find humor, but a comedy routine from an old Bill Cosby album kept running through my mind. He tells a story about God talking to Noah. Noah was questioning God about preparing for the great flood. God kept asking, "Noah, how long can you tread water?" It sounds crazy, but I kept thinking, "Holley, how long can you tread water?"

Suddenly, it was a miracle. A fisherman had seen the accident, and he came to our rescue. As he pulled me toward the small fishing boat, I lost my grasp on Sarah and saw her go under water. Just as miraculous as the fisherman's appearance, another man seemed to appear from nowhere and dove in from his boat to save Sarah. The fisherman laid me flat on the bottom of his boat and placed Sarah lengthwise on top of me. At the time, I remember thinking, "It's bad enough to be cut up like a sausage, much less have Sarah stretched out on top of me." But the reality was that the pressure from her body was acting like a tourniquet and keeping me from bleeding to death. The whole rescue was as if the hand of God reached down to take charge.

It was a painful trip to shore, but the long wait for an ambulance was excruciating. We both were losing a lot of blood as we lay in the bottom of the boat. When the ambulance did arrive, I lost consciousness as they picked me up from the bottom of the boat. The coolness of the air-conditioned ambulance revived me, and the ambulance attendant warned me that if I lost consciousness again, I might not regain it!

Long days, long nights, and lots of pain followed 25 surgeries during my three-month hospital stay. I was in traction throughout the whole ordeal. There were days the doctors weren't sure I was going to make it. I drifted in and out of consciousness the first few weeks. The boat prop had essentially filleted my left thigh, shattered my left hip and broken the pubic bone. Bacteria, medically termed "pseudo-monis," had invaded my system. As we say in East Texas, I was "one sick puppy."

In the beginning, the doctors truly believed my leg could be saved. I remember my dad fighting back the tears as he told me my leg was going to have to be amputated. As a Shriner, he had helped take care of many children at the Shriners Hospitals. He knew full well the impact this would have on the rest of my life. I knew, too, that a one-legged person would probably never teach dance, much less operate her own dance studio. I hope I never have to know the pain my father endured during those moments. I tried to make a joke — after all, they say laughter is the best medicine. "Well, at least I'll always be able to find a parking spot in handicap parking," I quipped. We laughed, and it relieved the tension.

Doctors amputated my leg two inches below the knee, but the infection was so bad that they could not close the wound. It was like torture treatment when they took me in for debridement, the cleansing of the wound. It was so painful that they routinely put me to sleep each morning while they inspected and cleaned away dead, infected tissue.

Some people will suggest there is no such thing, but I had tremendous phantom pain. I'll never forget it. I'd be sleeping and sit straight up in bed from the pain . . . it felt like an electrical current shooting through my residual limb. I would listen to music and mentally go through dance routines — trying to stay focused on anything to block out that bone-chilling pain. I didn't know then that the phantom pain would haunt me for years to come.

I can remember all my cheery-faced family and friends, hoping to say something that would keep my spirits up. "Gee, you look just the same from the waist up," one remarked. "Why, I saw a guy who ran all the way across the country on a wooden leg," said another. "A wooden leg . . . ugh," I thought. It was not an optimistic outlook for someone who had always felt her legs were her best asset.

When you lose a leg, you lose alot more than a limb. There is an initial loss of spirit . . . an inner spirit that you must rekindle to get going again. It's kind of your survival instinct. It helps you overcome obstacles and put things into perspective. I know I wouldn't have gotten through it all without that special inner strength. I think it's that inner spirit that helps me remember so many of the funny times, but forget the really painful ones.

And I couldn't have asked for a more loving, caring family. From the moment I opened my eyes in the emergency room, someone from my family was always there. My dad was there day in and day out holding my hand all the way to surgery. My mom spent every night with me in the hospital for three months. And my sisters, Shelley and Kelley, were literally thrown out of my hospital room while trying to protect me from one nurse changing my bandages.

I could depend on my sisters to keep me smiling. They knew I was lonesome for my collie, Muffey. Of course, the dog wasn't allowed in the hospital, but that didn't stop my sisters. While Kelley raised my bed so I could see out of the window into the hospital parking lot, Shelley helped Muffey wave from the family truck.

I went home from the hospital in a body cast from below my breast down my left leg. I looked awful. I went through a stage where I wasn't sure I'd ever go out in public again. But after a couple of months of being confined at home, I changed my mind. Most of my friends were home for the holidays, and I grew tired of hearing about the fun they were having while I sat home playing "pitiful Paula." I wanted to be with them, but I had one real dilemma — how to dress around my very inflexible body cast. My mom made me some maxi skirts that covered the cast. I looked like a cross between Mrs. Butterworth and the Statue of Liberty. Because I couldn't bend, I could hardly get into a car without a T-top. Honestly, my dad bought a van for the family just so they could tote me around.

While I was recuperating at home, the doctor sent a physical therapist to work with me to try to loosen up my knee. I was in a body cast and traction for so long that the knee the doctors had worked so hard to save was frozen and useless. Sarah, already a patient of this particular therapist, had told me how much she enjoyed and admired him. The first day Eddie came to my home, I met him at the door. I know I must have looked less than attractive . . . wearing a body cast, with no hair. My hair had fallen out from all the trauma and anesthesia. I don't know when I realized that I was enjoying the physical therapist more than the therapy, but Eddie and I both admit the attraction was there from the start. However, our relationship was strictly patient/therapist — until my last therapy appointment when Eddie surprised me with a bouquet of roses and wished me luck on getting my first artficial leg at a rehabilitation center in Houston, Texas.

The following week, my parents helped me move to Houston. I was very blessed because my mom and dad were always ready to help me any way they could. Mother spent every night with me for six months, but eventually

she had to go home to help my sister with her wedding plans. The plans, by the way, had already been postponed once because of my accident. When my family wasn't around, I would do just about anything to keep from asking for help. I was in my "thank you, but I can do it myself stage" while I was in Houston. I'd go to the grocery store and hop all over the store behind my grocery basket, instead of asking anyone for help. When I returned to my third-floor apartment, I'd hop up the stairs with one bag at a time rather than ask for help. If you want to be back on your own and independent, I guess you naturally make everything harder than it has to be. I still am fiercely independent, but I try not to cut off my nose to spite my face. Most people are delighted to help you.

Because of my fractured hip, I was unable to walk on my new prosthesis, so I was still getting around on crutches. When I went out with friends and people saw me on crutches, they usually assumed I had broken my leg. If I told them the real story, some acted like I was kidding. I think it was easier for them that way. While I was in Houston, I had my first date since the accident. I had just gotten my below-the-knee prosthesis, and my date knew I had an artificial leg. I was trying to make everyone feel completely at ease with my situation. We went to a concert. First there were what seemed like thousands of steps. Then, the seats were about 12 inches apart. "Oh, great. How do I sit down?" I thought. My knee wouldn't bend enough for me to sit normally, so I had to take my prosthesis off. I asked my date if he would mind helping me hold it during the concert. Are we talking awkward or what!

Eddie started calling me while I was in Houston. By October, we had dated more than six months and decided to get married. He's been behind me all the way and has encouraged me to "go for it" when it came to anything I wanted to try. There have been some real setbacks along the way because of my struggle to find a prosthesis I could wear, but he's been there through it all. Needless to say, he is an answer to prayer.

I've spent a lot of time on one leg. I tried to wear a below-the-knee prosthesis for eight years, but had severe pain and discomfort most of the time because of my short amputation and skin graft. Wearing a prosthesis wasn't like what I had expected. I knew there might be some limitations, but I had heard about other amputees who had returned to most of their previous activities. I not only was limited as to how many hours a day I could wear my prosthesis, but I also had to remove the prosthesis to sit in the back seat of a car or on an airplane — and whenever I would be sitting for an extended period of time. Needless to say, it often was easier to go places on crutches than to deal with the discomfort and hindrance of the artificial leg. I was under the misconception that once you have a prosthesis, you wear it 24 hours a day. Maybe I was expecting my prosthesis to replace the leg that had been amputated. I discovered there were a lot of things I could do without my prosthesis and decided if I was going to spend periods of time on crutches, I would just have to learn to manage any situation that came along.

Sure, I'd prefer to walk into a room and blend in with the crowd, not stand out as a one-legged person. There have been times I've panicked before going to a party or large social function. But I try to get a grip by telling myself, "I may be the only person there on one leg, but I'm going to be the best person there on one leg." As long as I feel good about myself and my appearance, I feel I've fought the battle and won. When I wallow in self-pity, it's no one else's fault that I feel uncomfortable because I've made myself uncomfortable. Sure, I've had my share of stares from John Q. Public, but I've found the best thing to do is stare right back at people until they realize I do feel their stares and don't appreciate them. If I hold my head in shame, then they have won.

I'm sure my two sons will probably look back on their childhoods one day and realize I did things a little differently from other moms. During both pregnancies, I had a lot of trouble with my prosthesis and I spent a great deal of time on crutches. I used to hop on one leg and hold my stomach at the same time. It's amazing that I didn't deliver two Mexican jumping beans! John Everett is now 7 and Jerrad is 5. They both think it's pretty neat to carry my prosthesis to "show and tell," and they never miss an opportunity to tell friends "my mom has a broken leg. She was run over by a boat." I think they love to shock people.

You know how they say, "if you fall off a horse . . ." That was my attitude about water skiing. I still loved the water even after the accident, and I sure didn't want my kids growing up afraid of water because of me. It took me a while, but I finally got back out there on a slalom ski. It made me feel like I was really "back." Back doing something I had always enjoyed so much before becoming an amputee.

During the eight years I kept trying to wear my prosthesis, my gait was poor, and I was in alot of pain. I had lost 80 percent of the movement of my knee — so essentially I didn't have a knee. The end of my residual limb was covered with scar tissue that was continually inflamed and kept me from wearing my prosthesis. Every time the skin broke down, I'd be back on crutches. Finally, I consulted another prosthetist. He recommended I have a revision surgery to amputate my knee. Eddie and I weren't sure that was the best thing, so the prosthetist started building me a new below-the-knee prosthesis. During the time I was being fitted for a new leg, I visited with some of the prosthetist's above-the-knee patients. They told me how they were running, biking and doing activities that I had been forced to give up. I was supposed to be better off because I was a below-the-knee amputee, but they were literally running circles around me. That was all I needed. I called Eddie and told him I'd changed my mind — I wanted the revision surgery.

Three weeks later, I had my knee amputated. I was excited about the possibility that I would be fully active again, and everyone was pulling for me. Six weeks after the surgery, I began walking on a temporary above-the-knee prosthesis. It was different from the way I had been taught to walk on my below-the-knee prosthesis, but I was determined. My first clue that something was wrong with my residual limb came one day when I stepped down on my prosthesis and felt a knife-like pain in the bottom of my stump. I couldn't move without pain. I returned to the doctor who ran a test, but found nothing. Finally, after months of heartache, I realized I was probably going to have to have another revision surgery. Out of desperation, my dad tracked down a surgeon in Memphis who specialized in amputations. The doctor recommended surgery. I was sure my problems would be over if he could fix what was wrong with my stump. Six weeks after he operated, the pain hadn't subsided. The doctor was shocked, and I was once again deflated. What had started out as a simple above-the-knee revision surgery had turned into a nightmare. I could no longer wear any prosthesis.

I was beaten and down-trodden. I remember getting a newsletter about a high-tech prosthesis. An article in the newsletter featured a girl who had been fitted for her leg the same time I was. Now, she was riding a bicycle — and I was still on crutches. Nothing I did seemed to work. I needed to take a break from the whole prosthetic fitting process. Even though I wasn't ready to throw in the towel, I made myself accept the reality that I might never be comfortable wearing a prosthesis.

One of the biggest let-downs was the lack of understanding by other amputees. Several times while I was on crutches, I had amputees approach me and take it upon themselves to clue me in that if I was smart, I'd "get an artificial leg like theirs." One experience in particular left me a little dumbfounded. I went to the National Handicap Snow Ski Finals as a spectator and was looking forward to spending time with other amputees. But a couple of times I had doubts about whether these people were friends or foes. "I don't know why you're not wearing a leg," said one amputee. "I never had any problem. Are you sure you're trying?" another asked. I was really ticked off. But I tried to remember that these people obviously never had any complications after their amputations or with wearing prostheses. In the end, I had a wonderful trip and wouldn't trade the encouragement I felt just by watching so many physically-challenged athletes competing and enjoying life.

Since I was on crutches for so long, I decided I would get a little creative. Eddie and I were going to a gala event known as the Rose Ball. I couldn't imagine getting all dressed up in a formal gown only to hang on to my ratty, metal crutches. So for fun, I took my crutches to a paint and body shop where I had them painted in high gloss black and trimmed in gold. Then, I glued on about 300 rhinestones. They turned out great! Instead of detracting from my appearance, they became a wonderful accessory. People didn't seem to notice I was on crutches. I had so much fun dancing on one leg that night that a week later a friend told me she thought I had been wearing a prosthesis. I fooled her!

The prosthetist spent hours and hours working to fit me with a new leg, but the tissue on my stump hurt even when I wasn't wearing a prosthesis. He finally was able to design a suction socket that pulled the painful tissue away from the bone. This kept me from putting pressure on the sore area when I walked. Gradually, I began to wear the leg.

But I'm convinced that it was the Lord who ultimately healed my leg. It was July, 1989, and the sore tissue began to ache so badly that I was forced to take off my prosthesis. Even with that, the pain grew worse. I'm sure I was having muscle spasms at the bottom of my stump. It hurt so much that I called the doctor for pain medication, and I sat up most of the night with my stump packed in ice. Miraculously, the next day the pain was gone. Something changed that night, and I've never had pain like that since. Finally, I was on my way to attaining all the goals I had originally set when I took the plunge and decided to have my knee amputated. For the first time in years, I was comfortable and really over my setbacks. Trusting in the Lord and alot of patience had paid off at last.

Now that I've been wearing a prosthesis successfully for nearly two years, it seems like it was all so easy. Sometimes I have to make myself remember how much pain I was in and how many times I nearly accepted that amputees were supposed to walk in discomfort. I've been asked if I would go through the revision surgery again, if I had it to do over. Yes, definitely yes! I go to bed each night thanking the Lord that I went ahead and had my knee amputated. I couldn't really use the knee anyway. It just took longer and the road was bumpier after the surgery than I expected. I don't think revision surgery is ever quite as simple as you think it's going to be.

But the surgery changed my life. I can now do nearly everything I was once convinced I couldn't! I love riding bikes with my kids, dancing with my husband, walking into a room on two legs, and wearing whatever I want to. I guess to sum it up, I'm still not running, but I'm walking better and farther than I would ever have dreamed. Now I know that Holley is really back.

The Oklahoma City Bombing ... My Story

DAINA BRADLEY, 20
*She was victimized in one of the worst
terrorist acts committed in the United States.
Her mother, daughter and son were killed and
her leg was amputated to rescue
her from death.*

I rose early to get my children, Peachlyn, 3, and Gabreon, 4 months, dressed and fed. My mother, sister, my children and I headed out early to the Alfred P. Murrah Federal Building on April 19 to get a social security card for Gabreon. Remembering the long lines, we got there early to beat the crowd.

The Murrah building was buzzing with activity as employees started their day, and customers formed lines. My mother saved a place in the line and my sister, Felysha, watched the children while I filled out paperwork.

Suddenly, there was a bright flash of light. The last thing I remember seeing was my sister picking up a pen, and then I was slammed to the floor with rubble piled on me and all around me.

I screamed. I could hear a loud whirring sound, which turned out to be severed electric lines. My daughter was screaming "Mommy, Mommy" and my son was crying. Other people in the building were moaning, crying, and screaming for help. It was crazy.

Daina Bradley publicly expresses her feelings about her losses for the first time since the Oklahoma City bombing.

Then, I heard a series of loud crashes as the nine stories of the Murrah building fell on top of me and my family. The floor I was lying on collapsed, and I slid to what I later learned was the basement.

I could no longer hear the voices crying out. I could no longer hear my mother, daughter or son. My sister moaned "Mom, help me", while I lay with my left arm pinned beneath the rubble and my right leg trapped under a slab of concrete. I could not help myself or my family, because I could not move. Soon icy water filled the space I was in, and I knew that if it continued to rise I would freeze to death or drown.

Emergency rescue workers arrived and started pulling people from the building. I could hear them, but I could not see them. I screamed for help as the terror of it all sank in.

A fireman arrived and immediately started talking to me. In a calm, caring voice he let me know rescue workers were trying to get me out. Finally, some hope in what seemed a hopeless situation. In an instant, that would all be shattered.

The screaming started again. There was another bomb, and everyone began running away. I begged for the fireman to stay. He promised he would return to help me.

He and the rescue workers left me for what seemed like forever, and I waited silently for the bomb to explode. I did not blame them for saving their lives, but I thought it was the end of mine.

It turned out to be only a bomb scare, and they returned to begin the painstaking work to release me from what felt like a tomb. I was trapped in a coffin-size cave with a slab of concrete pinning my leg and another huge chunk of the building only eighteen inches from my face. I was buried so deep in the debris, it took 1 1/2 hours just to lower oxygen and a blanket to me.

My arm was without circulation for the five hours it

took them to remove the rubble. There was some relief when my arm was finally loose, but freeing my leg was going to be even more difficult. They talked about amputation, and I said no. I didn't want to lose my leg.

The rescuers called in a team of doctors to save me at all cost. As my survival instincts took over, I realized there was no other way. I would do whatever it took to make it out alive.

I lost so much blood that doctors were unable to give me an anesthetic. They could only give me a pain killer for the operation that would save my life. The hole was so cramped that the smallest doctor had to crawl in headfirst. While lying on his stomach he quickly amputated my leg. I don't remember the horror of the operation, nor do I remember my screaming that the rescue workers say still haunts them. But I do know the doctors saved my life.

After I was taken to the hospital, I found out my sister was alive but in a different hospital. She was in critical condition and may have suffered severe brain damage. My mother and Peachlyn were not in any hospital. They were dead. My son Gabreon had not been found.

Suddenly, losing a leg was not the most painful aspect of my life. In only a few minutes, I had lost my mother, my daughter, my sister as I knew her, and possibly my son.

On what would have been Peachlyn's 4th birthday I attended my mother's and daughter's funeral. As rescue teams from all over the country worked around the clock to find any remaining survivors, I held on to the faint hope that Gabreon was still alive.

The funeral was a blur. My body was badly burned and bruised. I wore a bandana to cover my hair that was burned off. I had no strength. I just wanted to change back time. I wanted my mother, Peachlyn and Gabreon to be with me, or I wanted to be with them.

After the funeral I began going through the motions of a

240

Pausing for a moment of silence in honor of the victims, federal workers gaze up at the bombed out Murrah building in Oklahoma City.

living person. . . but I was not. Friends and family were taking the steps for me. The operation which took my leg was crude and I had revision surgery at the hospital. We had never known anyone who had lost a limb, so the search for a prosthetic center began. My aunt, a nurse, knew of a place where they made artificial limbs.

I arrived at the prosthetic center in the same dress and bandana I wore to the funeral, still not knowing if the life I was left with was worth living. Just talking took most of my strength. I felt like I had been lifted from my tomb in the battered Murrah building, only to be placed in another one I would never escape.

I was admitted to Jim Thorpe Rehabilitation Hospital for physical therapy on my arm and leg, and I made daily trips to the prosthetic center. The people and patients at the prosthetic center were nice. There were other amputees who showed me how I would be able to walk and even run in time. Everyone was doing what they could to pull me out of the fog I was living in. I was making some progress, like talking before being spoken to and even laughing.

After my stitches were removed, I was fitted with a temporary prosthesis. A very special one. My prosthetists found out I liked Mickey Mouse. Everyone at the center worked to get permission from Disney to have Mickey Mouse laminated on my leg. I couldn't believe they had done this for me. It was wonderful! I took my first steps only weeks after the accident.

Things were starting to slowly look up when I received news of my son. Gabreon's body was identified as one of what would ultimately be 169 victims found in the Murrah building explosion.

We prepared for another funeral, and the realization that both my children were dead sank in. The mental pain became more intense than any of the physical pain I had

Daina Bradley walks with Donna Jackson, of Laguna, California, who raised money for her future prosthetic needs.

experienced, but I was still trying to hold on.

This time I not only attended the funeral, I was able to walk to it. But walking didn't seem to matter as much when I would never see my children or mother again. Living became even more difficult. Deep depression set in and left me with no motivation. I was discharged from the rehabilitation hospital and tried to begin the tasks of daily life. I didn't care. I didn't even want to live most of the time.

I was angry at God and everyone else who still had their family. Why me? Why my family and my leg?

People around the country continued to reach out and help me. A lady from California, Donna Jackson, whom I had never met, raised more than $20,000 for my future prosthetic needs. No matter how hard I tried to escape everyone, I was pulled back by people like her who refused to let me give up and die. My dream of my daughter being my model and my son being my football player will remain only that, a dream, but my life is still moving forward.

I am still struggling and have only just returned to the prosthetic center. I know there is a long road ahead of me, but the thought of running and playing with children again helps keep me going.

Gabe Bruce, Gabreon's father and my fiance, has been by my side every step of the way. We share the grief of our losses, and he is a constant source of strength when I am weak.

Life with My Short Leg

SARAH WOOLWINE, 10
(AND HER MOTHER, LINDA)

*Born with a congenital birth defect, her parents
faced a decision—whether or not to amputate
her right leg so she could be better fitted with a prosthesis.
Sarah has never let the amputation limit her
and is active in a variety of sports and
recreation . . . just like any child.*

From Sarah:

Life with my short leg began when I was 20 months old. They amputated my foot, and some of the bones were fused together in my short leg. My friends seem to have always treated me well. They never laugh when I fall down. Sometimes I wish I didn't have a shorter leg. Sometimes people stare, talk about me, or just laugh at me. But most of the time, people are nice to me.

Even if you have a shorter limb, you can still play sports! Some of the most athletic people have a short limb. I play softball. I can hop faster than anyone in the whole school . . .

From her mother:

There is probably nothing more frightening than the anticipation of your baby undergoing an amputation.

Sarah was born July 3, 1980, with a birth defect that

Sarah Woolwine utilizing the OKC running cable.

left her without the calf of her right leg. Her foot was attached at the knee. I guess I knew shortly after her birth that some sort of surgery would be required. I knew it in my head, but I couldn't accept it in my heart.

Since I worked in a hospital, I researched Sarah's problem in the medical library. It's not something I'd recommend for other parents. I didn't fully understand everything I read and probably would have been better off going to the doctor with all my questions.

Sarah was first fitted with a prosthesis when she was six months old. She didn't have any trouble wearing the prosthesis, but I still was getting used to the idea.

With the aid of "go-go," as she called her prosthesis, Sarah was walking while holding onto someone at age 18-months, and had just begun walking by herself when she underwent the amputation at 20 months. Even that wasn't enough time to prepare for the amputation emotionally. I talked to the doctors. I cried. I got angry as I struggled with questions like, "How would she react?"..."What would her limitations be?"..."Would she be able to cope...and would I?" I was afraid how strangers might treat her and wondered if a prosthesis would even work.

Eventually, I came to the realization that her leg was not ever going to grow. She would have to have the amputation to be able to continue to wear a prosthesis and walk. I gritted my teeth, and we went ahead with the surgery.

Sarah was in a cast for eight weeks following the surgery. When the cast came off, she refused to look at, or even touch, her leg. She cried every time she caught a glimpse of that short leg. I didn't know how to help her, and she wasn't old enough to explain what she was feeling. I talked with a counselor who suggested I keep the leg covered with a sock at all times . . . even when she bathed. The counselor said eventually Sarah would accept her leg. It took about two weeks, but she did.

The prosthetist fitted her with a temporary leg, but it wasn't easy. Sarah screamed every time anyone came near her. She was terrified of strangers doing anything to her. She wouldn't walk so the prosthetist couldn't see what adjustments needed to be made in her leg. One day, I called the prosthetist and asked him to meet us in the office parking lot. While he hid behind a car, I played ball with Sarah. It was the only way I could think of for him to see her walk so we could get a proper fit on the leg.

I guess the amputation was just a very traumatic experience for Sarah. Even through that following summer, loud noises and strangers still petrified her. I think she remembered the doctor sawing off the cast and how loud it was.

As Sarah grew and progressed, many of my questions were answered . . . but they were answered one at a time. I discovered that the reality of Sarah's amputation was not nearly as bad as the anticipation.

She started preschool at a private school where she has continued in the elementary grades. She always has been with the same group of children, and they have been very accepting. I do remember the first year she was enrolled in a summer program, however. She had a difficult time because she didn't know how to fend off all the kids who were bombarding her with questions. We've worked hard on dealing with questions and stares.

Some days, Sarah just ignores the stares. Some days, she stares right back. I've always told her if a stranger asks her questions about her leg, she can answer if she wants, but she's under no obligation to tell them anything. Some people who ask questions are genuinely interested, but others are not. And little kids sometimes just follow her. I have, on occasion, asked a parent to come and get a child who persisted in following Sarah.

If Sarah is meeting a group of new kids for the first time, a group she will be seeing repeatedly, I encourage her

249

to get everything over with. I suggest she tell them, "This is me . . . I can do anything I want to . . . and I don't like to talk about my leg over and over."

She can do anything she wants to do, from gymnastics, swimming, softball to snow skiing. She rides a bike and participates fully in physical education classes at school. She can climb trees, shinny up poles, or hang upside-down on the jungle gym.

I still worry sometimes. I'm apprehensive like any mother who watches her child hanging from the jungle gym. I do get scared about what would happen if she broke her other leg. I'm not sure how we would cope.

But the toughest times are when Sarah gets depressed that she can't run as fast as she would like . . . or when one too many people asks one too many questions. I try to get through those times by letting her be angry if she needs to be. Then, we talk about what she is feeling, and I remind her of her special talents, courage and unique qualities.

In my eyes, Sarah has no limitations . . . only limitless possibilities.

Helping Myself by Helping Others

JACK M. EAST, 40

An accident on a rain-slick highway resulted in
amputation of his left leg below the knee.
Further medical problems later forced amputation
above the knee. Determined to return to a
normal life, he began researching the world of
prosthetics and founded one of the first
non-profit amputee support groups.

I t was a rainy June day in 1972. I was driving a delivery truck for a soft drink company that summer after my junior year in college. The Arkansas highway was slick. I lost control of the truck. My vehicle did a 360-degree turn, ending up in the opposite lane . . . going the wrong direction. I struck another automobile head on.

The crash caved in the front of my van around me. At first, I thought the empty soft drink containers had pinned me in the car. I didn't know my leg had gone through the front end of the van. I was trapped for more than 45 minutes. Fortunately, a medic was able to crawl into the van and apply a tourniquet to my leg. Otherwise, I probably would have bled to death. They literally had to saw me out of the vehicle.

"Get his leg," I heard one medic say as they lifted me out of the wreckage. It didn't dawn on me at the time what that really meant. At age 22, I was young and invincible. I'd

251

been in serious accidents before, and the doctor had patched me up. I just figured he'd put me back together once again.

They took me to the nearest hospital. From there, I was transferred to one of the state's major medical facilities. My leg had multiple compound fractures, and my hip and pelvis were broken. The doctors waited for my condition to stabilize before taking me into surgery. When I awoke in the intensive care unit, they told me they had amputated my left leg below the knee. They said I was very lucky . . . they had been able to save my knee.

In the days that followed, the doctors and nurses tried to encourage me. At the same time, they were programming me to think that amputation above the knee was the worst thing that could happen to you. They kept telling me how lucky I was to be a below-the-knee amputee.

I was in intensive care for two weeks before I was transferred to a private room. I remained in traction for my hip that hadn't yet been repaired. As the days passed, I was in horrible pain. Sometimes, I wished that I had died. But death would have been the easy way out. I didn't realize that my problems were just beginning. There was constant bleeding from the dressing — the doctors didn't know they had missed a bone fragment that had been driven into my thigh.

About two months after the amputation, they discovered an aneurysm. My blood pressure dropped to 40/0 before they could get me into the operating room. As they wheeled me into surgery, the last thing I told them was "Whatever you do, don't remove any more of my leg."

I awoke back in my room. I had tubes running up one side and down the other — so I couldn't move. The doctors and nurses hinted around about the surgery. "We had to do further exploratory surgery," one doctor told me. What did that mean? No one ever mentioned that I was now an above-the-knee amputee. I didn't find out until one of my round-the-clock nurses burst into tears and explained what had happened. I asked her to pull back the sheets so I could see for myself.

I really resented the fact that no one told me. I truly believe doctors need to be frank and speak in understandable language when talking with amputees. I think we have a right to expect that.

I had been given so much blood that my body began to reject the transfusions. I became very ill, and the doctors weren't sure I'd live. As a last resort, they performed what is called "a last call." The treatment was designed to reverse the blood problems. It threw my body into shock and then convulsions. When it was over, I began to show signs of improvement, but then the doctors discovered a blood clot. I opted for medication to dissolve the clot rather than return to surgery. The clot dissolved slowly. I was improving, but my weight had dropped from 165 to 116 pounds, so I was very weak.

I had been in the hospital for three months when I asked to see a prosthesis. It was several days later when someone from physical therapy came to my room and showed me a child's limb for an above-the-knee amputee. It was all they could come up with, but it wasn't much help to me.

As I entered physical therapy, the pain was horrible. I still had a hip contracture and several broken bones. But the doctors wanted to get me ready to go home, so I was up on crutches, walking with the parallel bars and exercising. Gradually, I regained some strength.

After my release from the hospital, my girlfriend and I moved into an apartment — and my life as an amputee began. It wasn't long until we decided to get married. At that time in my life, the marriage had no real chance. Besides all the normal problems that two young people go through, there is a lot of pain of recovery for a spouse and family after an amputation . . . it's not just the amputee who goes through grief over the loss of a limb. The marriage ended in divorce a couple of years later.

I was fitted with my first prosthesis about four months after my release from the hospital. All my other medical problems prohibited earlier fitting. Even with an artificial leg, I could only walk with crutches or two canes because of my hip problem. I turned to drugs and alcohol for relief from the pain in my hip. I didn't think I could get through it without them. I had been on strong pain medication while I was hospitalized, and the doctor sent me home with Valium. That only compounded my problem with an alcohol addiction that I didn't realize I had. Coming off Valium was a horrendous experience. But once drug-free, I felt like I had a new lease on life. It was then that I really began to accept what had happened to me.

I continued to have a great deal of pain in my hip. It was difficult to get around, climb stairs, or carry anything. I started looking for someone who could fix my hip. But my finances were in terrible shape, and I didn't know where to turn. Our State Vocational Rehabilitation System came through with some assistance, and my parents' insurance paid part of the cost. I scheduled total hip replacement surgery. The doctor only gave me a 50 percent chance of walking without pain and without the use of canes or crutches. It was indeed a miracle when I was walking without canes or crutches six months later.

The road to acceptance of a disability isn't an easy one. But I always had a desire to overcome and the willingness to try. I guess I was just hard-headed enough not to give up. The most negative thing the doctor had ever said was that I wouldn't walk. I could do that. I worked on perfecting my gait because I took great pride in how well I walked. Maybe subconsciously I wanted to camouflage my amputation . . . all I know is I wanted to be as normal as possible.

As I was improving, I began trying to get information about what was available to amputees — but there was little information to be had. I volunteered my time at the hospital to visit with other amputees. It wasn't long until I was planning a non-profit foundation to help amputees. In 1975, the American Amputee Foundation (AAF) became a reality. It was a long, uphill battle for funding, but I believed the foundation could provide a vital service to amputees who were looking for answers. No one was providing the kind of information amputees needed.

I met the woman who would become my second wife at the Arkansas Pre-White House Convention for the Handicapped. Nan Ellen and I attended the White House Conference on Handicapped Individuals in 1977. Nan Ellen was active in the disability movement because she had three young children with varying disabilities. We were married in 1979, and I began to learn how to be a father to three boys.

I continued as executive director of the amputee foundation. At the same time, I worked to complete my undergraduate and master's degrees. My private consulting business evolved as I pursued my education. While I was compiling information for AAF, you would think I could have easily located the latest equipment and products available to amputees. Not true. Even my own prosthetist didn't offer to educate me on the various sockets, feet, and knee systems on the market. At the time, I just assumed I was getting the best available prosthesis.

During 1983-84, I began developing skin sores that became infected. After several months of treatment and life on crutches again, I resigned myself to surgery to revise my stump. Doctors hoped to do something that would keep my scar tissue from breaking down so much. Through my research, I had heard about an Oklahoma City prosthetist. Since I would need a new limb after surgery, I scheduled an appointment. After several visits, I was fitted with the lightest leg I had ever worn. I had walked well in the old socket, but the new socket gave me more comfort and stability. Since it was lighter, it didn't require as much energy to walk.

I'm still troubled from time to time by sores on my stump. I think it's just the reality of being an amputee. It's difficult for skin to heal when it's encased in a plastic socket. And I have very thin skin since the revision surgery.

I've come a long way since the amputation, and it hasn't always been easy. I think it's important for amputees not to be afraid to re-learn and try things. You can't give up. You don't reach acceptance of an amputation instantly. I see it as an ongoing process. Just dealing with the awkward stares from people is one obstacle. I vividly recall my first venture to a restaurant. I was on crutches and didn't yet have a prosthesis. I stood out like a sore thumb — and people can be cruel with their comments. How people react hasn't changed over the years, but I have. I guess the difference is that I'm desensitized. I was very sensitive to those stares and comments when I first became an amputee, but I'm just not as sensitive to them anymore.

Sometimes I reflect back on those early days as an amputee. I felt hopeless and depressed. I just knew I was going to live life as a cripple. But things haven't turned out that way. There is a quality life to be had after amputation. Anything is possible.

For me, probably the best thing I did was start the American Amputee Foundation. Helping others gave me the strength to recover. I've talked with hundreds of amputees. They all have stories to tell . . . stories of struggles, strength and survival. From my experiences, and those others have shared with me, I offer these steps to recovery and acceptance:

1. Grieve over your loss.
2. Discuss and share your loss and recovery.

3. Seek out peer support and role models.
4. Gather information regarding your amputation.
5. Seek advice on prosthetic options from professionals and peers.
6. Commit yourself to the rehabilitation process, including therapy, counseling and prosthetic training. Remember: it takes time.
7. Don't be afraid to try old and new activities. Find out what your limits are.
8. Share your knowledge and experience with another amputee. You, too, may discover strength and healing as you help someone else.

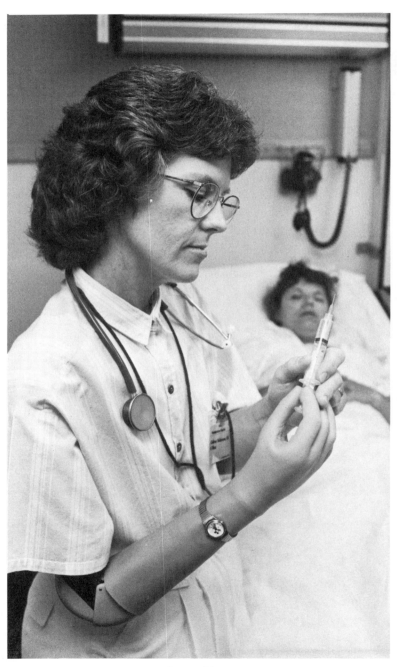

Colleen Valderama

Armed with Determination

COLLEEN VALDERAMA, 36
*She was a ninth-grader when the doctor's
discovery of a malignant tumor in her right arm led to
amputation at the shoulder. She hated the cosmetic
arm and hook, so she learned to do everything
left-handed. No one ever really denied her abilities
until she applied to nursing school. "People
just won't accept a one-armed nurse," she was told.*

A t age 14, I was active in my Oklahoma City junior high school band and drama productions. I was working on a backdrop for an upcoming play when a big piece of scenery fell, striking me on the right shoulder.

My parents had the doctor examine me, and he treated me for bursitis for about three weeks. But the pain wouldn't go away. It kept me awake at night. There apparently was no circulation in the arm. I would hold my arm under hot water . . . as hot as I could get out of the bathroom tap . . . just to ease the pain. When my mother discovered what I was doing, she took me back to the doctor. After an X-ray revealed a tumor, the doctor sent me to a surgeon for a biopsy. I had the biopsy on a Friday, in April, 1969 . . . by then, I was in horrible pain.

There was never any option other than amputation. My parents came to me and explained that the cancerous tumor would continue to grow and spread throughout my body if the arm was not removed. Without the amputation, I would be dead within six weeks. Actually, there was never a choice because I was hurting so much. All I wanted was for the pain to stop.

From the time of the biopsy, I was hospitalized and under heavy sedation. My family was there for me, as they were throughout recovery. I remember my older brother and sister, Hap and Jeanette, would just get really silly and make me laugh. They stayed by my bedside and helped keep my mind focused on something besides the pain. They constantly massaged my hand to ease the pain that remained with me day and night. The following Monday, the doctor amputated my right arm at the shoulder. The tumor was on the humerus bone, midway between the shoulder and elbow.

I remember waking up in the recovery room. I could see my cousin, who was a hospital intern, standing at the foot of the bed. My legs and left arm had been tied down, and I had a tube in my throat which made it impossible to talk. "Please untie my legs," I tried to say. I didn't understand why they were putting me through all that.

Later, back in my room, I was horrified . . . not that they had removed my arm, but that they had cut off my breasts. There were bandages from my clavicle down to my waist, and I thought my breasts were gone. No one ever mentioned it, and I was too embarrassed to ask. Boy, was I relieved when they changed the dressing, and I could see my breasts were still there!

The phantom pain was horrible immediately after the surgery. It was hard to believe that I could still feel the arm and the pain . . . as if it never had been cut off. For weeks after the amputation, this phantom pain prevented me from sleeping. The harder I tried to relax, the worse the sensations became, until I was in tears and near hysteria. After many agonizing weeks of sleepless nights, I began to realize the sensations weren't going to end, so I needed to find a way to live and sleep with them. Thanks to the patience and help of my mother, I began learning to focus on relaxation of my body and muscles until I became calm and less anxious. The phantom pain became more bearable as I relaxed. Finally I drifted into much needed sleep. I still use relaxation techniques to help me sleep when the phantom pain bothers me.

I didn't focus too much on my arm being gone those first few days. My grandmother had made me a dress for 89ers Day, an annual celebration in Oklahoma. She brought it to the hospital for me to try on. When I slipped it on, the sleeve on the right side hung flat. I think that was the first time I noticed my arm was gone. At the time, it didn't matter. I was so happy to see the dress that I didn't worry about a missing arm.

In the late 1960s, they didn't do much chemotherapy following amputations, like they often do now. But I went through a series of steroid treatments, and I was kept out of school during that time. I had to have a homebound teacher because the doctor was afraid my immune system couldn't handle any germs I might pick up at school. It was a very difficult time.

Two months later, my parents took me to the prosthetist to be fitted with a cosmetic arm and hook. That was a pretty nasty experience. We were shown to a rather dismal room where lots of artificial arms and legs were hanging on the walls. "This is gross," I thought. "I don't want to wear any of these." I flatly refused and cried as my parents took me home. I told them I was never going back to the prosthetist.

When we got home, my mother called our family doctor. He had a close relationship with our family and didn't mind telling me what he thought. He said I had to stop acting this way . . . that my parents had been through enough, and I didn't need to give them anything else to worry about . . . I had to rehabilitate myself and do whatever I could do.

I guess it was good advice, although I wasn't so sure at the time. Later, while I was in my room feeling sorry for myself, I decided I could either stay in my room forever — or I could join the human race again. I chose the latter.

It helped that I had two brothers and a sister who weren't about to cut me any slack. They made it plain that I could do things for myself, or I could sit around and feel sorry for myself for the rest of my life. They certainly weren't going to do everything for me. Now, my dad probably would have carried me everywhere and been my right arm. Looking back, it was a good thing he was busy with work . . . for both our sakes.

My one brother was ambidextrous and worked very hard to help me learn to write with my left hand. "Anyone, even someone as stupid as you, can learn to write left-handed," he goaded me.

Some of my friends in band and drama stayed in touch over that summer following the amputation. They didn't ask many questions at that age. They just wanted to see that I wasn't dying. It didn't matter that I was without an arm.

Things changed when I went to high school the following year. No matter who you are, high school is an awkward time, and it was even more so for me. I didn't make friends easily. Hap was a senior then. He insisted I join the pep club and attend other school functions; otherwise, I probably wouldn't have participated in anything. At the time, I thought he was being really mean to me.

I had been fitted with a special shoulder, cosmetic arm, and hook. I had therapy at Children's Hospital where they taught me how to move my arm up and down at the elbow. But because the arm was amputated at the shoulder, I didn't get a lot of use out of the artificial limb. Normally, the cable that makes the hook work is operated by moving the arm — but since my arm was amputated at the shoulder, I had no arm to move. I wore the prosthesis to school only once. "Forget it," I said after that. I always thought it was stupid to wear something that wasn't useful. I tossed the arm in the closet and informed my family that I wasn't going to wear it . . . no matter how much they begged.

I didn't date in high school. My brothers took me to lots of places with their friends, and I was one of the "buddies." It did hurt, however, when girls tried to make friends with me just to get introduced to my good-looking brothers. It was also painful when I didn't have a date for the prom. But for the most part, I was a feminist before feminists were "in." Frankly, I thought most guys were pretty stupid, and I certainly wasn't going to let a guy tell me what to do.

After I graduated from high school, I went through a vocational rehabilitation program. I had my sights set on becoming a nurse, but I was told there was no way I would be capable of being a nurse. Program officials suggested horticulture.

I wouldn't give up my dream. I applied to nursing schools at the University of Oklahoma and Central State University, but they wouldn't even talk to me once they found out I had only one arm. I remember a doctor who was examining me as part of a follow-up exam. He scoffed at the very idea that I wanted to be a nurse. "It will never happen," he said. Later, after I became a nurse, I was speaking to a group at a clinic where he happened to be in attendance. As I spoke, I looked him straight in the eye. "I can remember being told by a doctor that I would never get through nursing school," I said. "I'd like to let that doctor know that I did, and I'm doing quite nicely."

It was a long road. People were very "anti" when it came to a one-armed person. Handicaps just weren't accepted in the 1970s, and that made me mad. My ability to survive wasn't in my arms and legs. I had been brought up with the idea that you were more than your body . . . you existed because of what was in your mind and your heart. People only limit you when you accept their evaluation of you. I had to keep trying.

In 1973, I was accepted into the nursing program at Oklahoma State Technical University in Oklahoma City. The only stipulation was that I would have to wear an arm. School officials felt the public would accept me if I had an artificial arm and hook.

I agreed, but it meant relearning everything. I'd gotten used to doing everything with my left hand. It was hard to make myself use a hook. I had to pick up things, make beds and hold instruments with my hook. I had a supervising instructor who was always there to remind me if I forgot to use my hook. Yes, sometimes I spent more time in the lab than my nursing classmates. I'd do things over and over until I got them right. But once I mastered them, I never forgot them. I graduated from the nursing program with an associate degree in nursing in 1976. I was a registered nurse at last!

My first job was at University Hospital in Oklahoma City. The hospital was short-staffed the day I began work, so I was thrown right into the regular routine. People were amazed at how many things I could do. Most people just can't imagine life without two hands . . . it's as if they think it affects your mind because your brain would surely short-circuit without two hands!

Sure, there are things I can't do as quickly as I would like, but we all have our strengths and weaknesses. As nurses, we share the load. I help others when I'm better at something, and in return, they help me.

After a year on the job, I wanted to travel. I joined the Peace Corps in 1977, thinking I could travel and still make a difference.

The people in Brazil were surprised to encounter a one-armed nurse. They were not accustomed to people with handicaps, let alone one working as a professional. Normally, anyone with a missing body part or an illness did not work! People without limbs or those with disabilities were beggars in the streets. It was an opportunity to show people that I was more than just a person with a handicap. The people treated me with respect and courtesy, yet they looked at me with awe, because I was working as a nurse.

I spent the next several years working awhile and traveling awhile. I'd work to make some money, then put my things in storage, sell my car and be off. I guess having cancer at such an early age made me realize I'd better live for today. I traveled around Europe and tried to live in Spain several times in the early 1980s. In many ways, I lived life my own way. If I wanted to do something, I would go do it, never thinking "I can't" because I only have one arm.

I took a couple of years off from nursing to work in the family oil business. It was during this time that I met Alvaro, who became my husband. I was taking Spanish lessons from his aunt at the time. The fact that I didn't have an arm didn't seem to affect him. The hardest thing for us was the fact that we were both independent and pretty hard-headed. We struggle with that in our marriage even today.

We now have three boys: Chris, 2, Alex, 5, and Simon, 6. I've never had any real problem (yet) managing the children that two-armed mothers don't experience. As a mother, sometimes you need 10 hands to keep up! I remember during my third pregnancy, I cried because I didn't see how I would be able to hold on to another baby and still keep my other two boys with me. I soon found out that I did things just like any other mother with three kids. I tried to move fast and keep a firm grip on them at all times, even if I had to use my feet or mouth!

Now that I have a myoelectric arm, elbow and hand, the children are particularly fascinated. It doesn't bother them that I have only one real arm. I laugh when I think that my youngest is going to grow up thinking everyone takes off one arm and stores it in the drawer overnight!

Getting my myoelectric prosthesis wasn't easy, however. I had returned to fulltime nursing at Presbyterian Hospital in Oklahoma City when I went to the prosthetist to see about the possibility of getting such an arm. But it was quite expensive, and insurance company representatives flatly told me that they would not pay for it.

Frankly, I would have given up. What was I going to do if insurance wouldn't cover the cost? But my hospital supervisor wouldn't let me toss in the towel. "When you wanted to get into nursing, what did they tell you? Only you can decide if you want to do battle with them," she told me. A reporter for a local television station did a story on my problem. Money donations came in from across the state, and a firefighter in Altus even offered to give me his myoelectric arm.

I had heard of, but never met, Doug Bonds several years before from a nurse friend who had cared for him. He had battled the same kind of cancer I did and had lost his arm also. His cancer had recurred, so he wasn't going to be able to use his myoelectric arm. When he heard of my plight on the news, he contacted me immediately.

Doug gave me his arm, wanting to know someone would wear it and get good use out of it. It was a real joy to meet him and receive his special gift. It wasn't only receiving the arm that mattered to me — but meeting someone who had experienced many of the same feelings as I had over the years. We shared some humor that bordered on crazy, but we both agreed that's what helps you survive. He gave me more than an arm. He gave me the knowledge that he had overcome many hurdles and had never given up!

The prosthetist was able to use parts from Doug's myoelectric arm, but he still had to build a shoulder so I could wear it. The insurance company wouldn't pay for the shoulder either. It seems many insurance companies only want to give amputees the minimum required in a prosthesis . . . not what might improve the quality of life. I believe a person has the right to have the very best prosthesis available if you are determined to use it.

It took many calls from my attorney to get the insurance representatives to pay for the shoulder. I'm grateful for my friends at work who stood behind me and all those who donated money to help me get the arm. The donations have helped cover what the insurance didn't and will help pay for servicing the arm. I don't know what I would have done without that support system. I was ready to give up. When you are told "no" over and over, you get tired of it mentally and begin to wonder if it's really worth it. It becomes too much to deal with . . . like running up against a brick wall repeatedly.

The arm is like a part of my uniform now, and I have changed my mind entirely about the use of prosthetics. I never would have believed that the arm could make me feel this differently about myself. I love it when I look in the mirror and my clothes fit better. I've even gone out dancing . . . something I never would have done with a hook. The arm is not only cosmetically pleasing, but it's also functional.

The arm works off electrodes — when I flex my shoulder and chest muscles, the arm moves electronically. I can do a lot more than I ever could with a hook. Many times, instruments would just slip through the hook, but I have control and strength with my new hand.

Before, people saw my hook first. Now, they see my face first . . . they see me as a person first. I never have liked being described as "the one-armed nurse." I'm a person, not a nurse with an artificial arm. People at work say they can tell a real difference in me. The arm looks really natural.

At work, it's not "my arm," but "our arm." Everyone is

really excited for me. The first day I wore it, one doctor insisted on seeing how it worked. I was, and still am, learning how to use it, so I was hesitant when he wanted to shake hands. I did and the hand kept squeezing until he was in tears. The harder he tried to take his hand away, the harder my myoelectric hand squeezed. I had to relax so the hand would relax. I think he probably had bruises. There have been several instances when the hand wouldn't open. It's not funny at the time, but later I usually laugh.

Of course, there are some drawbacks with the new arm. I began to have more phantom pain again when I started wearing it and had to practice relaxation techniques to lessen the sensations. There is never going to be an artificial arm that will replace my real arm — there just isn't. There are electrical problems with the myoelectric arm, and sometimes I really get frustrated. I was at work once when the arm locked in the "up" position, and the battery just kept running. I was so mad that I wanted to break the thing. I was ready to throw the arm out the window, but I didn't. I counted to 10, took many deep breaths and tried again. But all in all, the arm is still better than the cable-and-hook system of 20 years ago, and it is certainly better than not having an arm at all.

I've come a long way since those days as a teenager when I refused to even discuss wearing a prosthesis. I wouldn't be where I am today without the support of my friends, co-workers and family. I'm glad they didn't let me give up, and I hope I never will.

My Family Kept Me Going

EMILY BAUM, *80*

Blood clots led to amputation of both her legs —
first one above the knee and later the other
below the knee. After the first amputation, she wanted
to give up . . . to die. But her family kept
encouraging her, and now she is
determined to enjoy life.

I knew I had a problem with blood circulation and hardening of the arteries, and my doctor had me on all kinds of blood thinners to prevent clots. But when I was 73, I began developing blood clots in my left leg. My heel became ulcerated, and I had a growing pain in the leg.

The doctors tried several bypasses in my leg, but nothing worked. My foot turned black, and I knew then I would probably lose my leg. The leg was amputated above the knee because that was the first place doctors could find good tissue and circulation.

After the amputation, I didn't want to live . . . I refused to eat. I wasted away to 90-some pounds. I didn't want to live and be a vegetable. It depressed me when I hopped up out of bed at night to go the bathroom . . . only to fall flat on my face because I didn't have a leg. Life just didn't seem worth the trouble. My children, the doctors, and a psychiatrist talked to me and encouraged me everyday. It was my children who finally talked me into living. Later, I was glad I'd made that decision because I just got along beautifully with a prosthesis and the aid of canes. I drove the car, lived alone, shopped and did everything I wanted.

I didn't know then I would one day lose the other leg. In fact, I was walking so well I thought I'd never have any problem with the right leg. The doctor was checking it regularly for any problems. Then in 1990, I developed an ingrown toenail that wouldn't heal. Ulcers began to form on my leg. I had a woman who came each day to put hot packs on my ulcers. Thinking the deterioration could be retarded, doctors tried several bypasses on the leg. They didn't help, and the foot began to turn blue. Gangrene was spreading rapidly, and I was told if I wanted to save my knee, an immediate amputation was necessary. In February of 1991, doctors amputated my right leg below the knee.

I went through many of the same feelings I had felt after the first amputation. I was determined I would not go through life as a vegetable in a wheelchair. I didn't want to be half a person. I knew I'd have to change my whole life-style with the loss of both legs, and I didn't think life would be worth living. Once again, it was my family that kept me motivated. The children gave me the will and the desire to live.

They remain concerned about my comfort and have all pitched in to help me adapt my home to make things easier for me. My son took the doors off the bathrooms to accommodate the wheelchair and rearranged my bedroom to make it easier to get around with the walker. My daughter reorganized my kitchen, placing pans and utensils where I could better reach them. I'm having some cushions made to raise the seats of some of my chairs to make it easier to get up from a sitting position. The children have even checked with the woman who helps me weekly to make sure she gets me out of the house frequently so I don't get depressed. I still have "down" times from time to time when I ask, "Why did I deserve this?" But the times are short, and I can usually pull myself out of the dumps by getting tied up in a book or television program, or by calling to talk to someone. My children phone at least once a week-sometimes twice — and that is a big boost.

I have a woman who comes four days each week to help me with the things I am not able to do. I think if I had someone help more often than that, I might become too dependent. I still do alot of things for myself, like bathing, laundry and such.

Even though the second amputation was only four months ago, I already have my below-the-knee prosthesis. I had to have it if I was going to walk, so I was pretty anxious. I get around with a walker now — I'll probably always use it. It tires me to walk a long distance, but I think once my new stump is completely healed that it will make a difference. I want to go to the mall to see just how far I can walk without the wheelchair. Of course, there are still things I regret that I will never be able to do again. I could have my car adapted for an amputee, but I may just give up driving. I haven't decided. My bridge club friends told me not to worry about driving — they'd take me to the store or to bridge club.

I had phantom pain with the first amputation, and I'm still having phantom pain in the right leg. I feel like I have a foot with a sore ankle. I just try to concentrate on something else when it bothers me — like a book or a TV program.

When I got my second prosthesis, I was on the television news. I was at the rehabilitation center and was totally unprepared for the interview — I even had to borrow a pair of slacks for the filming that day. (The news crew was amazed that someone who was 80, and had two artificial legs, could walk.) However, I was a little disappointed in what the media said on the air that night. What I wanted to tell everyone was that there is a whole new world out there for amputees or anybody who is disabled. There are wonderful rehabilitation centers where you can go for help. While I was at one, I saw so many people come in unable to eat, feed themselves, or walk. In the short time I was there, I saw the same people feed themselves and walk out of the center. So, it can be done. There is help, and there is hope...I'm proof of that. It can be done, but you have to want to do it! I did it and am getting along nicely.

Never Two Bad Days

ROGER DAKIN, 32

*To a firefighter, grass fires are routine. But out of
the smoke that day came a car that would
change his life. An accident left him without both his legs
above the knee. He refused to let the amputations
get him down and kept in shape
through weight lifting.*

I was just sitting down to a late lunch at a Sedgwick County fire station on that November day in 1989. It was 2:10 p.m. when the fire alarm sounded. Lt. Stuart Segraves and I rushed to put on our bunker gear. As we drove to the fire, we joked about missing lunch again . . . and all because of a grass fire. I didn't know that for me this would be more than a routine grass fire.

The fire scene was approximately six miles from the station. More than a mile away from the fire, we already could see thick, gray-white smoke. There weren't any fire hydrants out that far, so Stuart called for a second tank truck to help supply water.

At the scene, visibility was only four to six feet. We drove slowly through the dense smoke to try to find where the fire began. Stuart called the sheriff's office for traffic control. Once we located the origin of the fire, we drove back to the head of the fire to begin extinguishing the

*Roger Dakin taking a walk through the park
with daughter, Kristine.*

blaze. We turned the engine into the wind, about 20 yards in front of the smoke. Stuart jumped out and pulled the booster line while I charged the pump to get water to him as soon as possible. Routinely, I got back into the truck to drive so we could "run and pump." Stuart walked along the side of the truck extinguishing the fire.

But the smoke got thicker. I could no longer see Stuart in my side mirror. I set the brake, locked the wheels, got out and walked around the truck to locate him. He was about 30 feet off the roadway fighting the fire. I told him I could no longer see him, so he would have to yell or hit the side of the truck when he was ready to move.

I was thinking how exceptionally smoky the fire was as I stepped onto the roadway behind the truck. Out of the corner of my eye, I caught a glimpse of something in the smoke. The next instant, I was upside-down, pinned between the front of a car and the engine tail board . . . my legs were behind me embedded in the grill of the car. The impact completely knocked me out of my bunker boots. The engine was shoved forward 22 feet. The front of the car was pushed straight up into the air, and the motor was sticking up.

"Stuart . . . Stuart . . . help me," I yelled. He had trouble finding me in the smoke. That pain was indescribable. I just prayed to the Lord not to let me die. I wanted to see my little girl, Kristine, again. She was only 18-months-old.

After assessing me and the driver of the car, Stuart called dispatch. He told them he had a motor vehicle/ pedestrian accident with a firefighter down. On his author- ity, they launched a Life Watch Helicopter. Two more engines were dispatched for fire control.

I could hear the pump still running on the truck. Stuart returned with the medical kit to try to stabilize me. "Get my legs down off this car. Get me down," I kept telling him. "You know I can't do that," he said, as he tried to calm me. Had he moved me, I probably would have bled to death.

But as we stayed in the smoky roadway, I think we were both painfully aware that if that one driver had ventured through the smoke, another might. We could both be killed.

Within a few minutes, firefighter Alfred Pressnel arrived at the scene with the second tank truck. He pulled across the roadway sideways about 25 yards back to block further traffic. Alfred knelt beside me to take my pulse and check my respiration. He was surprised to find me conscious and alert. Alfred and Stuart continued to check my injuries. Remarkably, only my legs were hurt. But there were multiple open fractures and massive tissue damage to both legs. The left leg had been crushed to such an extent that it was hanging only by soft tissue.

Capt. Jim Shavers, firefighter Bob Conger, and the EMS unit arrived. The EMS team started two IVs and removed my legs from the vehicle grill. They rolled me onto a spine board and applied mast trousers, a shock garment that also would stop the loss of blood. I never looked down at my legs. That way I could get by thinking they were just broken.

The helicopter arrived, and they rushed to get me loaded. I had been at the scene of many accidents and wanted to be a good patient, so I tried to do as they told me. The pain was still there, but I was tired . . . I felt like I couldn't go any farther . . . I wanted to go to sleep. I knew I was experiencing shock. They kept telling me I had to stay awake. I wanted to go to sleep so badly.

The Life Watch technicians were in touch with HCA Wesley Medical Center in Wichita. "We're on our way with a code red trauma alert," I heard a technician tell the hospital. I knew that meant I was just short of dead.

We landed at the hospital just 20 minutes after the accident. They prepped me for the operating room. When they removed the mast pants in surgery, the left leg just fell off. Doctors worked eight hours to save my right leg. But after the operation, the bleeding wouldn't stop. I went back in for a second surgery to amputate the right leg.

In the intensive care unit, I was covered with a sheet held up in a tent-like fashion. I really didn't think about looking at my legs because I could feel them. There was crushing pain. "I wonder if I'll lose both my legs?" I remarked to my wife, Kathy. She was shocked. She thought they already had told me, so she went to get the doctor.

"Roger, we had to take them both," the doctor told me. "Okay, then what do I have to do now," I asked. He looked puzzled. "Do you understand what I said," he questioned. "Sure. I know both of my legs are gone, and they aren't coming back," I replied. "So, what do I do now?"

I guess I'd already made an unconscious decision about how I was going to deal with the amputations. I could get mad and depressed, or I could get over it. I chose the latter.

That doesn't mean it was easy. There were three more debriding surgeries to remove infection. And the phantom pain was incredible. It was really weird feeling such intense pain in legs that weren't even there. I averaged about four to five shots of Demerol each day for 70 days.

I had been in the hospital for a little more than two weeks when I began physical therapy. The therapist wanted to test my upper body strength. By the time I'd finished the session of cable crossovers, dips and a variety of balance exercises, she said I was already stronger than she would have wanted to make me. I was weak and had lost a lot of strength by my standards, but compared to the normal accident victim, I was quite strong.

I had been lifting weights for the last eight years. I usually worked out more than two hours each day—five to six days-per-week. At the time of the accident, I was 6 foot 2 inches, and weighed 220 pounds with only six percent body fat. So, I was in better shape than the average person.

The therapist also commented on my extraordinary attitude for someone who had been through such a trauma.

I told her I knew I could live out my life and be depressed and in a bad mood, or I could live out my life trying to cope and make something good out of it. The fact that my legs were gone would never change. I chose to be happy.

It's not that I didn't care about losing my legs. I surely did. And there's nothing—no prostheses—that can replace my real legs. Even with artificial limbs, there are still a bunch of things I can't do . . . like squat down. If I bend both the artificial knees at once, I fall on the floor. But I just don't think about that everyday.

While I was in the hospital, I had to tell myself not to be mean to the nurses or the doctors . . . not to take it out on anyone who just came in the room . . . and not to be mad at the lady who hit me. I just was in the wrong place at the wrong time. Plus, I'd been raised in a family that always went to church. My mother taught me that God has a plan for everything that happens, and "I can do all things through Christ who strengthens me." (Philippians 4:13) I had tremendous support from my family, friends and fellow firefighters . . . letters and cards came from churches and pastors I'd never heard of. They were all praying for me. They believed that would help, and so did I.

It was hard on Kathy. She had a really tough time accepting the accident. But as long as my spirits were up and I was "just Roger," she did okay. I wasn't sure about my daughter. I didn't let her come up to the hospital for more than a week after the accident, until I had all the tubes out of me. It would have scared her to death. But she was so young, she really doesn't remember me with legs. In fact, she sees pictures of me before the accident, and she says, "How can this be daddy? Daddy doesn't have legs."

I left the hospital January 11, 1990. My first outing was a trip to the gym the very next day. I didn't get much of a workout, but I did give it a try. People wondered why I went, and some of the guys just stood around and stared at me. But the fact that I had been in such good shape is what kept me alive. I wanted to get back into shape again. I'd lost 75 pounds. Granted, some of that was legs, but I wanted to get back to weight lifting. The guys at the gym were afraid I would roll off the bench, because it is difficult to balance when you don't have any feet on the floor.

Of course, getting the blood flowing again meant increasing the pain, but with weight lifting, you hit pain barriers all the time. You have to teach yourself to go ahead and learn to handle the pain. Over the eight years I'd been lifting, I had gotten to where the pain was secondary . . . I learned to block it out. I think that helped me at the time of the accident. I was able to have some control over the pain.

It was March before I got my first artificial limbs . . . stubbies, as they are called. They were real short, square-footed legs that help you regain balance and confidence in walking. They also helped toughen the stumps. I took right off walking on them. My prosthetist couldn't believe how well I walked on them the first day. I went home with the short legs to practice walking, standing, turning, and going up and down stairs . . . to get ready to try some taller, permanent prostheses.

One of the first places I went on my stubbies was the softball field. I had played ball and coached for years. I stood in the batter's box and hit the ball. I even tried running to first base.

I went back to the prosthetist for my permanent legs just after Easter. I put them on, and I was 6 feet tall again. It was odd because I'd kind of gotten used to looking up to people on my stubbies. Now, I looked down on some people, just as I had before the accident. The prosthetist told me it would take awhile to get used to balancing on the higher legs. But I started walking around the office complex with the aid of a cane as soon as I put them on. I was told to wear the artificial limbs four to five hours each

Roger Dakin still competes and bench-presses up to 400 lbs.

day to get used to them.

My first day home, I wore them 14-15 hours. I went to a softball tournament. I walked everywhere. I guess subconsciously I was trying to prove something . . . that this was not going to get me down. I had been told if I wore the legs too long, I might develop painful blisters. And I did. I think it was me against the pain. I was not about to let it beat me or let those legs beat me by making me fall down until I quit.

I had some real struggles with the new legs. It was a hot summer and my legs lost some volume, so I couldn't wear the prostheses because they just didn't fit. I remember one time I wore the legs to a softball game where I was scorekeeper. One of the legs kept slipping off. After the game, I came out of the dugout, took my leg off and threw it. I was really mad. Now, I've gained back some of the weight I had lost in the hospital, and the legs don't fit again. But I'm just waiting for the weight to level off so I can go to the prosthetist for adjustments. It is frustrating, and I get mad if the leg malfunctions. But most of the time, I'm fine and things are fairly easy.

I'm just not the "why me?" type of person. I won't allow myself to dwell on that. I know I will have bad days. But Lord willing, I won't have two in row. I guess the only thing I really feel bad about is not being able to go back to work as a firefighter. I do feel the accident robbed me of that. It was one thing I really enjoyed and wanted to do for a career. I won't go to work in a fire department office because that's not what I originally hired on to do. I hired on to help people. I liked doing that, and I enjoyed fighting fires. I do plan to go back to work, but it will have to be a job where I get up everyday looking forward to work . . . like I did at the fire department.

I hope something good can come out of all this . . . that I can help someone who has had an accident like me . . .

someone who can look at me and say, "Man, he has a good outlook on life, and I want to be like that." I believe once you get it in your head that you want to do well, you will. Every cloud has a silver lining. You just have to find it.

Twelve Steps to Acceptance

RON, 51
*A truck accident caused the loss of his left leg below
the knee. There were 12 long years of alcohol
and drug abuse, along with three attempted suicides,
before he surrendered his will and his life to the
care of God. With God's help, he finally accepted the
amputation and himself. Now he's pursuing a
career as a drug and alcohol counselor.*

I was an active person and enjoyed hunting, fishing,
camping, and just tramping through the woods with my
three children when I was home between my coast-to-
coast runs as a cross-country trucker.

In June, 1973, I was a member of a two-man truck team. I
must have had a premonition that something was going to
happen, because I didn't really want to make that trip. But we
were coming up on a contract negotiation period, and I was
afraid I might be out of a job for a time if we went on strike. I
needed the extra money I'd earn from the trip. My partner was
driving on an eastern Tennessee highway while I was resting
in the sleeping berth when the accident occurred. I awoke
underneath the truck with one wheel on my chest. Someone
kept screaming and I thought to myself, "Why don't they just
shut up?" I finally realized I was the one screaming.

A woman had crawled under the truck and was holding
my head up out of the diesel fuel. I kept feeling some sort

of mass under my shoulder. It was uncomfortable and I kept trying to move it. It turned out to be my left leg, bent and twisted up under me. As I lay there trapped underneath the truck for more than five hours, it became apparent to me that the leg would have to be amputated.

I didn't have a great deal of pain; doctors later said it was because I was in shock. I was conscious and talked coherently to the ambulance technicians on the 30-mile ride to the hospital. I remember telling them, "I've never been in a vehicle like this before, so how about turning on the siren?" They kept telling me to lie still — that I didn't need to see everything that was going on. I was taken to a hospital in Kingsport, Tennessee. Fortunately, it was a tri-state trauma center, so they were equipped to handle accidents like mine.

I had an eerie feeling as they rolled me down the hall on a gurney — there were all these faces looking down at me. They had an internist and a fine orthopedic surgeon standing by. The doctors told me I was going into surgery and my leg would have to be amputated — they weren't sure how high because the bones were crushed and they would just have to see how much of the leg could be saved. I signed the release forms and went into surgery not knowing how much of my leg would be left when I awoke. I was lucky...by pinning the bone, the doctors amputated at mid-calf and were able to leave my knee.

It's kind of weird after surgery. When you raise your head up and look down your bed, you normally expect to see two feet sticking up. But after an amputation, you raise your head and all you see is one foot sticking up. You see the other leg going down so far, but nothing at the end of it. It's hard to describe the feelings. So many things ran through my mind. "What's happened to me? What am I going to do now? How am I going to make a living for the family? I don't even want to live . . ." There were millions of questions, but no one who could give me any answers.

Doctors weren't sure I was going to survive, so they didn't focus much on helping me recover emotionally from the amputation. In addition to the amputation, my chest had been crushed, causing one lung to collapse, both arms and my other leg were broken, and there was significant damage to the internal organs. During my hospital stay, a woman who was a double amputee came to visit me. She told me that as an amputee, I could do whatever I wanted to do. That was the only counseling or help I received, and she was the only one who told me I could still do anything I wanted.

I was in the Tennessee hospital two weeks before I was flown back home to an Oklahoma City hospital. There I met an orthopedic doctor who probably did more for me than anyone. He made me mad. I hated that man. I guess he could sense that I was starting to feel sorry for myself. He was an old battlefield surgeon from World War II and went to work on me with a little reverse psychology.

I'll never forget how he grabbed the end of my stump, twisted it around and shoved it toward my face. "Look at this. This is what you're going to have to live with," he said. "You're going to be a cripple for the rest of your life. You're going to be out on the corner selling pencils to make a living."

It worked. Nothing he could have said or done would have made me more angry. "I'm going to walk out of here," I told him flatly. "I want a leg built so I can walk out of this place. I'm not going to ride out in a wheelchair."

A prosthetist came to the hospital to cast my leg for an artificial limb. I walked out of there 30 days after the accident. I didn't walk very well, but I walked. I swore then that I wouldn't let anything or anyone stop me. I practiced walking hour after hour and even wore a path across my yard in an attempt to walk with a stride so natural that most people wouldn't notice anything was wrong.

Learning to walk with a prosthesis was nothing compared to learning to accept the amputation. That, I just couldn't do. I was addicted to morphine when I came out of the hospital and a relative continued to get me the drug illegally. I had been a heavy drinker before the accident, so the morphine dependency came easily. My morphine supply ran out after a couple of years, so I turned to street drugs . . . whatever I could get at the time.

I combated what I first thought was physical pain with drugs and alcohol. Only later did I understand that what I was feeling was emotional pain. The pain came from many sources. My wife at that time told me I was repulsive to look at. She said she couldn't stand to see me lying in bed with just one leg. Whether it was my drug and alcohol abuse or my physical appearance, I had become repulsive to her. Worse yet, I was ashamed of my appearance. I didn't want people to know there was something wrong with me. I did everything I could to hide it. I tried to prove to myself that I was still whole. I wasn't going to be a handicapped person!

Compounding my feelings of inadequacy was the fact that my employer wouldn't let me drive a truck after the accident. The company wanted to give me a desk job. My supervisor called me a cripple and said there was no place for a "handicapped" driver with the company. Being told that nearly did me in. I overdosed on drugs and alcohol in two attempts at taking my own life and ended up in a hospital psychiatric ward for 90 days. I was just tired of me, tired of being put down, and tired of being called a cripple. Doctors told me then that I had an alcohol and drug problem, and if I would just quit, that would take care of many of my problems. But I didn't quit. I was drinking within 24 hours after I left the hospital.

My wife and my employer only reinforced the bad feelings I already had about myself. The bottom line was that I couldn't accept me. I didn't like seeing myself in parts. I let the feelings of other people dominate me, and they only reinforced the thought that was buried within me: that I was nothing. I could have adapted to the physical challenge of the amputation, but the emotional trauma wouldn't let me. Using alcohol and drugs was my way of hiding my feelings from other people. I hid my emotions and thoughts about being an amputee for 12 years, from 1973 to 1985.

I filed a discrimination suit against my employer, which took more than three years to settle out of court. During the suit, I took a leave of absence from the company. Ironically, the only job I could get in the interim was driving a truck in California. That was fine with me because I wanted to prove to myself that I could still drive a truck, which I did from the summer of 1980 until February, 1984.

My drinking and drug use continued — and eventually, I turned to cocaine. Once I had given up on myself, drinking and drugs seemed to me to be the only answer. But no matter how much I thought I was hiding from the outside world, I still had to face me on the inside. I nearly overdosed a third time in 1983.

I moved back to Cklahoma City in 1984. In 1985, I finally realized I needed help. I drove all the way to Shawnee, a small town outside Oklahoma City, to my first Alcoholics Anonymous meeting. It's funny — you don't want anyone to know you're going to an AA meeting, but it never bothers you when your name is in the paper for driving under the influence. I was reaching out. I just wanted someone to say, "Hey, you're okay."

I made the decision to quit drinking in July, 1985, and checked into a drug and alcohol treatment center that August. I was drunk when I checked in. I think that's probably the only way I could have done it at the time. I went through four days of "detox" and was in treatment a total of 30 days. That was the beginning of acceptance. I had to get off the drugs and alcohol before I realized all the pain was in my head — it was emotional pain, not physical pain that was killing me. I carried that injury for 12 years, and it hurt like hell all that time. But when I finally gave up and asked God for help, I finally quit hurting. I had to accept that this was the way it was — I was an amputee and that was not going to change. Part of that acceptance was learning I didn't have to hide my amputation from people.

"You've never told anyone about your leg being gone, have you?" one treatment center counselor questioned me. I said, "No," and he asked "Why?" I couldn't really explain to him, except I didn't want anyone to know. "Someday you will," the counselor told me. I think that was the beginning of understanding who I was . . . that just because I was an amputee didn't mean I was any less than the next person, and I could be just as much as I wanted to be.

I saw that same counselor again several years later. He was the guest speaker at an Oklahoma City AA meeting. I walked into the meeting in sneakers and shorts. He didn't say anything directly to me, but just looked at me and smiled, taking note of the shorts. I knew what he was thinking . . . "Someday you will."

For the first time, through a support group of other patients at the treatment center, I was able to talk about me . . . my fears and anxieties. Being able to talk about it made the difference. Many of my self-doubts and fears ceased being problems.

That doesn't mean acceptance came overnight. Just wearing shorts in public was a big deal to me. I had to work up to it. I started wearing them to work in the back-yard and eventually graduated to the front yard. Initially, I looked around to make sure no one was watching.

I had remarried in 1978. I can honestly say now that I never really knew my wife, Ruth, the first seven years we were married. But she was my biggest booster when I was in treatment. She has always accepted me for who I was. More importantly, she had patience until I was able to accept me.

After I was sober, Ruth and I joined the Catholic church. They were signing people up at church to walk in the CROP Hunger Walk. "Hey Ron, why don't you sign up?" one of the girls asked. Before I could answer, another woman said, "Oh, he can't do that." So, of course, I signed up. My wife asked what I had done. "I signed us up to walk," I laughed. We participated in that 10-mile walk for three consecutive years. I walk four miles a day now. I started that when I was preparing for the first CROP Walk and Ruth chided me, saying "You hardly walk to the mailbox and you're going to go 10 miles?" Of course, there are alot of people who practically fall over doing double takes when they see me out walking in my shorts.

Ruth has been a constant source of support, something I needed from the beginning. Having someone to talk to is so important. I have several support groups now, including AA and the church, but I think it's really important for amputees to have the opportunity to share with each other what they are going through . . . what they can and cannot do.

I have a lot of pride in me now. I'm proud of the many things I've been able to accomplish in the last few years. Now, I'm able to accept that an amputation doesn't mean I'm a cripple . . . it doesn't mean I'm disabled. I am only limited in some areas. And I discovered that sometimes I am limited only by what I think I can't do. I remarked to my prosthetist one day that about the only thing I really couldn't do was run. "Sure you can," he said. I tried it, and I can run, but it seems a little awkward. Right now, I run at night because I'm not ready yet to let other people see me do that. I still want to make sure I can do something right before I do it in front of anyone. Eventually, I'll get around to jogging in the daytime.

It's an ongoing process. You have to try some things to

find out you can do them for sure. Like dancing — it may not be easy and it may not be graceful, but I can still dance. Now a lot of people may think I can't dance, but I think I can dance. That's how I see me now. Before, I didn't even want to see me.

I've adapted the things I do to the point that I don't much think about being an amputee anymore. I've found that I need to be me, not what other people want me to be. I can't worry about their expectations. I've grown comfortable with who I am — I've accepted me. Sure, there are "down" days . . . days when I see someone walking with two legs and envy the fact that he has two ankles. That's negative thinking, and I have to get away from that. That's one thing I've learned through AA — when I get negative, I've got to get back on the positive side. I have a sponsor I call when I get down. I've found my problem quits being a problem when I can share it with somebody.

Now, I'm working at a hardware store and going to school. I literally drank my way out of college 32 years ago, but now I'm back studying sociology. I plan to go into drug and alcohol abuse counseling and hope to work in the penitentiary system. It's needed so badly in the prisons. People in there have problems they can't deal with, just like I had problems I couldn't deal with, but they don't have the avenues of help I had. I hope I can make a difference.

As a part of all I've been through, I found out I can do most anything if I try. I just didn't try for 12 years. Drugs and alcohol made it easier — easier to hide behind and easier to accept what others thought of me. Even now, everything isn't perfect. I work toward my goals, and I know I'm going to have problems. But if I can accept me today, then I can take care of tomorrow.

Editor's note: In keeping with the tradition of Alcoholics Anonymous, we have chosen not to use Ron's last name.

It Couldn't Happen to Me

VIVIAN THOMPSON, 47

*A diabetic since age 6, she knew she was at risk
for circulatory problems. But it wasn't
something she thought about until a blister on her foot
led to an infection that wouldn't go away.
It meant amputation of her right leg
below the knee.*

There is more publicity about diabetes these days, but still many people don't realize it is the third leading cause of death. And many don't know it often causes nerve damage that can lead to amputation.

I was diagnosed with diabetes when I was 6. The doctor prescribed insulin and a strict diet. Of course, back then they told diabetics to eat alot of food, and I was a picky eater like most kids.

In the late 1980s, I developed neuropathy in both my legs from the knees down. The doctor told me to be very careful about getting any cuts or scrapes on my legs. He explained that the nerve damage would make me less sensitive to the severity of a cut, and the diabetes could prevent proper healing.

It was summer, 1989, and I had bought a new pair of shoes. We went to my mother-in-law's house to visit, and I wore the shoes all day. Only later did I discover I had rubbed a blister on my right heel. I doctored the blister as anyone would, but it never healed completely. For the next year, I continued to have problems with the foot. Little cuts and scratches took forever to heal. In the summer of 1990, an ulcer appeared on the bottom of my foot for no apparent reason. My entire foot puffed up and turned red. It looked as if I'd twisted my ankle. Even the doctor thought so — and he sent me home to stay off my foot for a week.

The foot didn't get any better, so eventually I ended up consulting a rare disease specialist and a couple of other doctors. Two of the three said amputate, but one thought antibiotics could solve my problem. He told me to go home, get in bed and stay there. And I did. From August to mid-October, I was told to try different things, but nothing worked.

By late October, I could barely walk on it — and when I did, I could hear the bones crunching. I'll never forget that Halloween. I was looking forward to seeing my 3-year-old granddaughter, Brittany, in her costume. I really wasn't feeling well that morning . . . and as the day wore on, I got worse. When my family realized what was happening, they rushed me to the hospital. By the time I arrived, I was unconscious. The infection had spread throughout my bloodstream.

I underwent three surgeries. During the first, they cut the heel all the way around to see what was going on. My foot was total mush. About four or five days later, doctors performed a "guillotine" surgery, amputating the foot so the infection could be drained. About five days later, they cut off a little more of the leg and fixed the stump so I could be fitted with a prosthesis.

When they did the first surgery, I still had hope the doctors would be able to fix things. But the night before the first amputation, I started to think about how losing my foot was going to affect my life. After the amputation, I was on an emotional roller coaster. Somewhere in the back of my mind, I'd always known this was a possibility. I was certainly aware of the poor circulation problem and the complications that were caused by diabetes, but it never really hit home until it happened. "It can't happen to me," I thought.

After the surgery, I was enveloped by a big dose of self-pity. I just knew I'd never be able to take care of Brittany — and she is the light of my life. I knew I'd never be able to garden again . . . I felt like my life was over.

"You can get an artificial leg, and you can do this and that," everyone kept telling me. But I don't think I really believed them at first. Still, I hated to stay in bed, and I hated that wheelchair. I couldn't go to the bathroom without help — and it is a terrible thing to have to give up your privacy. But I was a fighter, and I was determined to do what I could. For instance, whenever I wanted to cook, my family would help me to a stool in the kitchen.

My family was the greatest support to me. "You can do it if you want to," they told me repeatedly. Eventually, I guess it all soaked in. But what really jolted me was a question from Brittany. "Grams, are you going to go get a new leg?" she asked. I knew then I needed to get a leg . . . if not for me, then for her.

I got my temporary leg in November, 1990. I felt like a bird let out of its cage. Being able to stand on my own two feet and walk was the most wonderful feeling in the world. It's something we all take for granted.

Learning to walk with the prosthesis was no problem. But I don't think I would have let anything stand in my way— I wanted to walk so badly. And I haven't had any skin breakdown. The prosthetist was worried about possible skin problems, so he made a special sleeve that fits tightly over my stump to protect it and keep it from rubbing against the socket.

I can't get around like I used to. I can't garden on my hands and knees like before . . . and our hilly yard makes it hard to get around. But I put my prosthesis on first thing every morning, and it's the last thing I take off every night. I am able to do most things I want to do.

I think learning to accept an amputation is an individual thing. The best advice is to lean on your loved ones, your friends and the Man upstairs. Ask God to get you through it. You have to accept that life is never going to be exactly the way it was before. I know I'll never have that leg again, and there certainly will be things I'll never be able to do again. But I can have a full life . . . and I intend to.

A Spirit That Wouldn't Quit

Donald "Butch" Wyman, 37

Alone on a mountain cutting trees for lumber to build a new home, he was trapped when a mammoth–size oak tree fell on him, crushing his left leg. Faced with certain death unless he freed himself, he cut off his lower leg below the knee with a pocket knife. His "I can do" attitude has helped him deal with the loss.

M y wife and I were going to build our dream home in the Pennsylvania woods. To cut the costs, we decided we would do as much of the construction ourselves as we could. As an employee of a strip mining company, I was used to taking down trees to clear an area. The company let me borrow the equipment, and I stayed after my regular shift to cut some trees that would be turned into lumber for our home.

The woods became quiet as the others on the strip mining crew headed home late that July afternoon in 1993. I turned to go back down the hillside with my chain saw, never expecting that the serenity soon would be shattered, and I would face a life or death decision.

I had my eye on a big oak tree. I had cut hundreds of trees, so I should have known better. The top of that particular tree was slightly bowed because it had been wedged between several other trees on the ground. As I

295

Donald "Butch" Wyman

cut, the trunk suddenly snapped! I was knocked to the ground, and my lower left leg was pinned under the tree. The tree was more than 30 inches in diameter. As soon as it hit me, I knew I was trapped. I couldn't move my leg, and there was no way that tree was going to budge.

I couldn't cut the tree away because of the diameter, so I started digging around my leg hoping I could open up enough space under the tree to pull it out. At the same time, I was screaming for help. I'd dig a little and scream a little. But my cries for help rang hollow in the woods—no one could hear me. I kept frantically digging, first with my chain saw blade to loosen the soil until it ran out of gas, then my hands to scoop away the dirt . I just knew I could do it—until I hit a rock. Then, I had to deal with the fact that there was no way I was going to free my leg.

I was kind of panicky, but I knew I couldn't let myself lose control. I didn't want to pass out. Part of the bone was sticking out of my blood-soaked pant leg. A pool of blood was beginning to form on the ground. I don't know what made me think of it as an option, but it came to me that since my leg was already broken, I could cut through the flesh and leave my leg there. I pulled out a pocketknife. It was horribly dull, so I sharpened it on a piece of rock and cut my pant leg away to see how bad I was hurt.

I prayed for a little while. I decided I could either stay there and maybe bleed to death, or I could go for it. I decided I had to go for it. I took the rope off my chain saw and tied it around my leg like a tourniquet, hoping that would deaden the feeling in my leg. I scratched the knife across my leg, and it wasn't too painful. As soon as I started to cut though, I hit a nerve, and it was just like there wasn't a tourniquet at all. I didn't think I was going to be able to do it. For a few minutes, I wasn't sure what to do. But there really was no other option. I had too much to live for—my wife, Janet, and son, Brian. I closed my eyes and began to cut. It was an agonizing pain, and I'm not sure why I didn't faint at that point. I just tried to concentrate. Finally, my leg was free!

Leaving the lower part of my leg pinned beneath the tree, I began the uphill climb to my bulldozer which was about 135 feet away. I was hanging on to the tourniquet as I crawled up the hill and into the dozer. I used the dozer to drive myself the remaining 1500 feet to my truck. Once in the truck, I used a metal file to push in the clutch when I shifted, all the time holding on to the tourniquet to suppress as much of the bleeding as possible. As I drove, I was praying to find some-one—anyone—who could send for help. No one was home at the first farmhouse I came to. I passed yet a second vacant house before I saw children playing in the yard of another. I pulled over and started yelling for help.

As the farmer neared my truck, I screamed, "Help me. I'm bleeding to death. I cut my leg off." I kept trying to lift my leg up off the seat to show him. He ran inside to call an ambulance, but I knew we were still a good distance from the hospital, and time wasn't on my side. I asked him to drive me to meet the ambulance. We took off, but by that point I was growing weary. Knowing I had to stay awake, I began retelling my story of all I had been through to get that far. We met the rescue squad, and they immediately wanted to give me something for the pain, but I declined. I wanted to know what was going on and to stay in control. One of the rescue people asked where to find the rest of my leg, so I hastily sketched a map to help them locate it. That gave me hope that the leg could be reattached.

But it wasn't meant to be. They found the leg and delivered it to the hospital only about 30 minutes after I arrived. It was unsuitable for reattachment because it had been too badly crushed by the tree. The doctor joked that I was not a very good surgeon. As luck would have it, one of the best surgeons in the country was at Punxsutawney

Hospital. He had experience with amputations during the war. After he cleaned up my self–amputation, I was left with between six and seven inches of leg below the knee .

I was worried about my wife and how she would react. I asked the hospital not to tell her I had lost my leg. They called Janet and told her I had been in an accident and injured my leg. Maybe it was a sixth sense or something, but out of the blue she asked, "He didn't loose his leg, did he?" They didn't confirm that for her until she reached the hospital.

Janet and Brian have been there for me all the way. I kept a positive outlook, and I think that helped them, too. Some people ask how I kept my spirits up after losing a leg. I figure things happen in life, and you just go on from there. I lost a leg, but I was just happy to be alive and to be there with my family.

I was hospitalized for six days, and was scheduled to go to a rehab center about 30 miles away. Probably the hardest thing to understand was all the media attention. They were camped out at the hospital, and fortunately, the hospital public relations staff kept them at bay that first week. Janet and I decided that they weren't going to go away, so we picked out several we thought were reputable and agreed to tell the story. We figured if we shared the story, the media would go away. At first I was reluctant, but as I realized how my story was helping other people, I almost felt obligated to share the details.

In fact, when I say I never let the amputation get me down, there actually were a few days when I dwelled on "Why me, God?" I can remember being in the rehab hospital on a Saturday – no treatments, nothing to do, and Janet had errands so she didn't visit that day. I began to think about how Brian and I used to run in the backyard. I could visualize us racing, and myself with no leg. I had to deal with the idea that those days were gone forever.

As my story became highly publicized, I began to get

stacks of mail. There were letters from people all over, all saying pretty much the same thing—that they had troubles in their lives they didn't think they could handle until they read my story. It was then I came to a realization that God was using me as a tool to help other people with their troubles. What they didn't know was that their letters also were helping me.

Exactly a month after the accident, I was fitted with a temporary prosthesis. Even though it was a little uncomfortable, it was great to look down and see two feet on the floor. Of course, I had expectations that this was going to be a miracle leg, and I was going to put it on and take off walking. It wasn't quite that easy. Even after two weeks of pretty much taking baby steps to relearn how to walk with the prosthesis, it was not really comfortable. My surgery was so recent, and I had a lot of healing to do to get past the tenderness and the nerve endings that had been cut. My prosthetist tried to encourage me not to take it too fast, but I was determined to be walking for my wife's birthday that month, and I did exactly that.

I continued to use my temporary prosthesis, and, as I healed, the leg felt better and better. I returned to work three months after the accident and was fitted with my permanent prosthesis in January, 1994. I actually got two legs. One is a more rugged sports leg that I can wear to work. It's durable and has a shock absorber and spring foot. My second leg is designed to look like my real leg, with closely matched skin tone and simulated hair.

I guess I've looked at the loss of my leg as more of a minor setback. I knew from the outset that somehow my family and I would get through this ordeal, and we'd go on from there. Mine is a story, though, that if I heard it, I'd say," I can't believe that. I could never do that." But I did. What it all boils down to is an overpowering will to live. I just couldn't give up.

Shattered Dreams

BRENT POLANCHEK, 27

*He was living out his lifelong dream of working
on the railroad when a boxcar sheared off
both of his legs at the upper thigh level. Now, with
two artificial limbs, his sights once again
are set on becoming an engineer.*

I took my first ride on a train when I was four or five, and I was hooked. That's all I ever wanted to do — be an engineer.

As soon as I turned 18, I started putting in applications and sending letters everywhere in hopes of landing a job on the railroad. It took more than seven years, but in July, 1988, my dream came true. I began working as a brakeman for the railroad in Portland, Oregon.

By June of the following year, I had worked my way up to switch foreman. I was working the graveyard shift, usually on the job from midnight until noon. This particular night, it was only 15 or 20 minutes until quitting time. I didn't know then the next few moments would forever change my life.

It happened in an instant. One second I was standing; the next I was on the ground. I'll never forget the sound the wheels of the train made as they ran over me, like metal

Brent Polanchek, bilateral above-the-knee amputee, showing his enthusiasm after his first climb back onto the engine with his new prostheses.

crunching a 2 X 4. Like in a dream, the cars kept coming — one, two and then, three. But I was conscious, and I knew exactly what had happened. I knew that my legs had been cut off.

The third car dragged me more than 60 feet. It finally stopped, but I still was pinned under the one wheel. I raised my head and saw one of my legs in the middle of the track, a couple of feet away.

I thought, "This is it. I'm going to die." All I wanted to do was go to sleep as the paramedics struggled to keep me awake and worked to keep me alive.

I don't remember the helicopter flight to the hospital. I only remember the pain of sliding off the carrying board onto the operating table. I woke up in a hospital room. I didn't know if it was the same day or days later. I don't remember the few minutes before the accident or about 10 days afterward.

I'd always said if something terrible like this happened to me, I'd rather be dead. I wanted to kill myself.

The sense of loss was overpowering . . . lying there in a bed, knowing I didn't have any legs, that I couldn't walk, and I couldn't run. I knew I couldn't go back to being a brakeman or a switchman anymore. And I knew no matter how badly I wanted them back, I couldn't have my legs back.

The doctors were encouraging. From the very beginning, they told me I could be fitted with artificial legs that would let me walk again. I listened, but the fact was when I went to sleep and when I woke up, I still didn't have any legs. I felt my life was over. My family tried to help keep my spirits up. I did fairly well when they were there during the day, but after the lights went out and I was alone, I wanted to somehow slip off into the next world. I wanted to kill myself. If there had been any way — a pair of scissors or a gun — I would have done it. I thought of pills, but I didn't have any and I couldn't get out of bed.

I was on morphine, which took the edge off the pain, but couldn't relieve it entirely. The pain of the original amputation was surpassed only by the pain after the skin graft operations. They had taken all the skin off my back to patch my legs and the fingers on my left hand, which also had been amputated by the train wheels. The pain was incredible . . . like lying on a cookie sheet with a gas flame underneath.

Several days after the second skin graft, I was loaded into a wheelchair for my first ride outside the hospital since the accident. Tears ran down my face as I got my first glimpse of grass. Green grass. I could see it, but I couldn't get up and go over to it. I cried because I knew even with artificial legs that I'd never again be able to feel the tickle of the grass between my toes.

I cried alot those first few weeks. Maybe that was therapeutic. I needed to get the grieving out of my system. Calls from friends I hadn't heard from in a long time would trigger yet another round of tears. The memories of things we did together . . . things I'd never be able to do again . . . came flooding back.

While I was in the hospital, a workman was installing an intercom system. He told me about a friend who also had lost both of his legs. He gave me Roger Charter's phone number. I called him. During the first part of the call, I cried and he listened.

"You can do it . . . there is hope," Roger told me. "You can get fitted with legs and do alot of the things you used to do. Just don't give up."

Talking to Roger and others gave me hope. I sent for information from the prosthetics facility where Roger had been fitted with legs. I saw a videotape of Roger running. "My God, look at that guy. He's lost both his legs, and he's not walking — he's running," I gasped. Something changed inside me. I saw Roger and other people who had faced the same kind of catastrophe that I had, and I knew I wasn't alone. If they could make it, so could I.

I was dismissed from the hospital even before my legs were completely healed. I didn't know then that I would be in for yet a third skin graft on my right leg. It was six months before my legs were healed and I could consider getting my first prostheses.

At the time of my accident, my fiancee Kathy and I were looking forward to a big November wedding. I couldn't imagine that she would still want me, but she said I was still the same person, whether I could walk or not. We moved the wedding date up and were married in a small ceremony by the Justice of the Peace, August 22. I couldn't have made it through those first weeks and months without her.

I had talked with a couple of prosthetists while I was in the hospital. One offered very little hope, telling me that my residual limbs were so short that I was going to need big belts and metal hip joints to even hold on a pair of artificial legs. I wanted to punch him out. I'd seen Roger run. I wanted to be able to slip my legs on and go. To be honest, I thought it was going to be easier than it was. Somehow in the back of my mind, I thought a prosthetist was going to make me a pair of these magical legs, and I was going to put them on, stand up, and go cruising.

I wanted to go to the Oklahoma prosthetist who had fitted Roger, but a local prosthetist assured me he could do anything they could do in Oklahoma City. And looking at the practical side of it, he was close if I needed anything fixed.

I was fitted with my first legs in January, 1990. But even after a few months, I could wear them only 30 minutes at a time. And the pain was excruciating. I know the prosthetist wanted to help me, but he didn't have a lot of experience fitting amputees with so little of their legs left.

It was July when I arrived at the Oklahoma Sabolich Center. Within a few days, I was up on stubbies. First I walked with canes, and I was surprised when the prosthetist told me to walk without them. And never in my wildest dreams did I expect to be climbing stairs. In those little short legs, I went up and down the stairs outside the office. Those stairs were bigger than me. I wasn't sure about it at first, but once I did it, I knew nothing could stop me. I felt like my life had been handed back to me.

To be an engineer, you've got to climb stairs to get up on the engine. And I was climbing stairs. I knew that maybe not that day or the next, but in time, I would realize my dream of being an engineer. I knew I could do it.

With my desire and the help of my prosthetist, I knew I could do whatever I wanted. I finally could see that keeping a positive attitude was paying off, despite the months of agony and frustration. I'm not kidding myself. I know there still will be down days, but those are becoming fewer and farther between. Some days, I still wake up and think, "Geez, another day without legs," but the next day will be better.

Alot of positive things have happened since the accident. I have spoken with and grown to know many wonderful people, other amputees, whom I wouldn't have known otherwise. I think I can finally see the light at the end of the tunnel, and this time it's not a train.

Now, I'm just living for the day when the phone will ring, and it's going to be someone calling me like I called Roger. It's going to give me the opportunity to tell that person what I went through, and I'll be able to help someone like Roger and other people helped me.

Turning Obstacles into Stepping Stones

RICHARD TERRY, 53
*It was almost seven long years of pain, in and out
of the hospital, as doctors attempted to save his leg.
He refused to let the ordeal get him down.
Even when the doctor said the leg needed to be
amputated above the knee, he vowed to keep a
positive attitude and prepared for life as an
amputee by finding out about prostheses.*

Monday morning rush hour traffic in Houston is murder. But I was making good time in the fast lane as I headed for my office in May, 1983. At age 46, I was in the prime of my life . . . both financially and familywise . . . and I felt great that morning.

I had no idea that the carelessness of another freeway driver would soon turn my life topsy-turvy. I noticed the cars on the opposite side of the highway had come to a standstill, and I was grateful my lane of traffic was still moving. Without warning, the next instant I was facing a large truck grill embedded in the front of my car.

Apparently, the driver of the dump truck hadn't noticed the traffic stopping. Instead of rear-ending the vehicle in front of him, he swerved into oncoming traffic . . . into my lane . . . into my car. As my car came to an abrupt halt, so did much of my life.

I was trapped in the car for more than 45 minutes.

Fortunately, an off-duty nurse was in a nearby car and witnessed the accident. She took her scarf off and tied it around my head, cautioning me not to rub my face. I didn't know that the impact had caused my eye to pop out or that my head was filled with glass. I had a fractured skull, and by the time I arrived at the hospital, I had no feeling from the neck down.

Even though my right leg obviously was crushed, it was not the main focus as doctors placed me in intensive care. Two neurologists examined me and determined there was no problem with my neck or back. It was about a week before the nerve damage subsided and I began to feel my body again. But as I lay in intensive care, I really had no idea how badly I was injured . . . was it bad enough that I might die? It seemed ironic that as an executive for a large retail drug firm, I was on the road or in the air constantly . . . I practically lived on airplanes . . . yet this accident took place within three miles of my home.

I spent more than a week in intensive care. My leg was so badly swollen that doctors couldn't operate. As my more-than-two-month hospital stay wore on, I underwent several plastic surgeries. Doctors were able to put my eye back in and restore my vision, but the glass just kept working its way out of my head. I didn't know then that this would be the first of a continuing series of hospitalizations, and it was only the beginning of many operations on my leg.

My leg had been severely crushed. The shin was totally shattered, the bone almost in crumbs. Initially, doctors put metal implants in my leg, hoping new bone would grow to those and the leg would grow back. They took bone from my pelvis to graft onto the leg to help with new growth. I went home with steel rods running through my leg with compression bars attached.

I had every reason in the world to be depressed. I was in a wheelchair . . . the driver who hit me was uninsured . . . I couldn't return to work . . . doctors had no idea how long it would take my leg to heal . . . and I was in pain. But I'm just an optimistic person. My wife and I both are positive thinkers, highly motivated, and full of energy. I would not let this accident get me down. I suppose it was a little frustrating for my wife since I still wanted to do everything for myself, but everything wasn't so easy from a wheelchair. I laugh now to think how she sometimes left the house when she got tired of seeing me fumble around.

When I say I was independent, I mean I wanted to do everything myself, and that included mowing the lawn. I rigged my power mower so it would pull my wheelchair and I could tend to the yard. It threw me out of the chair about 20 times, but I remained determined. I wouldn't give up.

My brother, David, is a doctor, and he kept me advised of what I might be facing. He told me from the start that if osteomyelitis, a bone infection, set in it would be difficult to arrest. I'd probably lose my leg.

Doctors diagnosed the infection three months after the accident, but they didn't give up hope. I'd go back to the hospital two times a month to have the leg opened and the infection cleaned out. In addition, I had drainage tubes in my leg that I had to clean every day. I flushed the tubes with hydrogen peroxide. Intense pain was with me day and night. I have a high tolerance for pain and did fine during the day. But at night, I had to have strong pain medication to sleep.

My wife and I bought a small ranch in Madisonville, outside of Houston. It gave me a place to get out . . . not to be confined to just a bed and patio. Away from the city, there were no sirens, no fences . . . and I discovered the chirping of the birds for the first time in a long time. The ranch was one way of maintaining my sanity. While I was in the hospital after the accident, my company said my job would be available, but I would need to relocate to California. That was no problem, but I knew I had a long road to recovery ahead of me.

In addition to all the physical problems, my wife and I were dealing with the financial burden of being hit by an uninsured motorist. I had carried the minimum insurance coverage for underinsured and uninsured drivers just like most people. That certainly wouldn't cover all I would need. It could have gotten me down, but I was damn glad for what I did have. I chose to dwell on the positive.

Yet, I guess I still wasn't myself. The heavy pain medication was affecting my thinking. I realize now what a stress that was on my wife. I got to a point where I actually preferred to be by myself. I'd be alone all day while she was at work. When she came home, having someone else in the house was just one more thing to deal with.

The doctors repeatedly took grafts from my pelvic bone and applied them to my leg, but the infection just ate the bone away. Eventually, they had taken all there was to take from my pelvis, but the leg was no better. The pain continued to escalate for five years, as I bounced in and out of the hospital for surgeries on my leg. In early 1989, my knee literally fell apart, and I went in for a knee replacement.

By the spring of 1990, my doctor told me there was nothing more to be done. Instead of growing, the leg was getting shorter. He recommended amputation but wanted me to get the opinions of three other physicians. They concurred; it needed to be amputated above the knee.

I wasn't surprised. I guess I realized I had just been postponing the inevitable. During the long months of my convalescence I had thought about what my life might be like if I had only one leg. Now, I began to give it serious consideration. In the month that preceded the amputation, I spent a lot of time working out in my mind how I would stand, drive, bathe and do this and that. I asked my brother about a good prosthetist. I certainly didn't want something I'd have to lug around the rest of my life. He recommended the Sabolich Prosthetic and Research Center. So even

310

before I lost my leg, I flew to Oklahoma City to find out everything I could about a prosthesis . . . how to get one and what I could expect.

I was glad I took two to three weeks to ponder life as an amputee. I was lucky I had that time. Some amputees don't. By the time I had the surgery, I probably was better prepared mentally than 99 percent of the amputees. I'd had ample time to think about it. I knew that I soon would have a better quality of life and be more mobile than I had been for the past seven years.

The surgery went well, but the phantom pain that followed was incredible. The first two days after surgery were agony. I guess because I had been in such pain for so long, my brain just kept sensing the pain even after the leg was gone. It was just as real as if the leg were there. Sometimes I'd even have to look down to make sure the leg was gone. I spent five days in the hospital, and the pain began to subside but never entirely went away.

I was sent to a rehabilitation hospital. They wanted me to stay a couple of weeks, but after five days I felt I knew the exercises well and could do them at home.

I never dwelled on the loss of the leg . . . only on the new mobility I had to look forward to. The only distressing thing about the amputation was the phantom pain. After I was home from the hospital, I still needed pain medication at night. Even with that, sometimes I had to put my Walkman headphones on and turn up the music as loud as I could stand it to take my mind off the pain.

I healed quickly, and the stitches were removed within a couple of weeks. Then, I went to be fitted with a temporary leg. I was determined to do it by myself. I put on my backpack, grabbed my crutches, and flew off to see the prosthetist. I had no problem with the temporary leg. I wore it all the time, morning to night. Once I got used to the balance on two legs again, I set the crutches aside.

I suppose one thing that kept me going was the old cliche, "I cried because I had no shoes, until I saw the man with no legs." That kind of fits me. I look around at people who have no legs and people confined to wheelchairs. There's always someone else who is worse off than I am.

Most recently, I returned to the prosthetist to be fitted with a permanent leg. Of course, that is a misnomer of sorts since the leg won't last a lifetime. Like any mechanical thing, it will need replacing from time to time. I won't have them put the cosmetic covering on just yet, however. I want to make sure the leg is working for me in every way. I want to work with it until it becomes a part of me.

Once the leg was amputated and I was on my way to walking on two legs again, my wife commented on the change in me. The stress of watching me struggle to keep my real leg was finally over. "It is like having the ol' Richard back again," my wife said after I regained my mobility.

I quickly discovered after losing my leg that shorts are the easiest pants to wear. I know showing an artificial leg in public might bother some amputees, but it doesn't bother me. I don't let stares bother me, although when people keep peeking and turning away, I have the notion to walk over and ask them if they want to know about my leg. The only thing that really bugs me is at the cafeteria. I suppose out of kindness, they keep sending someone to carry my tray. Even when I tell them, "No thank you," they still follow me to my table. I guess they think I'm going to fall, but I do quite nicely.

In fact, I don't expect many things to change. I've always believed you can turn most obstacles into stepping stones if you approach them the right way. I plan to go back to work the first part of next year. I expect to do what I've always done, except maybe a little slower. I may not run up the steps . . . I may just take two at a time.

I'm Not Handicapped

DONNA PARDUE, 35

*At first, doctors thought it was nothing more than
a broken foot. But it never healed. After
years of medical treatment and excruciating pain, half
her foot was removed. The pain would not
cease, and months later her leg was
amputated below the knee.*

I was working as a secretary in Tennessee in November,
1981, talking to a client on the telephone. It was a
typical day at work until I reached to get a computer
printout off my desk.

I leaned back in my chair to reach the printout. As I
did, the roller on the chair caught the edge of the mat
underneath. I screamed as the chair flipped, sending me
into the air. I did a complete flip. As I tumbled to the floor,
I felt a surging pain in my left foot. The pain was so intense
that I couldn't even crawl back to my phone.

I was taken to my doctor, who said I'd broken a bone in
the center of my foot called the metatarsal. He set it in a
cast and told me to return in two weeks. I figured I could
live with a cast for that long. Little did I know this was to
be the beginning of seven painful years that would ultimately leave me an amputee.

When I returned to the doctor, the bone hadn't healed.

313

It was the same story when they X-rayed it three weeks later. I was still in a cast after six months, on crutches or using a wheelchair.

As the months wore on, everyone wondered if the doctor had done something wrong. It was so disheartening. The pain was too severe to be just a break. I was on Demerol and Phenigren for the pain. But everytime anyone touched it or if the weather changed, it felt like someone was tearing my foot off. I'd end up in bed for days. I begged the doctor to do something. I couldn't bear the pain, or so I thought. I didn't know what pain was until I had a bone graft.

The doctor took bone out of my right foot and put it in my left foot. I was hospitalized for a month at a rural medical facility outside of Nashville. Later, doctors gave me a walking cast that I ended up wearing for a year. The foot still refused to heal. I was told to walk as much as I could, but that only caused the foot to swell. I was disappointed and didn't understand why it was taking so long to mend.

The pain was relentless. I begged the doctor to cut my foot off, get rid of it and the pain. "I'd let your foot rot off before I'd amputate. You're too young, and I think it will eventually be all right," he told me.

He recommended trying a new device called a bone stimulator. I was the second person in the U.S. to use the stimulator. It had worked on a pro basketball player. The stimulator wires are embedded in the bone, come out of the foot and are hooked up to an electronic box. They must be surgically removed. It meant 13 more weeks in a non-weight-bearing cast. It didn't work. They tried it a second time with minimal results. My foot remained in a cast, and I was confined to a wheelchair through 1986. In 1987, the doctors decided to leave it alone to see if it would heal on its own.

By now, I was sick of doctors. They all had different opinions. I was sick of the hospital and, most of all, that cast. In 1988, doctors came up with a brainstorm. They would remove all the joints in the foot, replacing them with plastic joints. That would do it. By this time, all the joints had atrophied from being in the cast so long. So, they replaced the joints, gave me a new cast, and I waited.

I'd always been an active person. As a child, I'd played basketball and volleyball and was a cheerleader. As a young adult, I was a model and also enjoyed jogging. When the accident occurred, my son was 7 years old. My husband is a police officer and works nights. I tried to keep up with most of the cooking, cleaning and everyday tasks, but this put a tremendous physical, emotional and financial burden on my family. It was hard, even for my family, to understand why I was in such pain from a broken bone.

I was told I'd have to wait longer to see if the joint replacement was going to work. But in the meantime, the whole ordeal was taking a toll on my body. I stayed sick all the time. I ended up in the hospital with pneumonia repeatedly. The foot was poisoning my whole body.

Five doctors agreed that the foot had to go. Four recommended amputation above the ankle, but one thought he could save the ankle. In February, 1989, half the foot was removed. I never prayed for death like I did after that amputation — I can't describe the pain. I also was unprepared for what it was going to look like. It was not a pretty sight, but I was willing to put up with it if it worked.

It didn't. Within two months, the rest of my foot started to turn black. I went back to my doctor who told me there was nothing wrong with what remained of my foot. "Lay those crutches down or you'll be crippled the rest of your life," he said.

I returned to my medical doctor and begged him to help me. He sent me to the Mayo Clinic. Doctors said the leg would need to be amputated, probably above the knee. How could that be? I just went through one amputation. Was it for nothing? Was I going to be an invalid all my life just because someone messed up or because of some freak of nature?

I ended up with a vascular surgeon, one of the five doctors who said I needed the amputation. I needed someone who would pay close attention to the nerves. When I went into surgery, I didn't know how much of the leg would be cut off. The doctor was going to cut until he found good nerves and vascular circulation. It could have been above the knee. When I awoke, I had a nice, lengthy stump below the knee. It healed perfectly.

For years, I'd prayed for an amputation . . . anything to get rid of the pain. But you're never really ready for it, no matter how prepared you are. You feel like your life is over and you're no good to anyone. And you wonder, "Why did I deserve this?"

The reality of it all didn't hit me until I was recuperating at home after the surgery. As I rolled off the side of the bed, I caught my reflection in a full-length mirror. There was nothing there; no ankle, nothing to set down on the floor. I was ready for my life to be over. I locked myself in the bathroom and cried for three or four hours.

Trying to do anything was frustrating. At least when I had half a foot, I could balance. Now I struggled to do even simple tasks. "It's so easy for you to just get up, walk into the kitchen, and put a glass in the sink. I have to struggle to do it," I told my husband bitterly.

There were times I wanted to die. I'd thought about killing myself a couple of times over the years as I endured the constant pain. With my husband working nights, I always had a loaded gun for protection. I thought of using it again after the amputation. The nights were long, and as I lay in bed, I felt so helpless . . . so useless. I think I would have killed myself had my son not been in the house.

I watched a lot of late-night television, including programs that asked for donations for starving children. I'd watch and think, "My life isn't really so bad." The time finally came when I had to quit kicking myself in the backside and do something with what I had left. Other people walked on artificial legs all the time. If they could do it, so could I!

My surgeon had a prosthetist make me a leg. I didn't know at the time that you need to shop for a limb the way you do for a car or a home. My first leg had an ankle the size of my thigh. I'm a small person — and weighed only 89 pounds at the time. The leg was huge, and it weighed about 8 pounds. I could barely pick it up, much less wear it! I tried to wear it around the house, but I continued to use my crutches. I was determined to wear it, but when I did, it rubbed on the bone in the front of my leg.

A physical therapist from a home health care agency visited me regularly to work on building up strength in my leg. One therapist told me that mine was the worst artificial leg he'd ever seen. He got me the number of a prosthetist he'd heard of in Oklahoma, and I called for information. I'd almost given up on the idea of ever walking again and had resigned myself to living a life on crutches. Now I had a ray of hope!

I was really anxious to be fitted with a leg I could use—one that would let me walk and run. But my stump was so tender I couldn't stand to have them touch it or even put on a stump sock. They couldn't cast my leg for a prosthesis because it was so tender, so they sent me home and told me to rub and pat my stump to make it tough. I had my doctor arrange for a physical therapist. I rubbed it. My son helped me. We worked day and night because I wanted that leg. The temporary leg wasn't great, but I could walk on it without my cane. I still had pain, and I needed to toughen the limb some more. But I now had real hope.

I guess one thing I learned at the prosthetist's office was that I am not a handicapped person. I'm an amputee, and

317

there is a difference. I also discovered I am not alone.

I used to think all I went through was some sort of punishment. But I know there was a reason. God had a reason. The Lord has been my strength through all this, along with my family. I know I'm meant to help other people. And I like talking with other amputees because I wish I'd had someone to talk with when I had my amputation.

My number one goal now is to jog again. My son, Doug, is very athletic, and I want so badly to run with him. He wants to be an Olympic contender, and I told him I'd be there to walk with him. Also, I live near Barbara Mandrell, but you have to climb a mountain to see her house. I'm going to climb that mountain . . . with my new permanent leg.

I have a 5-year-old niece who, everytime she saw me after the amputation, would say, "But Aunt Donna, you said you were going to get a leg and you'd run with me." When I got the first leg and had to tell her I couldn't wear it, she didn't understand.

When I got the temporary leg, I went to visit her. Her mother called to her in the backyard. I walked around the outside of the house to meet her, and she bawled and bawled. She'd never seen me walk in her lifetime. I told her, "The next time I see you, I'll run with you." It's important to her. It's important to me.

Working Through the Anger

RICHARD REYNOLDS, 58

A prominent businessman and mayor, no one would guess that he is an amputee. At age 44, bone cancer forced amputation of his left leg below the knee. During the year that followed, he endured chemotherapy and dealt with an anger that nearly consumed his life.

I was a runner. I ran every day to stay in shape, but my ankle kept bothering me. The nagging pain in my leg ultimately made me decide to see the doctor. Thank goodness I was a runner and kept irritating the leg . . . so it forced me to do something about it.

The pain was caused by a tumor in my ankle. The doctor could tell from the X-ray that the tumor had grown into the bone. It most likely was malignant. But he assured me what it wouldn't be . . . osteogenic sarcoma. That type of bone cancer generally is found in children younger than 18 or adults more than 65 years of age . . . usually. I was 44, but the final diagnosis was osteogenic sarcoma.

My physician in Norman, Oklahoma, sent me to a doctor at the Oklahoma Health Sciences Center in Oklahoma City. The doctor there said my leg needed to be amputated seven inches below the knee. Originally, I'd been told the leg would have to be removed above the

Richard Reynolds, Mayor of Norman, Oklahoma

knee. At the time, I didn't know anything about amputations and didn't realize the difference in losing one joint or two. I didn't realize how lucky I was.

When I first was told I had cancer and would lose part of my leg, I was scared . . . not so much that I would die, but of the unknown. I didn't know what I was facing. Just the thought of having a portion of my body cut off was difficult to accept. Something like that reinforces all the negative feelings you have about yourself. I was afraid I'd be less of a person . . . be less acceptable to other people.

Besides fright, I was consumed by a terrible anger. I tried to cover it up with humor sometimes, but I was angry — with myself and with everybody else. I didn't know why this happened to me. I didn't deserve it. I vented my anger at the doctor, my family, people at work . . . everyone and anyone. I wasn't a pleasant person to be around. And it was an anger that didn't go away overnight.

About 10 days after they discovered the tumor, I went into surgery for the amputation. When I awoke, I was in a lot of pain. I had a cast on my leg along with ice packs, and they kept me pretty sedated. It wasn't so bad when I was in medicated "never-never land." I had pain from the surgery and some phantom pain. I never could quite figure out where the phantom pain was coming from, but it didn't go away easily. I still have a little phantom pain even now.

My leg was in a cast for the first two to three weeks. I had to sleep on my back, and I felt like I was in a strait jacket. After the cast came off, I was more comfortable. And six weeks after the amputation, I was fitted with a temporary prosthesis.

About the same time I was getting the leg, I began chemotherapy. Initially, I was hospitalized, but later I took treatments on an outpatient basis. When you have something like cancer, your whole life revolves around it. I'd have treatments for five straight days. They started me on five different drugs and later reduced it to three. The drugs all made me sick. I'd be totally out of commission during the treatment days. I'd get up . . . throw up . . . and go back to sleep. But I was determined not to let the chemo run my entire life. I was back at work as soon as treatments were over . . . until the next round.

I had owned a Norman car dealership for a number of years, and I didn't like to be away from work. I lost my hair after the first round of chemotherapy, but I refused to wear a hat or a wig even to work. I'd never worn either before, and I didn't intend to start. Losing my hair was one thing, but the chemotherapy also strips your color. My color was so ghastly. Even my hands were blue. I went to a business meeting and guys I'd known for years didn't even recognize me.

As I lost the leg, began chemotherapy, and tried to resume some normalcy in my life, I was still tormented by anger. I think working through the anger was probably as difficult as working through the physical aspects of the amputation. I knew I had to do something to resolve my problems. Suicide. I thought that might be an answer. I figured out every imaginable way . . . gun, gas, drowning. For the first three months, I dealt with that scenario over and over in my mind. But I came to the conclusion that I could not do that — I couldn't take my own life.

One day my doctor visited me while I was at the hospital for chemotherapy. I lashed out at him. I don't even recall what I was complaining about . . . something going on in the hospital. He listened. "You know you're not going to die. You don't have to worry about that," he said reassuringly. That made a big impression. I didn't think I was scared of dying, but maybe I was harboring that fear subconsciously. Somehow, him telling me I wasn't going to die helped make my anger more manageable.

As the months of chemotherapy wore on, I'd be expecting to begin treatments on a certain day, only to be told that my white cell count was too low. Treatment would have to wait a week. My body just wasn't recovering fast enough between treatments. It kept my life pretty mixed up — and it was just one more aggravation that kept me angry. But that was only part of it. Everytime I went for a chemo treatment, I had to sit in the waiting room and listen to all these sick people talking about their ailments. "I am so tired of listening to these people. I've got my own problems," I told a nurse. "You know why they talk like that, don't you?" she replied. "That's their lives now. That's all they know. They don't know anything but cancer and dealing with their health problems."

But she understood my need to get away from that. She suggested I come for treatment in the early morning before the center officially opened. She knew what I was going through.

I knew I couldn't go on being angry with my kids and everyone else. I had to face up to the fact that I had lost a leg and that I had to go through chemotherapy. Once I got to that point, the anger started to subside. It helped that I had a good friend at work I could talk to. She listened as I talked it out. I think every amputee needs someone to talk to. You just can't go through it alone.

I came to realize that I could sit there and cry and lament over this thing, or I could put it away . . . make it less important in my mind and get on with the things I really wanted to do. It seemed fruitless to sit and cry. No matter how hard I cried, I wasn't going to grow another leg. It was a waste of time and energy.

The amputation, the months of chemotherapy, the anger — the whole ordeal took its toll on my family. The kids dealt with the amputation pretty well once they knew I wasn't going to die. But my wife couldn't accept it. She'd just turn her head and wouldn't look at my leg. I guess that was the only way she could handle it. We never talked about the amputation. Our marriage ended in divorce in 1980, four years after the amputation.

The end of chemotherapy was a milestone. The anger was finally coming to an end, and I started getting well again. I guess the only thing I worried about in the back of my mind was how I was going to get along with my prosthesis. But I did well. I have a regular socket that fits like an old glove. The only problem I've ever had is holding the leg on. I wear an elastic sheath, but if it touches my skin, I tend to blister. So I wear extra socks to protect my skin and the leg has a tendency to slip out of the socket because of that.

I've been amazed at the changes in technology over the years. When I first got my leg, I'd have a pain in the right hip after walking alot. But now, I have a new foot that has a spring in the toe. I don't have to work as hard at walking, and there is no pain.

And I have walked alot, especially when I decided to run for mayor in 1986. Seeking public office was something I'd always wanted to do. I'd reached a point in my business where I felt I had the time. I hit the campaign trail on foot. I'm now serving my second three-year term as mayor of Norman. I campaigned door-to-door during both elections.

As mayor, I'm constantly in the public eye. Not everyone knows I am an amputee so when I did a television show on amputees about three years ago, alot of people were surprised. Even today, sometimes I'm taken aback when people ask about the television program and say they didn't know I had an artificial leg. It makes me feel good they don't notice. They just take for granted I have two legs.

I discovered I could do most everything I wanted to do. I don't run much any more, but I ride my bike and keep up with guys who are a lot younger than I. I've even done some dancing.

I think the toughest thing about being an amputee is

the unknown. You don't know what to expect because you've never been an amputee. You need to cry and work through all the emotions, but you also need someone to talk to about it . . . another amputee. I was once asked to go to the hospital to talk to a young man who had lost his leg in a motorcycle accident. No one had ever told him that he could get up and dance again one day. He thought at age 20 he was a goner and he would be bedridden for the rest of his life. He was shocked when I told him he'd dance again . . . if he wanted to. When you learn that your life really isn't going to be all that inconvenienced, that's a big turning point.

Chuck Tiemann

Miracles Still Happen

CHUCK TIEMANN, 35
*He was working as a lineman for a rural electric
company when a live wire sent 7,200 volts of
electricity through his body, ultimately resulting in the
loss of his left arm and right leg. Refusing to be
sidelined by the amputations, he now puts the latest
prosthetic devices to the test.*

I recently finished the grueling Bay to Breakers race in
San Francisco, a 7 1/2-mile uphill pavement pounder
that challenges even the most able-bodied runner. My
time wasn't as good as I had hoped, but I finished the race,
and I know I'll better my time next year.

The fact that I ran the race at all may have surprised
those who don't know me. But for me it was another opportunity to show that amputees can lead normal lives. That's
something I've done since I became an amputee in 1980.

It was a typical, windy spring day in May. I was working as a lineman for Kay Rural Electric Company in north
central Oklahoma. We were upgrading part of the electrical
system. Nothing had gone right all day. The job wasn't
ready when our construction crew of five arrived. I shut off
the 762-volt line, while another crew mate was to kill the
7,200-volt line. There was a mix-up in communication.
The line with 7,200 volts was not dead.

I climbed the pole and can remember reaching out and touching the line. I screamed. There was a bluish flash. Then, everything went black. The next thing I knew, the crew foreman was with me atop the 35-foot pole. He and another crew member had started pole-top rescue. I was conscious as they lowered me down a hand line.

I was scared to go back to sleep after they got me off the pole. I knew I was hurt. I felt I had to keep talking and call the shots. They put me in the line truck and arranged to meet the ambulance. First, the truck was stuck in the mud, and later we had a blow-out, forcing rerouting of the ambulance. I remember the winding roads . . . the blue silos . . . and the trees flashing by, and I just kept talking.

A favorite hymn popped into my head, and I repeated the words from "Love Lifted Me" over and over in my mind. It gave me a sense of peace and by the time we arrived at the Ponca City hospital, I knew everything was going to be fine. Ironically, the Sunday before, my wife and I had chosen to study the Bible at home rather than attend church. We turned to the book of Job. We did not know then how precious those lessons of patience would become over the next ten weeks.

Doctors at the hospital emergency room said I had to go to a burn center in Oklahoma City or Tulsa. My family was nearer to Oklahoma City, but that burn center was full. It was perhaps a blessing in disguise, since we later found out that Tulsa's Hillcrest Burn Center was rated as one of the top in the nation. Even with that, the prognosis was not good. The doctors were honest. They said I had only a 10 percent chance of surviving the first 24 hours.

Their first goal was to get me through that critical period and to save the arm and leg, if possible. The accident affected my left arm, which touched the line, and my right leg, which was grounded. The electricity had blown off my right metatarsal bone.

The first night, doctors split open my leg and arm. My limbs were very swollen, and they had to cut away the charred, dead skin. There was no discussion of amputation at that point, partly because electricity stays in your system as long as two weeks and can keep burning away the tissue.

Fortunately, I beat the odds. I came through the first night, and the doctors continued their efforts to save my limbs. I underwent skin grafts — there was intense pain with each of the surgeries. We fought for six weeks to keep the arm and leg, but the limbs were deteriorating. They turned black and hard. I know what it means to say a limb is dying. The smell is rank, much like spoiled bologna. I'm glad they did all they could to try to save my arm and leg because I never felt cheated. When it came time to discuss amputation, I was ready. On June 10, 1980, doctors amputated my right leg below the knee and left arm below the elbow.

I went through some real emotional changes after the amputations. When you lose a limb, much less two, you feel ugly and mutilated. I wondered how I could ever again live in a two-armed, two-legged society.

The man in the next bed was a big inspiration, even though we came from different backgrounds and had different values. He had lost a leg earlier in his life, and was hospitalized then for burns sustained in a house fire. I also had a great deal of support from my family and friends. I received well-wishes in 542 cards from people throughout the community. But one of my greatest sources of strength was the Bible. I kept looking for that miracle verse. The Lord didn't give me the answer right away. He made me read the first four gospels before I got to Romans 5:3-5, verses that I stand on, which say: "We can rejoice, too, when we run into problems and trials for . . . they help us learn to be patient. And patience develops strength of character in us and helps us trust God more . . . Then, when that happens, we are able to hold our heads high no matter what happens and know that all is well, for we know how dearly God loves us . . ."

The nurses were good to me. Someone always stopped by just to chat, and my physical therapist even came in on Saturdays. I tried to learn everything about taking care of myself. I watched carefully to make sure my limbs were wrapped properly because I didn't want any infection.

Originally, the doctors told me I'd be in the burn center six months, so I was thrilled when I went home after 69 days. But it was hard to leave the hospital because I had made so many friends among the patients and staff. I spent the first night at the home of my in-laws.

It wasn't long until I went back to work at Kay Electric and even climbed a few poles. I think I had to prove that I wasn't handicapped. I would do crazy things in those early days to prove to the world that Chuck Tiemann wasn't handicapped. I'd always been active in sports, and I love baseball. I felt like this was the bottom of the ninth with two men out, and I was up to bat. I didn't want to let anyone down.

Four days after my release from the hospital, I celebrated my 25th birthday. I was never so glad to see that quarter-century birthday. My wife, Terri, and I decided we had so many friends and family members who wanted to see me that we'd throw a big birthday party. We had more than 200 people. They just came in the front door and went out the back. Even though I didn't have my limbs, it was a real celebration.

I knew from the very beginning that I would get an artificial leg, but I didn't know what I would do about my arm. My first goals were to do the regular daily things like walk and hold my toothbrush . . . things I'd taken for granted in the past. My brother had a friend who begged me to try a myoelectric arm. Many amputees are first fitted with a hook and later, if they do well, with a myoelectric prosthesis. But Terri and I talked it over, and we were convinced a myoelectric was the way to go.

I guess a visit by a man who wore a hook was what really made up my mind. "You've just got to have an 'I don't give a damn' attitude when people stare at you in the grocery store. Kids especially will stare and say, 'Oooohh, look at that man with the hook', " he told me. "But there's a good joke you can use at cookouts. You can surprise your guests and pick up the hot grill." I knew there had to be more to life than that. I wanted a myoelectric arm.

I had a prosthetic leg five weeks after the amputation, and within a couple of weeks, I was walking two miles each day. Because I worked hard at perfecting my gait, alot of people couldn't tell I had an artificial leg. I watched video-tapes of my walk, I practiced in front of a full-length mirror, and Terri checked my posture. I wanted to walk as naturally as possible.

I guess you could say I am the perfect amputee, if there is such a thing. My amputations were below the knee and below the elbow, which are the best levels for adapting to and using prostheses. But, having lost one of each, I can say unequivocally that I would rather have lost both legs than an arm. The loss of an arm is so much more visible. And learning to use an artificial arm is harder and requires more patience than working with an artificial leg.

Still, I worked hard at using the hand, and within three months I was doing things the man with the hook never dreamed of. I was picking up everything from popcorn to five-gallon buckets of water. Every time I'd learn something new, I'd call my prosthetist and say, "Guess what I just did."

I was ready to get everything back. I wanted to see what I could do — and do everything the best that I could. Terri was, and is, my backbone. She encouraged me all the way. I remember once after I had my prosthetic leg, I was sitting in the living room and asked Terri to get me a drink of

331

Chuck Tiemann gives daughter, Kim, a big swing.

water. She pointed her finger at me and said, "No, I won't. I'm not going to do anything you're capable of doing for yourself. I didn't marry a handicapped person, and you're not going to be that way. You've always loved sports, and you're going to do that, too. Sure, you're going to be like a baby, and you'll have to learn things over, but you're going to adapt, and you're going to do it. Do you understand me?"

I said, "Yes, ma'am." I appreciated that. We'd been married five years, and that probably was the first time I really respected her for who she was.

Terri was right. I'd always been an athlete, so I tried out for the softball team. The guys said, "We know you can hit, you can run, and you can catch, but don't you think it would be better if you coached? You could fall and hurt yourself." I didn't want people to treat me differently because I had lost an arm or leg! If I had dropped the ball before, it was no big deal, an error. But if I dropped it now, they thought, "Well, he's lost an arm, and that's the best he can do." It seems amputees can't make errors if they want to fit into society again.

Because that was the way I felt, I was always trying to prove myself. After I got my arm, I was really fired up. It was a modern day miracle. I went to Enid, Oklahoma, to show it off. I was trying to impress one orthopedic surgeon when he turned to me and said, "What the hell are you going to do, Chuck — try to change the world?" I told him, "No, but I'm going to change my little corner of it." But from that point on my attitude changed. I realize now that I was going too fast.

Still, I want to be all that I can, the best that I can. I believe firmly that if you say you can — or you say you can't — you're right. So, I've been dubbed sort of a guinea pig for the latest in prosthetic devices. Whenever a manufacturer has something new that might make life easier for amputees, I try it. I feel like whether it's good or bad, whatever I do today is going to affect what's available in the future. If somebody didn't do it, we'd all still have hooks and wooden legs.

Artificial limbs have changed so much since I was first fitted with prostheses. My first leg weighed seven pounds, while the one I have now weighs only a little more than two pounds. Now the leg is totally adjustable, and I have a flexible foot. Actually, I've got three feet — one with a cowboy boot on it, one with a dress shoe, and one with a tennis shoe.

Of course, I like to test a prosthesis the Chuck Tiemann-way. I don't like the manufacturer or prosthetist to tell me what I can't do with it. They told me my leg wasn't waterproof; that if I stepped in a hole of water when I was hunting it was okay, but not to submerge it. I wear the leg water skiing and dry it off when I'm through. I've never had a problem. A prosthesis needs to be dependable. More than that — it needs to be good enough to make an amputee equal to a guy who has both legs.

I left the electric company in 1984 and returned to school to pursue my degree. That always had been the plan. I received a degree in rehabilitation counseling, but I discovered I didn't have the patience to work with people who weren't motivated or willing to try, so I returned to school for a teaching degree. I taught only one year because of the lack of support for education by the state legislature. Now, I'm working my way up at Security Bank in Ponca City, and I honestly like my job.

But one of my first loves is talking to groups, like school children and other amputees, about what it's like to be an amputee. I talk to kids about my "toy arm" or "toy leg." I let them touch the artificial limbs. The kids can relate it to Barbie or G.I. Joe, and they are fascinated. Now, if they stare, it's because they are in awe — not because I'm some deformed man with a hook.

The most recent addition to my leg prosthesis is the Sense-of-Feel System. It lets me "feel" my foot on the floor for the first time since the accident. It's not perfected, but I was among the first group of amputees to give it a try. With the introduction of the system by my prosthetist, I realized another of my lifelong goals — to meet Joan Lunden. I was a guest on Good Morning America to help demonstrate how the Sense-of-Feel System works. I found that Ms. Lunden was as genuine and gracious as I had always thought she'd be.

I have a number of other aspirations. Someday, I'd like to publish my own book on using prosthetics and possibly do a movie for Disney and meet some of those ingenious people who design those mechanically-animated dolls and characters. My greatest goal is to establish a fund for the distribution of state-of-the-art prostheses for children.

I pray that God shows me the way and gives me the strength to do the things He wants me to do. I have been successful only because I love life and because God is in control of everything.

Laurie Arrigoni

Never Let It Define You

LAURIE ARRIGONI, 27

*At age 16, she was diagnosed as having a malignant
tumor in her knee. Her leg had to be amputated
above the knee. But she never let the loss of a
limb keep her from the dream of owning a
New York City boutique.*

I'd just gotten my driver's license. That was the most important thing in the world to me at age 16 as a high school sophomore. It was Memorial Day weekend. I was planting flowers in my mother's yard.

I noticed a pain in my knee. I didn't think much about it at the time. But the soreness didn't go away, and the knee became swollen. I'd been treated for a knee injury when I was playing high school sports, so I figured it was nothing serious. My parents made an appointment for me to see the orthopedic surgeon who had treated me previously. By the time I saw him a few days later, the knee was so tender I could barely walk.

The doctor X-rayed the knee and said it was probably a bone infection. At least that's what he told me. He wanted to do a biopsy. I had more important things on my mind — final exams and the prom. I'd been invited to the prom by the hottest guy at school, and now I had to call and turn him down because I had to have a biopsy.

The doctor told me the tumor was malignant. So, what did I do? I got out my high school biology book to check that out. I still didn't think much about it. It was beyond my comprehension that you couldn't just remove the tumor.

In mid-June, I began an aggressive program of chemotherapy at Memorial Sloan Kettering Hospital. I know some people will say something like that is devastating, but it didn't hit me like a ton of bricks at the time. It was more like a process, one step at a time. I went along, sorting it out with the doctors. My parents were there for me all the way. I didn't know it at the time, but they were doing a lot of background research on my condition.

Doctors amputated my leg above the knee on July 9th. The pain after the surgery was excruciating. But the amputation was something that was over. Not so, with the chemotherapy . . . it made the surgery seem almost secondary. I really concentrated on just getting through the chemotherapy. It was relentless — like there was no end in sight. I felt if I could survive the chemotherapy, I could survive anything. And I could get through life without one leg.

It was a tough summer, though. Most of my friends were getting summer jobs for the first time, but I was in the hospital. After the surgery, I had an immediate-fit prosthesis. When I woke up, I had a pole and cast so I was up walking within a couple of days. When school started that September, I didn't miss a beat. I was back in class even though I would miss a week at a time to take chemotherapy. I had a great group of friends and a family who never treated me all that differently.

My mother kept wanting me to go to the prosthetist to be fitted with a permanent leg, but I kept putting it off. I was busy with school and my friends. My mother was a nervous wreck because I was driving to school — but you don't need a left leg to drive! I got my first permanent leg six to eight months after the surgery. I can't remember a day that I didn't get up and put the leg on and walk around.

When I was feeling good, I led a pretty normal life. But there were weeks with the chemotherapy that I couldn't get out of bed. Originally, doctors told me I would have chemotherapy six to nine months, but it ended up being 14 months. I was hospitalized once because my blood count was so low. The doctors at Kettering are pretty hard core and pretty straight with you. When I woke up that Saturday, I flippantly asked my doctor what he was doing there on his day off. "Well, you almost died last night, so I thought I'd better check up on you today," he told me.

Maybe I was naive, but I don't think so. Somehow I just always knew that I was going to get through it. My mother and I went through it together. And I think I had some sort of inner strength that helped me all the way. Still, there was no expressway to the end of chemo.

Of course, when my blood count was low, the doctor would send me home with instructions to stay away from places where I might pick up a virus or infection — like movie theaters and shopping malls. So, where did I go on Friday night — to the movies with my friends, of course.

I finished my junior and senior years in high school and applied for admission to Boston College. One of the high school guidance counselors kept trying to steer me to a local college — maybe she thought I needed to be near a doctor or my home for some reason.

I have to admit that going to college wasn't as easy as I expected. Boston College has a huge campus, and there was lots of snow that started in November that year. The snow and ice reached a point where I just couldn't walk around anymore. I had lost one leg, and I sure didn't need to break the other. I can remember calling my dad and telling him I wasn't sure things were going to work out at school. He offered to buy me a golf cart. I told him "No, no, no." I didn't want something that set me apart. I wanted to be normal.

Eventually, I learned the ins and outs . . . which staircase to avoid because of the flood of people . . . and where to get keys to elevators. And a friend of mine who was an athlete gave me a tip for making it around in the ice and snow. He suggested cleats. I'd never thought of it before. Of course it worked, so I walked all over on the ice that winter with cleats strapped to the bottom of my boots. I found I could make do; there were little ways.

During my sophomore and junior years, I worked at Saks Fifth Avenue. I graduated from Boston College in 1985 with a bachelor of arts degree, and I set my sights on opening my own business. I don't think my amputation changed the direction of my life much. I never wanted a career in ballet or anything like that. I just never let the loss of the leg define what I wanted to do or be. After working and getting some further retailing experience at a couple of New York boutiques, I opened my own boutique in 1987. Called Sola (meaning "on your own"), my shop is located in Manhattan.

From the beginning, when I went to work, I never looked at my leg as a handicap. There would be those typical questions on job applications, asking if I had any physical impairment that would prohibit me from performing my job. I answered "no." I can stand on my feet for eight hours a day just like anyone else. In fact, I can do it better than some people. Owning my own shop hasn't changed how active I am either. It's not a desk job — I've never had a desk job. In fact, my shop has a spiral staircase down to the stockroom. Some people are surprised when I say, "It's no problem!"

Of course, being in the fashion industry, looks mean alot. I have to wear short skirts . . . I live in New York. So, I have a beautiful foam leg. Sometimes I think maybe it looks better than the real leg. I'm very visible, and the store is open seven

340

days a week. I like it that way. It's what keeps me going. I've always been a great walker, and I walk well with my prosthesis. I walk to work, I shuffle through the crowds to ride on New York subways; I don't just sit around.

Sometimes, people ask what I did to my leg. I've never really come up with a good answer to that question. If you tell them you lost the leg to cancer, they turn red-faced and feel like they've made a grand faux pas. I tried making up things that I thought would make it easier. I told one guy that I hurt it hang gliding in Mexico. Wouldn't you know it, he was a hang glider and started asking me questions about the sport! That answer just didn't seem to work. If it's a cocktail party, I usually just say, "Oh, nothing; it's fine," and go on.

I've learned to run with my artificial leg the last couple of years. I have some friends in an amputee support group, ASPIRE, and we go to the gym for a vigorous workout three times a week. We exercise right along with all the able-bodied folks, and it's a lot tougher workout than many of my two-legged friends can do. I have a sports leg now that I wear for running or when I go to the beach or participate in something more active. The sports leg is not as cosmetic, but it looks okay and it can take a lot more abuse. Of course, it wouldn't be the thing I'd wear with a skirt.

I choose to wear flat shoes even with my skirts. Some women have interchangeable feet or adjust their feet for different heel heights. There was a time when I wore 4-inch heels, but I never felt comfortable and I never walked as well. I wear flats even if it's a black tie affair. I have the perfect pair of little black satin flats. High heels aren't important to me.

Actually, my foam leg looks so good that it's really funny when I go through the metal detectors at airports. I always tell them that I have a brace that will set the alarm off, so they have me step to one side to do a hand search.

341

One security official kept looking at my leg, touching it. "Where is it? I can't see it," she said.

It seems that prostheses just get better and better every year. I can remember my first leg. It was an old wooden leg with hinges. I don't know how I got around on that thing, but the leg never slowed me down. Whether you're an amputee or not, I've always believed you set your own limitations — it's all up to you.

Never Say I Can't Walk

GABRI BUCKINGHAM, 20
*As an 18-year-old college freshman, her life was
filled with promise until the discovery of a
malignant tumor in her pelvic bone. She endured
months of grueling chemotherapy, as doctors
hoped to shrink the tumor. Ultimately, her left leg had
to be amputated at the pelvis. Her doctor said
she'd never walk again.*

I had finished one semester at the community college in Powell, Wyoming, 20 miles from my hometown of Cody. I was just back on campus after Christmas break when I noticed pain in my inner thigh. I thought it was a nerve spasm and figured it would go away. But it didn't.

My mom worked as a receptionist in a doctor's office, so she made me an appointment. The doctor checked me for vitamin deficiencies, but the results were normal. I was referred to an orthopedic physician, who thought it might be the sciatic nerve, but he couldn't find anything.

I returned to school, but the pain grew worse. I could barely limp to class. All the time, I was doing aerobics, thinking that would loosen it up. I returned to the doctor when the pain persisted; he X-rayed the leg but didn't find much. He off-handedly mentioned a shadow on the X-ray. He said it might be a benign tumor or a cyst.

Maybe we should have known then that something was

wrong. The doctor didn't want to touch it. He wanted us to go to Billings, Montana, for further diagnosis. I just wanted to go back to school.

My mom and I made the trip to Billings to see the other doctor on the first day of spring break. We talked about it on the trip. I think we were both kind of scared of what we might find out. We had to wait all day to see the doctor. He was the first doctor to mention cancer.

When he said the word — cancer — my mom and I started bawling. I felt like the walls of that little examining room were closing in on me. The doctor said a biopsy was needed. If it was a benign tumor or a cyst, it would be removed. If it was cancer, they would need to determine its size and how to treat it — it would mean removing part of the pelvic bone. He wanted us to go to Salt Lake City, but we didn't want to fly all that way if it was just a cyst. He finally agreed to do the biopsy, after consulting with the Salt Lake City surgeon on the best placement of the incision in case I needed further surgery.

He wanted to do the biopsy the next day. We returned home to gather our things and call the family. I told my boyfriend, Mike. Mike and I met during the fall semester at school. We had dated four or five months, and our families had grown very close. Mike, my mom and I set out for Billings the next morning. Later in the day, other family members came to be with us.

I didn't know what to expect. I was scared. After surgery I awoke early from the anesthesia. Before I could even focus, the doctor told me it was cancer. I cried, but I really didn't know then what it meant to have cancer. I was in alot of pain because they had to cut through alot of muscle to get to the tumor.

It was that night before I talked with Mike. He took it really hard. I think he thought I was just going to disappear right before his eyes . . . that I was going to die. Mike stayed in the room with me that night, while my mom slept in the waiting room. Mom said she'd come in and Mike would be standing by my bed staring at me as I slept.

I never was afraid Mike would walk out of my life because I had cancer, but he was afraid I was going to leave him. He thought I wasn't going to want him around — that I was going to dump him.

Since it was cancer, I was referred to an orthopedic surgeon in Salt Lake City. We stayed with a friend of my mother's and that made it easier. It seemed throughout my treatments that there always was something, or someone, there to give us strength.

The doctor eased my some of fears when he said I had osteogenic sarcoma, a very common kind of cancer in young people. He had treated it before, so that made me feel good. No one mentioned amputation. The doctor planned to remove part of the pelvic bone. I would have a limp, and the leg would be a little shorter. We were optimistic.

The following day was consumed by tests from morning to night. The last test revealed the tumor was bigger than the other scans had shown. The doctor told me to go home to begin chemotherapy; surgery was impossible at that time.

We went back to Cody. Mike and his friend, Lee, came up to be with me. We stayed at the Ronald McDonald House in Billings and watched movies that night. My mom and the three of us stayed in a room with two twin beds. Mom wouldn't have allowed it any other time, but that night she let Mike and me sleep in the same bed. She slept in the other bed, while Lee slept in the floor between the beds.

I checked into the hospital and started chemotherapy the next day. I don't remember much about the first round of chemo except that I got sick. Mom stayed with me at the hospital. One of my older sisters took care of me after I was released from the hospital. Three days later, I had to see a

Billings oncologist, who said I needed a type of chemo-therapy that required close monitoring of blood levels. It couldn't be done in Billings, so we'd have to go back to Salt Lake City. We flew out the next day.

That second treatment wasn't so bad. I really didn't get sick. They put me in a room with a girl a year or two younger, who had the same type of tumor and the same chemotherapy. She was ahead of me in the treatment. She slept through most treatments, but once we did talk. She was scared she was going to lose her leg. I felt really bad for her because someday I'd be well, but she'd be walking around on crutches for the rest of her life. I was really naive. I didn't have any idea that I could lose my leg, too. It never entered my mind.

My hospital roommate and I became very good friends, and we still write to each other. But the best part of that hospital stay was that her mom was with her. It helped my mom alot. Finally, there was someone who could under-stand . . . someone who could answer some of her ques-tions. She was as scared as I was and wanted to protect me, but she couldn't if she didn't get some answers.

Most of my 11 treatments were in Salt Lake City. My mom, Mike and I made the trips. Mike's dad encouraged him not to take a summer job so he could be with me. His family, as well as mine, was very supportive.

The worst part of chemotherapy was losing my hair. When I noticed my hair falling out, I only washed it every three days, brushed it once in the morning and plastered it with hair spray. I could only take that for a week. I took a shower one day and I pulled as much hair out as I could. I called my mom and asked her to come home and shave the rest of it off. I wore women's baseball caps — in every color I could find. I couldn't stand my wig. It wasn't me. It was hard because people stared. Eventually, I decided I wouldn't let the cancer rule what I did and keep me from going out and having fun.

By the next-to-the-last treatment, the pain was totally gone, and I didn't limp anymore. We thought that was a good sign. The doctors wanted to see if the tumor had shrunk. But it hadn't. The tumor board was to meet and consider three options: radiation, chemotherapy injected directly into the tumor, or amputation. That was the first mention of amputation. We went home to wait for their recommendation.

The doctors agreed amputation was the only option that could assure getting all the cancer. I thought, "All right, if I have to have an amputation, I want it done now, next week." But they wouldn't do it because my blood count was down. They finally set my surgery for August 4, 1988, in Salt Lake City. The day before my surgery, we went to the amusement park. I put the amputation out of my mind. As long as I was with someone, everything was okay. The more I was alone, the more I thought to myself, "It's all your fault; maybe if you weren't thinking these things, you'd be all right. Maybe you want to have cancer."

When I arrived at the hospital, there was a shortage of nurses, and the ward I was supposed to be in was full. I ended up in the neurological ward. I wanted a private room, so my mom and Mike could stay with me, but only a double room was available. That night, Mike was telling me goodnight when a nurse asked if I wanted to stay in the VIP room. It was great . . . plush carpeting, mahogany wood, marble counters in the bathroom and a view of the entire city. I tried to relax . . . just to spend some time with Mike. Then, my doctor came in and bluntly told me there was a chance the cancer was inoperable. If I awoke with a leg after surgery, it had spread too far to amputate.

The doctor expected the surgery to last four hours, but it took eight. He did a hemi-pelvectomy, removing the pelvic bone on the left side, along with the leg. I had no bone below my rib cage.

I came out of the surgery screaming. I don't remember pain from the incision, but I had terrible phantom pain. They had used my thigh muscle to fold back and reconstruct a stump where my hip had been, so it felt like my leg was twisted behind my back. In the middle of the night, I'd try to pull my leg out from underneath me, but of course I couldn't because it wasn't there.

The whole ordeal depressed me. I don't think anything can really prepare you for the phantom pain. They've taken away your leg, but you still have pain as if it's there. The physical therapist had a hard time getting me out of bed. I was mad, not that I had lost my leg, but that I was having all the phantom pain. I don't know if the pain killers helped, or if it went away on its own. Eventually, the intense pain went away. I still have phantom pain, but nothing like that.

My orthopedic surgeon said there was no way I'd be able to walk with a prosthesis without crutches. He'd never seen a person with a hemi-pelvectomy walk. He didn't want me to get my hopes up only to be disappointed.

I went back to school on crutches, and I got special permission from the school to use a four-wheeler on campus. I still had six follow-up chemo treatments. It was really hard going back to school where I had been popular and having people see me like that. It does a lot to your self-esteem. I wanted to tape a picture to my shirt that showed me when I was whole . . . when I had a leg and hair.

You grow up fast when you have cancer. Sometimes I wished I could take away the cancer and be who I was before. Sometimes Mike and I would fight. I think when your life is consumed by fighting cancer, after so long you forget how to have fun. I forgot what it was like to go out with my friends, to go to a dance, to laugh with them, and joke with them. You kind of have to relearn that while your life has revolved around cancer, the lives of your friends have kept going. It's really hard, and I still have to work at it.

I became proficient at using the crutches. It wasn't until the spring of 1989 that I thought the doctor might be wrong about me never walking with an artificial leg. I felt really strong, and I could still control the thigh muscle that now formed my hip. When I was in the hospital for one of my follow-up chemo treatments, my original orthopedic doctor checked me. He agreed. He thought I could walk with an artificial limb. And after he looked at my spine, which was curving badly from standing on one leg all the time, he said I had to get a leg even if I couldn't use it without crutches. Otherwise, I faced life in a wheelchair.

Even when Mom and I made the trip to Oklahoma City to get my prosthesis, we weren't sure whether I'd be able to walk. I remember the prosthetist coming in and showing me all the different parts of the leg and different feet. He asked if I had any questions. "Well, am I going to be able to walk?" I asked. "What are you doing here if you aren't?" he replied. We were beaming.

It wasn't easy though. I expected to get this leg and go. The second day I had the leg, I went to the mall. With this leg, if you bend down, you have to go all the way back up. I bent over to look at some watches and fell down on the floor. My mom wouldn't help me because she knew she wouldn't always be around to pick me up, and I had to learn to do it myself. It took awhile to learn my limitations. Most of the time, I use my cane. I can walk without it, but it's my security.

After I was walking, I made it a point to talk to the doctor who told me I never would walk. "Don't ever tell anyone again that they cannot walk. It just isn't fair to them," I said. He said he was sorry. He'd never seen anyone like me walk before.

I finished my fourth semester at the community college

in Powell after I got my leg. Then, Mike and I transferred to Northern Colorado University. During the summer, I worked with physically handicapped kids. I plan to graduate with a psychology degree and eventually work in a hospital as a counselor for cancer patients, especially amputees. I know what I went through. It really helps to have someone to talk to.

The 38 people who shared their lives, their vision and their strength in this book, had one thing in mind — to help you through a difficult time.

It's not easy. Acceptance is hard work. To go on and overcome isn't simple. It takes all the physical, emotional and spiritual energy you can muster.

Even if today is the worst day you have ever had, don't give up. Hold on with all you have. You will feel differently in time. Don't focus on the negatives. Stay in the positive.

I hope that what we have shared helps you see the light at the end of the tunnel and it reminds you that you are not alone.

John Sabolich

Glossary

AE — An amputation above the elbow.

AK — An amputation above the knee.

Anterior — The front part of your body.

Adherent Scar Tissue — Tissue that is stuck down, usually to the bone.

Atrophy — A reduction in muscle mass and strength.

BE — An amputation below the elbow.

Bilateral — A double amputation, involving 2 limbs.

BK — An amputation below the knee.

Congenital Anomaly — An abnormality at birth, such as a missing limb or malformed limb.

Cosmesis —A word coined in the prosthetic field and used to describe the outer, aesthetic covering of a prosthesis.

Disarticulation — An amputation through a joint; commonly the hip, knee, ankle, elbow, wrist or shoulder.

Endoskeletal Prosthesis — A prosthesis built more like a human skeleton, with support and componentry on the inside, and a cosmetic covering on the outside.

Exoskeletal Prosthesis — A prosthesis that is hollow on the inside, with a hard outer surface, to bear weight.

Donning and Doffing — Putting on and taking off a prosthesis.

Hemi-pelvectomy — An amputation where approximately half the pelvic bone is removed along with the leg.

Hypertrophy — An increase in muscle mass and strength.

Ischial Tuberosity — The large sitting bone.

Lateral — To the side of the body; away from the middle of the body.

Medial — Toward the mid-line of the body.

Myoelectrics — Literally, muscle electrics; technology used in prosthetics for upper-extremity amputees; used in prosthetic hands and elbows to control the prosthesis via muscle contraction utilizing electrical signals from the muscles to the prosthetic device.

Neuroma — The end of a nerve left after amputation. It continues to grow in a circular pattern after amputation and can sometimes be troublesome, especially when trapped in scar tissue.

Partial Foot — An amputation of the front part of the foot.

Preparatory Prosthesis — Stage between temporary and permanent prosthesis, using transparent diagnostic test socket and special fitting techniques to accurately fit the prosthesis so problems can be eliminated before it is cloned for the permanent prosthesis.

Prosthesis — An artificial part of the body. In the case of an amputee, usually an arm or leg.

Prosthetics — The systematic pursuit of providing cosmetic and/or functional restoration of missing human body parts.

Prosthetist — A person involved in the science and art of prosthetics; one who designs and fits artificial limbs.

Posterior — The back side of the body.

Pylon — Often what is referred to as a pole in a temporary prosthesis; the weight-bearing support shaft in an endoskeletal prosthesis.

Ramus — The middle portion of the pubic bone, in the crotch area.

Residual Limb — Remaining portion of a limb after amputation.

Shrinker — A prosthetic reducer made of elastic material and designed to help control swelling of the residual limb.

Socket —The part of the prosthesis into which the residual limb fits.

Stump — A word commonly used to refer to the residual limb.

Supercondular Suspension — A method of holding on a prosthesis by clamping on above a joint.

Symes — An amputation through the ankle joint that retains the fatty heel pad portion.

Temporary Prosthesis — A prosthesis made soon after an amputation as an inexpensive way to help retrain a person to walk and balance while shrinking the residual limb.

About the Author

As National Prosthetics Director of NovaCare at the NovaCare Sabolich Prosthetic & Research Center, in Oklahoma City, John Sabolich is committed to the development of advanced, technological prosthetic devices to better serve amputees. He is a Certified Prosthetist/Orthotist. His interest in prosthetics began at age 13 when he started working summers and weekends at the prosthetic center founded in 1947 by his father, Lester J. Sabolich. The center is now one of the largest in the United States, with branches in Tampa, FL; Edison, NJ; St. Louis, MO; Atlanta, GA; and Wichita, KS, and attracts patients from around the globe.

Features about Sabolich's research and its practical applications in the prosthetic field have been carried on television news programs, in newspapers and magaines worldwide, including Good Morning America, ABC News, Dateline NBC, CBS This Morning, CNN, American Medical Association News, USA Today, The New York Times, Life Magazine, National Geographic, Reader's Digest, Popular Electronics, Redbook, Medical Tribune, Popular Science, Omni and many others. He has received international recognition in publications in Russia, Germany, France, Canada, China, Japan, England, Italy and Brazil.

Sabolich earned his degree in prosthetics and graduated first in his class from New York University. He is a past examiner for the American Board for Certification in Prosthetics and Orthotics and has taught special prosthetic courses at the University of California, Los Angeles. Currently, he is a clinical instructor for the University of Oklahoma Orthopedic Surgery and Rehabilitation Department and an adjunct associate professor for the University of Oklahoma Health Sciences Center Physical Therapy Department. Sabolich has also authored numerous articles for professional journals.

A noted lecturer nationally and internationally, he was invited by the People's Republic of China to tour and lecture at the country's major teaching hospitals. He was a key speaker at the Sixth World Congress on Prosthetics in Japan. Sabolich's research has served as a catalyst for changes in prosthetic designs worldwide.

Located in Oklahoma City, OK, the NovaCare Sabolich Prosthetic & Research Center, is the hub of research and training for the over 140 NovaCare prosthetic facilities in the United States.